PAST RITES

Claire Stibbe

United States of America

Past Rites

Copyright © Claire Stibbe 2016

This is a work of fiction. Names, characters, places and incidents either are the product of the author's imagination or are used fictitiously, and any resemblance to any actual persons, living or dead, events, or locales is entirely coincidental.

All rights reserved. No part of this book may be reproduced or transmitted in any form or by any means, electronic or mechanical, including photocopying, recording, or by any information storage and retrieval system, without prior permission in writing to Noble Lizard Publishing.

Published by Noble Lizard Publishing, USA

ISBN-10: 0-9906004-8-3
ISBN-13: 978-0-9906004-8-0

Printed in the United States of America

Cover artwork by Author Design Studio

Other books in the Detective Temeke Series
The 9th Hour
Night Eyes

www.cmtstibbe.com

Acknowledgements

My thanks to New Mexico for providing the inspiration for the Detective Temeke series. To my mother for giving me a safe and loving home, and to my father who gave me his love of language and books.

Special thanks to the Albuquerque Citizen's Police Academy, to the Bernalillo County Sheriff's Department and all the officers and detectives I have worked with, especially for their dedication and sacrifice. For the invaluable services of Twisted Ink Publishing, The 13th Sign and An Tig Beag Press. A huge thank you to Kingdom Writing Solutions and to editor Sandra Mangan for molding the clay into something worth reading.

As always, I owe the greatest thanks possible to Jeff for his love and support, and to Jamie for his encouragement and humor.

Claire Stibbe
Albuquerque, New Mexico
December 2016

ONE

Gabriel dropped the poker and reached for the camera. He had planned this night for a long time. It might seem a despicable act to some but what others thought didn't bother him in the least. He had been hounded for the greater part of his teenage years but now he was deaf to every insult, every condemnation, every dismissal of his right even to exist.

At high school there had always been whispers in the darkness, boys in the gym or on the soccer field, and girls in the corridors. They had said things, wanted things, demanded things.

Then Demon whispered to him. "You don't have to suffer this. There are things you can do. Permanent things. I'll help you."

It was a harmless comment on the face of it, but there was something in the tone that let Gabriel know nothing would ever be the same. Demon was wild, exciting, insane. Right from those very first words, the life Gabriel once knew was forever gone.

They say patience is a virtue so Gabriel waited until

after high school graduation. He knew the girls and boys would all go to the same college because they were the very best of the gene pool. He bided his time, watching for that special moment when the mind conjures up the worst of those memories and the body breaks loose in a perfect gush of hatred. That exquisite moment when there's no turning back.

Catching sight of the poker on the carpet and his pale reflection in the full-length mirror made him flinch. He looked like a man who had a skin disease and who never saw the sun, chest speckled crimson, even down to the gloves and military boots.

He lifted the camera. Gabriel relished the sound of the motor drive; it reminded him of a howitzer. Fast, heart-pumping, like a model working it to the last drop. He photographed the girl on the floor, the living room, the view of the park from the window and a dangle of dead mistletoe inside the front door. The things Asha once saw, things she once felt. Precious things locked up in another head now, a head that yearned to be part of her.

There... captured and sealed.

Haunting his prey had been the fun part, until Gabriel was so pumped up with anticipation he couldn't hold it in any longer. He sent Asha five Calla lilies in a black vase with a typewritten card that said, *You light the lives of those you touch. But none as much as mine.* It was funny now he thought of it, especially the quick scrawl on the back. *Saturday. Eight o'clock. Your place. P.*

The flowers were on the mantel with a note propped up against the vase. Asha was expecting a visit from a law student she had the hots for. Dark hair, blue eyes, everyone's crush. Even at school.

It explained the stylish sheath dress she wore. The pearls and the burgundy lipstick. It also explained why Asha hadn't gone out with her friends to an all-night frat party with two hundred dancing drunks, a freshman's idea of a hot Saturday night.

Gabriel couldn't remember how it happened, how he tore the life out of another human being or how he severed two of her fingers with a knife he'd found in the kitchen. It was the release before the blackout that worried him. He had no idea how long he had been there.

All he did remember was taking the key and letting himself in. A typical south side house, two bedrooms and a large open hall that led to a kitchen. Asha had been playing the piece she always played on a small Steinway grand. Chopin's Prelude in E minor, fittingly depressing and suited Gabriel's black mood.

She never heard the soft clang of the iron poker, nor did she feel the heavy thump against her skull. She may have heard a voice, excited and loud that made no sense. She may have heard nothing at all.

Blood pooled out from under her head, a dark stain on a Persian rug. Gabriel now couldn't stand the sight of her. Those singular eyes mirroring a full image of him.

It was the Smarts that made all the difference. Tiny little pills that made him happy. Made him float on thin air. They awakened him to the book he had come to find.

Only it wasn't there.

There was a blue shower curtain in the bathroom. Rolling one hundred and twenty some pounds of dead flesh in the vinyl wrap wasn't a problem. Dragging it out to the van was exhausting.

He went back inside, took the poker and wrapped it in a towel, wiped the piano, walls and furniture with a damp cloth. The blood had soaked into the deep pile carpet, camouflaged within a red medallion design, and as for her fingers, they were safely hidden where no one could find them.

With the knife, he carved a name on the kitchen door frame, one inch beneath the first hinge. *Mahtab*. It would mean nothing to the finder. But it meant everything to him.

Taking the typewritten note from the mantel, he replaced it with another. *Come away, come away with William Tell, stick an arrow up his ass and run like hell.*

Asha's mentally incompetent roommate would think she had gone on a long vacation and would likely celebrate her absence with a round of applause.

She would hear from Asha of course, because Gabriel took that smart-looking Mac from Asha's bedroom and made it his own. He would pretend to be Asha, out-of-town Asha, party-animal Asha, Paddy-mad Asha.

Gabriel was good at manipulating the system. It was probably why he had so many enemies. If he hadn't been a scholarly stick insect, he might have been popular at school.

No, he would never be one of the elite. They made that plain enough. It wasn't about what he'd done or what he hadn't done. It was about luck, about uncertainty, about the cards a person was dealt.

Gabriel would do whatever possible to prolong the fantasy. Because luck, uncertainty and cards were not enough.

TWO

A few minutes past four o'clock on a bitter Sunday evening and outside, the day had prematurely aged into night. Detective Temeke lay on his couch, feet resting on a weight bench, smoking a cigarette. He stared through the window at the sunset, now a pale streak on the horizon. On a clear night, he could see as far as the computer factory on 528 and the smoke stack that spilled into a gray sky. But not tonight.

A snow-heralding wind prowled along the driveway, blowing the last of the winter leaves into the neighbor's yard. The forecast had issued a storm warning, alerting drivers of the possible closedown of I-40 and I-25 in the event of severe blizzards. Fortunately, Temeke didn't use either. It was up Alameda all the way to Ellison, provided his car didn't trace another counter turn in the ice before Northwest Area Command.

He was glad he didn't have to drive downtown to those cracked pavements, dirty sidewalks and old fashioned slot boxes for parking. Where old newspapers got caught up in dirt devils, gyrated down the middle of Lomas and snaked onto Fourth Street. The old folk who read them peered between the net curtains of their derelict houses, living proof that not all of Albuquerque had been transformed by gentrification.

The good news was, he would be reviewing cold cases starting tomorrow and reporting directly to his brother-in-law, Luis Alvarez. At least he had the autonomy of pursuing his own cases without the usual red tape. But if he was honest, leaving Homicide was like being catapulted into space with only thirty minutes of oxygen. He'd felt the dread then. He felt it now.

Put the old bugger in a closet and lock the door – wasn't that the whisper on the streets?

His partner, Malin, told him he needed a support group, told him he couldn't be in law enforcement if he was going to drink and smoke. Especially in the office. What kind of example was that?

He'd kicked the booze all right. Well... almost. Bought a cat, an outcast British Blue he'd picked up at the pound. He and Dodger were two of a kind.

Cocking his head sideways, he listened to the crackle of flames in the fireplace and the soft chime of Dodger's identity disk. It was the rattling he couldn't work out until his cell phone skidded sideways between the ashtray and a potted cactus. The cat bounced off the couch in a fit of rage, got as far as the fireplace before collapsing in an exhausted heap.

Temeke grabbed the phone, fingers fumbled with the buttons.

"Got a moment?" a voice muttered.

It was Captain Fowler, treacherously smooth with hot lava bubbling beneath the surface. In a word, he was a sod.

"Your commander wants you in at nine o'clock if you still want a job. Got a cold case he wants to discuss."

Temeke consulted the view outside his window. It was

pitch black out there, temperatures in the low twenties.
"When you say cold, how cold?"

"Delgado. 2007." Temeke had to press the phone closer to his ear to catch what Fowler was saying. "Mrs. Delgado called this afternoon. Said her younger daughter didn't come home last night. Found a note in the pocket of a pair of jeans when she was doing the laundry. After what happened to Alice a few years back, she wanted us to take a look."

"Any idea what it said?" Temeke studied the glowing end of his cigarette.

"She didn't say. Wanted to talk to you."

It didn't surprise Temeke that Mrs. Delgado wouldn't talk to an insensitive git like Fowler, but she must have given him a reason. "And she asked for me because...?"

"Read your name in the newspaper. The Oliver case."

That was the trouble with being a well-known detective in the Duke City Police Department. Everyone wanted a big part of your life. The time-off part. "Girl's name?"

"Lily Delgado. Nineteen, five-seven, a hundred and twenty-five pounds. Missing? Maybe not after inheriting a crap load of money."

"Tell Hackett I'll be in at eight."

Temeke hung up and mashed the remains of the cigarette in the cactus pot, pressing it deep into the soil.

It had been a week of reports, car thefts and drunks. Old files, new files, cases-that-got-under-your-skin files. A box of black three-ring binders that had found their way onto Unit Commander Hackett's desk over two weeks ago had now found their way onto Temeke's.

He remembered the Delgado case even down the photograph of a young woman on the front page of the newspaper. A redhead, a suicide, an aggressive investigation. The medical report confirmed an overdose of amphetamines and alcohol – if he remembered correctly – but it was possible they had missed something.

He poked another cigarette between his lips and dragged a match along the top of the coffee table, blew a smoke ring and watched it drift toward the cactus, separating between two spiny shoots. The house was spartanly furnished, cold, uninviting, nothing like it was when Serena had been there. Dumbbells on the hearth where a brass coal scuttle once stood and eleven bottles of amber ale piled in a pyramid on the mantelshelf. Letters still lay on the kitchen table, untouched, unopened since the day they arrived from her attorney and that was over a week ago.

He almost laughed, but not as much as he did when she told him she was leaving. A striking woman in a red dress, standing by the front door with a mound of suitcases she expected him to carry. It was lucky he managed to squeeze them all into her car on the first trip, he couldn't have handled it if she had come back for the rest. He'd lost the love of his life.

Reluctantly, he picked up the phone and called Malin Santiago. She was the only partner he had ever had who could put up with a bawdy, cynical, chain-smoking Brit like him and somehow infuse some hope into his bald skull.

"Marl," he said, imagining the apologetic smile, her half-hearted condolences. She knew about the divorce papers he refused to sign and the house he refused to sell. "Fowler just called. Looks they're reopening the Delgado case."

"He told me this afternoon. Said the girl's tall, skinny. Nice looking."

"It takes a horny old sod to notice." Temeke could hear the sound of dripping water on the other end of the line and the echo in her voice. "So, where would you go, Marl, if you were tall, skinny, nice looking?"

"LA. Where all the models go."

"Most of them end up bussing tables for a living."

"Someone with a large handout wouldn't be working in a restaurant, sir. If this girl's a looker, she'll have an agent and might already be the new face of *Rogue's Bazaar*. She had an older sister."

"Alice. Committed suicide at school on her nineteenth birthday."

"Any family background, sir? Reporting officer?"

"Alan Delgado, Albuquerque's top racing driver, was killed on NAPA Speedway in 2006. Public refused to believe it was an accident, refused to believe their star was dead. Apparently one teenager, who was sitting in the Turn 1 grandstands claimed he saw the two drivers in an altercation half an hour before the race. The surviving driver denied any such disagreement."

"So no foul play?"

"None that I can see. It was one of Jack Reynolds' old cases, only Jack's dead and there's no one else to ask."

Temeke knew the police had monitored every murmur, every move, every breath for months after that terrible day and still couldn't come up with a reason other than depression. They'd gotten hints over the years, carefully planted lies that made you itch under the skin. But nothing solid you could hang your coat on.

"We'll go and see Mrs. Delgado tomorrow and it wouldn't hurt to call a few modeling agencies either. And it wouldn't hurt to get out of the tub, Marl, before you turn into a bloody raisin."

Hanging up, he ground the cigarette in the ashtray and stood up to stretch. He noticed the motion sensor lamps flick on and off in the neighbor's yard and saw Fats Riley sauntering down the driveway toward his mailbox. His dog did a fine impression of an air raid siren as it sprinted after a drift of junk mail. It was the same every night.

Temeke felt an unusual urge to see Alice Delgado's picture again, to study those eyes, read what was in them.

He imagined that lowered chin, faraway gaze, strands of Titian-colored hair playing around her jaw. Not smiling, yet she was strangely haunting, beautiful come to think of it.

She reminded him of someone.

THREE

Late on a full-mooned Sunday night, Gabriel Mann walked along the street in a fierce wind. Dressed in coveralls – a sheath of protection against a biting cold – throwaway clothes that didn't matter, throwaway clothes that would soon be spattered with blood.

Shadows were playing tricks under a lambent moon and he thought he saw Demon, the grinning gargoyle he had learned to trust. The man with a hundred names, the man with the irresistible charm. Made him feel he was worth something for once.

The adrenalin made his back and fingertips itch. It always happened when he remembered the words. Unkind words, foul words, gnarled words, like an arthritic hand digging its nails into his brain. Nothing had ever prepared him for such cruelty.

Slipping into a trance, he imagined the stinging cold outside the ranch home on Cornell Drive, the one he had studied for so many months. Rough-faced brick sprinkled with snow and a gray vine that covered half the structure. On that day, Demon had assured him the spare key was exactly where the girl always left it. Behind the vine and hanging on a tiny nodule to the left of the front door.

"Make sure you get free of her afterwards," Demon had whispered, as if he stood right there beside him now. "Otherwise she'll follow you for the rest of your life."

But she broke my heart, Gabriel wanted to say. *She*

broke my spirit.

"Well, that doesn't matter now, does it?" Demon said. "After all, that's why we're here. To make it all better. As for the book... finders keepers."

Gabriel snapped out of that dark place, reached up and swatted away the last of them, those leathery things with yellow eyes that ripped at his hair and cheeks. They had been hissing around all day, beating and tearing his mind to shreds, and he thought he felt blood trickling down one eye but it was only sweat. The attacks had worsened and sometimes his muscles felt as if they were on fire. If he found the book, he could destroy it and the ghastly thing that had come out of it.

"You can't stop me," Demon reminded. "When will another opportunity like this ever come up? You're losing your nerve."

Gabriel was losing his mind.

He tried to detach himself from the thing that taunted him day and night, an extra mind that could never be removed, heart and mind dependent. These were only some of the vital things they shared.

It's not like we're twins, Gabriel thought. We can easily be cut apart."

"Oh, you'd like that, wouldn't you?" Demon said. "Ridding yourself of the one true friend you've ever had. There will never be anyone like me."

Gabriel nodded. There would never be anyone like Demon, although he did wonder if there was such a thing as a procedure to free him from Demon... a spiritual severing. It would end in the death of one and the survival of the other and the more he thought about it, rage flared up inside him and he braced himself for the explosion to come.

There was one thing that set him apart, one thing that gave him the monopoly in every game. He could define a conversation across a crowded room by watching lips, tongue and face. They all told a story. They all gave so much away. It wasn't that people hated him. It was that they felt unnerved by him. And that made Gabriel feel powerful.

"You were pathetic at school... *Pathetic*," Demon said. "Little goody two-shoes. Didn't like socializing, didn't like all the fun things they did. Wasn't exactly a *fit* was it?"

"I did fit."

"Not really. Not like a real person. Gumption, is what it's called. You wouldn't know what that means. To think you were such a tattletale."

Gabriel sensed he was on a downhill slide, sinking lower and lower into that fiery pit and each time he felt his feet burn, he'd try to scrabble out again. Tried to reach for the pills that made him feel so alive.

"Want to have some real fun?"

Gabriel nodded. That's what he'd got all dressed up for, wasn't it? That's why he took the pills.

"Well, then. This is going to be a glorious night."

What Demon didn't mention was that everything would turn black soon and Gabriel wouldn't remember a thing.

FOUR

Malin smelled the unmistakable scent of cigarette smoke as she slipped behind the wheel of the Explorer. The tailgate still rattled from a rear-ender they'd experienced on a previous case and she was reluctant to leave it in the shop. The last unit had returned without a GPS or the mobile computer mounting on the dash.

She arrived at Northwest Area Command at a quarter to eight on Monday morning. The clouds were the color of ash and there was the unmistakable scent of wet brick. It would thunder soon.

After swiping her card in the reader, she found Sergeant Moran behind the front desk, framed by a wide pane of bulletproof glass and shaping a bicycle from a pile of paperclips. He had an ear to the holding cells in the back where a drunk was shouting about how he'd been flying high for two days and how it kicked like a 12 gauge when it came on.

"Is it just you and me today?" she asked.

"Looks like it." Sarge took his feet off the desk. "Temeke tells me you can mimic just about any accent? Do German?"

"US accents, Sarge. And I'm not that good at those."

"Great news on last night's sweep. Makes you proud to be DCPD. We made the front page."

Sarge shook open a newspaper, smoothed it down against the counter and read it out aloud. "*Federal, state and local law enforcement officers executed twenty arrest warrants last night one state warrant, search warrants on eleven residences and twenty-three people in custody. All charged with racketeering conspiracy and conspiracy to murder.* Of course, there's always one who doesn't approve of the travel plans or the destination. According to Officer Jarvis there was quite a noise in the back of the prisoner transport van. Pat 'Yellowman' Mendez was wondering if they could drop him off at the Indian Pueblo Cultural Center for some fry bread."

"They got him?" Malin was jumping.

Sarge pointed toward the holding cells where distant yells were being ignored. *Sons of bitches! I'm gonna gut you. Hell, yeah!* Mendez was one of the leaders of the Syndicato de Gato Negro and so thickly tattooed he was beginning to look like a political cartoon.

"So, where's the party?" she asked.

"They're all in the Fat Duck. Temeke said if you don't want to go there are a couple of boxes on your desk that need sorting."

Malin thought of Temeke and his high, carved cheekbones, a big feral cat and black as midnight. She'd be lying if she pretended she hadn't noticed.

No fraternizing with employees, she promised herself. But if he ever asked her out, she would be hard pressed to say no. He wouldn't, of course. He was still in love with his ex-wife.

Temeke's humor always focused on embracing the underdog and if he could pull Commander Hackett down a peg or two he'd do it. There was sarcasm in everything he said and a liberal sprinkling of self-deprecation which seemed to give him the license to hand it out. She was the only one in the office who understood his gags and she was also the only one who wasn't offended by them.

Malin rushed upstairs to the office she shared with Temeke and took off her scarf and coat. A stale waft of cigarette smoke lingered from the night before and she wondered how long it would be before Hackett had another meltdown about the smell. Temeke was killing himself with all that nicotine and the worst part was he didn't seem to care.

She sprayed the room liberally with a can of mango tango scented air freshener, tired of tacking *no smoking* signs to the walls which Temeke clearly ignored. He'd torn down the last two in a fit of rage and cussed with words she'd never heard of.

What is a *wanker* anyway?

She stared out of the window where the view plunged two stories down to a snow dusted rear parking lot and an automatic gate. Three Ford Interceptors and two cruisers. One of which had a damaged front bumper from a recent PIT maneuver and Temeke's jeep which had several tears in the fabric roof, possibly done by a squirrel.

She didn't feel like eating burritos and making small talk with the officers in the Fat Duck, so she opened the first of two storage boxes marked Alice Delgado. Pulled out three black binders and set them on a table under the window. Took the first one apart, page by page, typed up a fresh spreadsheet, had her own routine.

She opened the ICRIIS database, an acronym for Integrated Criminal Investigation and Identification System, and checked for any updates on their CAPTURE administering program. The first incident report had been written by Detective Reynolds and according to the 911 verbatim report, Alice Delgado had been found dead in the tub, wrists slashed with a knife. Labeled a suicide.

She flipped through the pages at a furious clip, through the autopsy report signed by Dr. Vasillion, the crime scene photographs, a forensic report from Matt Black, and court transcripts, until she found the suicide note.

It was hard to accept that a girl could take her own life, much easier to accept someone else had done it. How deep does that stinking morass of depression have to be before you sink to the bottom, slicing yourself up good and deep?

The doctor ruled out the use of a razor where the margins would have been more regular. Said it was a fillet knife because the wound was linear, no tissue bridging.

Malin didn't care how Alice did it, suicide wasn't an option in her world. She had never been depressed, at least not close enough to taking her own life and the very thought of cutting herself made her squirm.

The note was short, one paragraph that made no sense.

To become a true sister a woman must make herself mistress of everything in the world, evil as well as good, pain as well as pleasure, cruelty as well as mercy. Only then will she be in perfect balance to the power of infinity.

It indicated an evil force, a blood pact Alice may have been part of, something that had contributed to her death.

It also brought back a memory from Malin's time at the Camden County Police Department in New Jersey, a drug the high school students used. Methylphenidate, a central nervous system stimulant used as a study aid, dangerous, life-threatening and highly addictive. They called it Smarts.

Malin thought about a dozen things, but settled on the simplest. There was evidence to prove Alice had indeed taken her own life, but there was nothing to prove she had been alone at the time.

Malin called Suicide Prevention, asked them if Alice Delgado had ever made any calls before she died. There were none recorded and no one remembered her name. And worse, there was no mention of a psychiatrist on Alice's file.

Malin turned on the computer and scanned her email. Temeke had been most thorough. Not only had he left the Delgado files on her desk, he'd emailed two old press releases. Told her to print them out and put them in Alice's file.

May 13, 2006. American Champion Racing Driver, Alan Delgado was killed today while racing on NAPA Speedway. He was hit in the rear fender by fellow driver, Tony Aimes at Turn 2. Delgado's car burst into flames on impact. Although emergency personnel quickly reached Delgado, he died an hour later in hospital. Alan Delgado is survived by his wife Valerie and two daughters, Alice and Lily.

May 13, 2007. Alice Delgado, daughter of former American Champion Racing driver, Alan Delgado, has been found dead, aged nineteen, in an apparent suicide. Duke City Police said she was pronounced dead at the scene shortly after officials responded to an emergency call around eight p.m. local time.

The dates were the same, only one year apart. Malin tried to be disciplined in her thinking and hit *print*.

As the printer whirred to life, she took a magnifying glass from the top drawer and scanned the faces at the graveside on the first photograph. There wasn't anyone she could single out, no one who gave her that unexplainable feeling of being out of place. Eyes downcast, likely tracing the movement of the casket as it descended gracefully on a lowering frame. If she hoped for a glimpse of a killer, it wasn't there.

A short strawberry blonde in a veil, eight men in suits, seven teenagers of both sexes and a teenage girl sitting beside her mother, hands clenched. Both faces were fixed on an antique blue casket and Malin could almost hear muffled sobbing, the very picture of pain and grief.

She leaned back and stretched her legs. There was something, though, something that burrowed under her skin and made her stomach roll. It felt as if she had swallowed a particularly gristly piece of chicken and she pushed the photograph away.

The second photograph was the same, so were the third and fourth. The fifth showed a different expression on Lily's face, eyes down this time as if she turned slightly to acknowledge the hand on her shoulder. A young man, seventeen, eighteen. Kind eyes. Malin checked each photograph for variations, all labelled from one to forty-seven, copyright to the *Duke City Journal*.

A few weeks ago, she and Temeke had watched another funeral through a rain speckled windshield and just as the casket was lowered into a muddy hole, Temeke had said something about killers returning to admire their handiwork.

Slipping the printed press releases into the file, she took the cell phone out of her pocket and laid it on the desk. If Temeke called, the thing would rattle louder than a beer can. She couldn't remember a day when the sun shone as brightly as it had in the summer, or a day where she felt less hopeful. But this year things were different. They were starting to feel different too.

FIVE

Sun shone through the office blinds, casting diagonal shadows on the walls, strange shapes Malin tried to analyze, even in that zoned out state.

She heard Fowler's nervous, grunting laugh from next door, a vulgar gumshoe, the type that made you feel dirty inside. The gap under the door had a way of filtering out the worst of Hackett's fits and by the aggressive pitch it was Fowler who was in the stocks today.

Three major cases in the course of four months. Not unusual in a city with one of the highest crime rates in the United States. A city with Spanish heritage, a city beyond the ordinary. Old Town, the gleaming walls of the Bernalillo County Court House, The Anderson-Abruzzo Balloon Museum, San Felipe de Neri Church and so many architectural triumphs she associated with home. But there was a mood in the weather, the landscape, the people. As if the whole earth had been zipped up in a body bag.

"Bored?"

The voice almost made her jump. Captain Fowler's face peered around the door frame, a vision of brass and black, and cologne that echoed the iconic scent of Pine-Sol.

"Thought you might need some company," he said, shutting the door and sitting in Temeke's chair.

Malin pursed her lips, slid the cell phone closer to the

keyboard and turned on the recorder ap. She had to force herself to think, force herself not to look Fowler in the eye.

"Since your office is within walking distance of mine, I thought I'd drop in," he said.

Malin shuffled the photographs in a neat little stack and put them back into the file. She searched a list of modeling agencies on the computer, selected the fourth on the list and finally scored a hit. Lily Delgado, second from the left. She ignored the sound of a cleared throat.

"You look nervous. Know how I can tell?"

Malin didn't. Nor did she care. She was waiting for Temeke to take her to the Delgado residence and she wasn't about to let Fowler in on her case.

The sound of cracking knuckles set her teeth on edge and her heart began to beat a little faster. He tipped back in his chair, a subtle move to disguise his defensiveness – he was well on the way to pissed.

"I can tell, because you get all red and rattled when I'm around," he said, leaning forward suddenly. "Interested in lunch?"

"Yes I am. But not with you, I'm afraid." Malin studied the redhead on the computer, the arched eyebrows and a hint of resentment behind those watery eyes. If it hadn't been a headshot against a cream stucco wall she would have guessed the girl's hands were curled into two tight fists. She was rather attractive.

"What's that stink?" Fowler said, snapping open a Swiss army knife to clean his nails. "Perfume?"

Malin nearly rolled her eyes. How like Fowler to think a short squirt of air freshener was all about him. She kept tapping the keys as if she wasn't listening, hoping he'd disintegrate into thin air.

"Ever had kids?" Fowler asked.

"Nope."

"Ever been married?"

"Are you married?" Naturally, Malin assumed he was.

"My personal life is none of your business."

"Ditto."

"Your personal life has gone viral. What was it a New Jersey captain once said? Oh, yeah, sleeping with you was like humping a tranquilized carthorse."

"The captain you're referring to never had the pleasure." The words gushed out of her mouth like water through a cracked dam and she almost snarled as she said them.

It was the sudden laughter that caught her by surprise. Deep and guttural as if there was a glob of spit lodged in the back of his throat.

"Got a thing for Temeke, haven't you. Course, you should know he'll be canned before long. Homicide's running bets he can't solve this case in nine weeks. All that drinking and smoking. Think I don't know what else he's doing? But nobody comes a close second, do they? Nice sense of rhythm these black people."

"Is that right?"

"I don't know," he said. "You tell me."

Again the eddy, the cramping stomach. She was suddenly angry, the type of angry when you're looking around for a spare telephone cord and wondering how long death by asphyxiation takes. A few minutes, she thought, which was a long time when every cell in your body is gasping for air.

"Someone's helping you, aren't they? Giving you a bit of extra tuition after hours. Be careful on that computer, Santiago. Never know who you're talking to."

Malin gave him a long hard look. "Do you use chat rooms?"

"What?"

"Chat rooms... do you use them?" Malin studied a brow creasing with three deep lines.

"Why would I use a chat room?"

"Because eighty-five percent of all police work is searching on the internet and the other fifteen is searching in all the wrong places. You're in the wrong place."

"What are you talking about?" The Swiss army knife snapped shut.

"Women are like speeding tickets to you." Malin narrowed her eyes and logged out of her computer. "You come up behind, flash your lights, pull them over, take more than their license and registration, and then tell them to have a nice day. Talking of viral, the girls at the Journal call you Jack Flash. Nothing like a pistolino going off when you least expect it."

Fowler's smile changed from a long thin line to a big O, and he stared like he had sleepwalker's eyes.

"If you'll excuse me," Malin said, grabbing her cell phone and heading for the door.

She didn't turn back when he called after her, didn't tell the impact sergeant where she was going either. The air smelled like rain and the outside wall of the building pulsed with the reflection of an emergency beacon. A black Charger pulled up, strobe light streaking on the dash.

"Boy, am I glad to see you," she said to Temeke as he swung off the door frame of Lieutenant Alvarez' car.

"You look flushed, love. Doesn't she look flushed, Luis?"

"It's Fowler," Malin interrupted.

Luis shouted something about parking his car round back and drove off in a cloud of smoke, brakes screeching as he made a U-turn.

Malin caught the fragrance of citrus, the same scent she remembered when she had fallen asleep on Temeke's shoulder in a helicopter once.

"I'll haunt that stanky-ass Romeo until the day he sticks a gun in his mouth and pulls the trigger." Temeke stepped back suddenly and seem to study her for a while.

"Do we need a rape kit?"

"Where were you?"

"In the Duck. Where do you bloody think I was?"

"It felt like I was being held hostage. He just doesn't give up."

"I'll ask a couple of the lads to have a go at him. Damage his morale... knees—"

"Don't even think about it!"

"Please yourself. Good will to men and all that swaddling."

"Talked about my computer." Temeke's face seemed to screw in concentration and she felt a frisson of unease. "Look, I know you never believe anything I say. So I taped it. He asked me if I was getting some extra tuition after-hours. I thought he was being suggestive, but now I'm wondering if he's stalking me."

Temeke rammed a cigarette in his mouth and blistered the end with his lighter. "Listen, love, Fowler's a cock of the walk, looking for a promotion and not caring who he treads on in the process. He wants you out. He wants me out. But I'm damned if I'm going to let him do it on his terms. He should have other things to occupy his fertile mind."

"You mean Detective Suzi Cornwell?"

"I do. Word is she's been looking for a transfer. Just bought a Pulte home nearby in Boulder Trail. If it takes the searchlight off you, love, then all the better. Now, drive me to the Delgado house and keep your mind on all those questions you're going to ask."

"You do the asking, sir." Malin didn't feel much like talking. "I'll look around."

Better inhale the last of the fresh air, she thought, as they headed toward the car. Gripping the steering wheel, she watched Temeke as he took one last drag of his cigarette and threw it in a wide arc over the back wall.

"No," he said, pointing in the air, "this calls for a little strategy."

Malin shook her head, put the car in gear and realized she was embarrassing herself. "Probably not worth talking about small fires. They usually go out all by themselves."

"Not if some stupid bastard starts pouring gasoline all over the place like they apparently did this morning." There was a sour look on his face. "Who's Fowler's assistant?"

"Sandra Buckingham, why?"

"Smart bird that Sandra. Time she brought him some lunch."

SIX

The wind soughed through a stand of cottonwoods, bordering a small group of houses off Camino Vega Verde on the west side of the river. Bazan Loop was a cozy neighborhood with a variety of large adobe style houses with tar gravel roofs.

The Delgado house was a two-storey villa with dark wood shutters and a roof straddled with terracotta tiles. Temeke estimated it was well over three thousand square feet sitting on a half-acre lot. The number 283 was barely visible behind a palm tree at the front gate and the yard was immaculate, suggesting the presence of a Homeowner's Association.

He studied a painting on the kitchen wall of two heavy draught horses pulling a plough through long trenches of soil and then glanced through an archway at the spacious living room beyond. The aroma of fresh coffee made his mouth water and the stocky woman who handed him a cup was in her early fifties, brightest eyes he'd ever seen.

"It's been over a week now," Valerie Delgado said. "I saw Lily last Friday evening at a little before seven. She went out to get the mail and never came back."

"So, where did you find the letter, ma'am?"

"I was doing the laundry." Valerie pointed at the kitchen counter, to a single sheet of paper which appeared to have been torn from a notebook. "And I found this."

Temeke's eyes locked on the page and he instinctively

put his hand out. "May I see it?"

He saw Valerie hesitate, knew how it must have felt to surrender anything from a family member. The writing was cursive like every school student's.

I can make anything happen just by wishing it. Look what happened to Alice? You wouldn't want that happening to you. D.

"Who's *D*?"

Valerie's eyes dropped to the floor, breaking the visual connection for a second. "I don't know anyone called D. I even looked through her address book."

"Alice have any suicidal symptoms, depression?" He passed the note to Malin.

"After Alan died, she said she heard voices. Said there were things flapping around in her room and on the staircase." Valerie went silent for a while, noticed the tilt of Malin's head and the tight frown. "Frightened the life out of Lily. This note sounds like a threat, Detective."

"Would you say the girls were close?"

"Very."

Temeke followed Valerie into the living room, eyes grazing over six silver framed photos on the mantelshelf. Family pictures, individual headshots, nothing out of the ordinary.

"Alice's death must have been a shock," he said, taking a seat next to Malin on the couch. "Lily behave differently after that?" It was a direct question, one that Temeke felt he needed to ask.

"Her headaches got worse, probably stress. She'd stay out late, but she'd always call." Valerie dabbed her eyes. "I've left messages. I think she must have been kidnapped."

Temeke studied that pale face and wondered how many nights she lay in bed replaying events, daring it to be a kidnap because she couldn't bear it to have been any other way.

"She could have run away," he said. "Young people do."

Valerie frowned and bit her lip. "She had everything, Detective. A President's scholarship to Gibson. A loving home."

"You spoke to Captain Fowler?"

"He was a little rude. Said the note wasn't proof of anything and it certainly wasn't worth sending out good detectives."

"Yet he sent us." Temeke shot a look at Malin who was bagging the note. "Should have filed a complaint, ma'am. Still can, you know."

Valerie wiped a curl of auburn hair from her cheek and attempted a smile. "I just want all of this to go away. All the nightmares. Is there anything you can do?"

"There's always something we can do," Temeke murmured, abandoning his cup on the coffee table. "Full birth name?"

"Lilith Ann Delgado."

"Do you have a picture of her?"

Valerie lifted down one of the photographs from the mantel, only this one was tucked behind the rest and framed in ebony. Two girls sitting on a wall, both frozen in a faraway stare. Temeke studied the first. Lean, with a narrowly sculptured face and thick, red hair cut to the jaw in a swinging bob. Lily Delgado.

It was Alice's face that brought a prick of unease. Wisps of hair gusted across a striking face and narrow eyes that seemed to judge her audience from beyond the grave. She wasn't smiling either. Cheeks dotted with the same freckles Lily had, only that's where the similarity ended. He handed the picture to Malin.

"Who took the photo?"

"Her father," Valerie said.

"Evidence." He waited for her approval, searching those eyes as if there was only a faint residue of pain. "When was this taken?"

"A month before Alice died."

"School?"

"Los Poblancs Academy. I thought both girls would do better in a private school. There was music and drama, things we couldn't offer them."

"If you don't mind telling me, what are the fees now? Roughly?"

"They were seven thousand a semester when Alice started. Ten thousand now."

"Quite a jump."

"I wanted the girls to have the best education." Her eyes watered as she said it, chin pointing to the ground.

Valerie Delgado clearly had money to burn, he thought, giving the house a thorough look this time. "We'd like to see Lily's room, if you don't mind."

They followed Valerie upstairs to a medium sized bedroom overlooking the back yard and a lavender field. Clothes hung over a wing back chair, regal, he thought, like a queen's throne. Keys, purse, make-up, perfume, all there on the dressing table. Nothing obvious missing.

While Malin familiarized herself with the contents of the closet and chest of drawers, Temeke studied Valerie Delgado. You could tell a lot by a mother's face.

Intuition was a prompt that frequently told him something he already knew, and now it was telling him Valerie wasn't too keen on Malin digging around her daughter's belongings. If he had lost a child, he'd be leaning over a police officer's shoulder, willing her to find something he'd missed.

"Did your girls have any boyfriends?" he said.

"Not Lily. Alice liked someone. Nothing came of it."

Her reference to *someone* indicated a crush, a short-lived liaison that merited no further scrutiny. "I understand Lily is now the beneficiary of a sizeable trust fund, her father being the donor. Who was the trustee?"

"A rep from Midas Mutual and a friend of Alan's. It was money held in trust with substantial accrued interest. Alan's will was very specific. He knew car racing was dangerous, made ample provision for his family in case of an accident. Alice would have received the same amount had she lived."

He could smell the faint trace of orange blossom... patchouli, a fragrance his wife adored. "What perfume did Lily wear?"

It was an intimate question and one Valerie would have no trouble remembering. She mentioned a well-known brand with a happy name. There was no sign of a bottle on the chest of drawers.

Temeke knew world renowned racing drivers received at least six figures and as for the house, it was worth a buck or two. "Anyone call you? Lily's friends... someone she was close to."

"One friend called to see if I'd had any news. Asha Samadi."

"The pianist?" Temeke recalled sleek dark hair, a grand piano and one of the best concertos he had ever heard.

"Played two years ago at Popejoy Hall." Valerie gave the flicker of a smile and nodded. "I had three hang-up calls yesterday. Call it a mother's intuition, but I think it was Lily."

"Could have been a salesman," Temeke said. It slipped out, and it stung. He could see it in her eyes. "But we'll look into it."

"I know it's her." Valerie gave Temeke a look of such implicit trust, he didn't have the heart to contradict her. "The man who's got her... He'll let her go soon, Detective. When he's ready."

It was bad enough Temeke had to dredge up the past

and here he was thinking of a way to convince her Lily had likely taken off with all that money. "Does she have a car?"

"It's in the garage."

"I'll take a look," Malin said. The en-suite bathroom no longer held her interest and she slipped out through the open door.

Temeke could see Alice's room was untouched, south facing and blinds drawn to keep the sun off. He gave the bookcase a cursory glance, opened the closet door to find her clothes had been covered with garment bags, shoes and boots neatly arranged on a stackable rack. It was pitiful to see.

He sensed the uncanny silence that even the barest whisper of the air conditioner couldn't hide. Alice's residue was there, still in charge, still directing the show, probably witnessing each victim's suffering and final death.

"Her clothes are all there," Valerie said, pointing to the chest of drawers. "I can't bring myself to look at them."

She turned her back and waited in the corridor. It gave Temeke the time he needed to open each drawer and gaze upon the intimate leftovers of a dead girl. All flawlessly folded with no sign or feel of anything hidden.

There was an array of china cats on a corner shelf and a black Mimbres vase crafted by an ancient culture known for their stylized imagery of animals and human figures. Books, stacks of them.

Valerie led him back to the kitchen and sat at a wood dining table, finger absentmindedly tracing grooves and saw marks on the surface. Temeke decided the piece was nothing more than a fashionable take on salvaged lumber and he studied that polished finger as it caressed a large bolt in the joint. A homey aroma of spruce wafted from a cultured stone fireplace and on the mantle, a votive candle flickered in a draft.

"Were you expecting any visitors on Friday evening?" he asked.

Valerie took a while to shake her head, hands lying flat against the tabletop now.

Under different circumstances, he might have taken in the beauty of the house and a crackling fire, sunlight filtering through floor-to-ceiling windows and a skylight that provided a nighttime opportunity to gaze at the stars. Dust motes circled around a grieving mother and a detective who tried to reconstruct the events of that fateful day.

"Tell me something," he said. "Lily have any idea how to live on the streets? Because if she has, she'd have an awareness of danger, heightened instincts that could help her survive."

"She's an innocent, detective. She has no idea about anything."

Temeke nodded, but couldn't entirely agree with the assessment. All young people had some idea about something, and very few were innocent. "We're extremely concerned for Lily's safety. There'll be a full investigation and we'll be drafting men from other units to help. Before I take such steps, I want to eliminate the person you think who's got her. Do you have a name?"

"I didn't mean to make it sound like I knew him."

"Let me be blunt, Mrs. Delgado. It will save time. You mentioned something about a man letting her go when he was ready."

"I was just imagining it was a man. That's all. I don't know anyone who would do such a thing."

"Right. If you hear anything, you'll let us know? We'll call you in a day or two. You take it easy now."

He found Malin in the hall, followed her outside and grabbed a smoke from his jacket pocket as they walked to the car. "Anything?"

"There's a laundry closet behind the kitchen, more

cupboards, mainly towels, detergents and a door marked *broom closet*. It was locked. The photo album in the master bedroom was interesting."

"Digging deep."

"Just a feeling." Malin leaned back in the driver's seat and he heard the click of her seatbelt. "A Halloween party they had a few years back. Usual ghouls, pirates, princesses, a tiger, four emo boys. Lily wasn't dressed as anything. Just thought it was odd, that's all."

"I know how she feels, all trussed up like a turkey for the sake of an old wives' tale." Temeke looked back at the house as they pulled out of the driveway. "See any sign of Lily's perfume?"

"Not the one you were asking about. Makes you wonder if she took it with her."

"A bit odd Mrs. Delgado mentioned a man. Why would she think Lily's been kidnapped?"

"What if she had Lily kidnapped?"

"Nah, she's got enough money of her own. And those weren't crocodile tears."

"You believe her?"

Temeke sucked on his cigarette and squinted. "Naturally, I'm a gullible fool and swallow everything without question. Of course, I bloody believed her."

But Malin's comment made him think.

"Almost an entire family wiped out in less than three years," he muttered as he flicked the cigarette through a crack in the window.

"Two cars in the garage, both unlocked, sir. A white BMW 4 Series registered to Alice Delgado and a black Lexus IS 350 F Sport registered to Lily Delgado."

"Better get them impounded for a thorough workup, Marl."

"There's a study at the back of the house," Malin said, resting the palms of her hands against the steering wheel. "Bookshelves, desk, filing cabinet. There was a book beside the computer, pages marked with a red pen. *Medium Minds*, it was called. And there was a one-eight-hundred number on a pad, so I dialed it. The call connected to a psychic called Kirsty Atwell."

"I hope she told you where Lily Delgado was."

Malin gave a small chuckle. "With two family members gone, I think Mrs. Delgado's quite familiar with parapsychology. I also think these psychics earn a fortune from broken women like her."

"Looks like the whole lot of them are flying with the bloody pigeons."

Malin slowed down at the stop sign on Alameda and gave him a long hard stare. "All of them, sir?"

SEVEN

It was six o'clock on Monday evening when Gabriel parked his van about fifteen feet from the front gate of a well-lit cemetery. The place was empty now. No more people milling around like there had been yesterday.

He peered through his zoom lens, watched the backhoe cutting into the cold, hard ground and read the stone marker that leaned against the trunk of a large cottonwood. Gray polished marble inscribed with a fitting epitaph.

Poonam Eva Kapoor, 1978 - 2013.
There is no death, only a change of worlds.

The worker stopped the backhoe and seemed to be looking for something. Glanced around the cab and tried to find the remote control that had once been clipped to his visor. He shook his head, raised the boom and bucket and headed off toward the open gate, unable to lock it now. Never gave Gabriel's van a second glance, just slid down the road, red soil dribbling from the loader.

Gabriel looked down at the remote control which was now sandwiched between the hand brake and the console. Memories played with his senses, making him laugh, making him cry. Then he studied the grave through the lens and the shovel leaning up against the tree, and he began to conjure spirits in that dark mind of his. It wouldn't do to let Demon in. He saw and heard, and he knew enough already.

Gabriel had read *A Time to Thrill*, a book on convicted murderers on death row in Tehachapi State Prison, where one inmate stated that killing his first victim was like a trial run before the real deal. The trial run was the one that gave him the worst nightmares and the biggest rush. The real deal fueled all that pent-up anger and turned out to be nothing less than a hacked up mess.

Gabriel never wanted Asha to be a hacked up mess. she had been the quiet one, the girl who refused to take part in the torment, the girl who stood at the back and did nothing. But in so many ways that was worse because Asha could have saved him, could have been kind.

Gabriel shivered, felt the change in the wind, the sudden stench of something rotten. He pinched his nostrils to stop Demon leaking from the trees, the ground, the graves, because when he came he consumed him and Gabriel didn't want to be consumed anymore.

"What we know from the dark ones we learn by someone's experience," Demon whispered. "Take me, for instance, I was five when it happened, when the first of the dark ones blew in under the bedroom door. I wasn't afraid. I knew what it was. So, I opened my mind to let it in. If you open yours, you can see what I see."

It worked every time. Because Demon was clever, always snickering and goading and stimulating the senses.

"Because it's so beautiful," Demon said, likely anticipating Gabriel's hesitation. "Of course, the truth-seekers don't think so. They're spineless. Barking up the two-branched tree. But you're different. I promised you'd be perfect and you are."

And then he laughed like he always did. "You just don't get it, do you? If you want to be in the driver's seat, you have to let me in."

Gabriel had always been of a different mind until the

storms came. Some were big; some not so big. And then after a time he gave in, even when the words carried a sense of the ridiculous. The first time it happened he floated, an off-the-ground floating that took his breath away.

Tonight, he was very much on the ground, smelling only a residue of that nightmarish stench. Nothing special about a van parked on the broad shoulder outside the front gate, probably abandoned because it was old.

Now came the hard part. He drove into the cemetery and parked under the tree. If it wasn't for hours of chest presses, dumbbells, pushups, squats, a whole routine, he would never have been able to haul that hideous load through the grass to where an open grave yawned up at a starry sky. Lurching and gasping, he rolled it toward the edge and watched it flop against the bottom.

"More exercise," Demon reminded with a laugh to his voice.

A shallow pile of dirt still lay on the graveside and, six shovelfuls later, the body was patted nicely into its surroundings. There would be no hint of it when the mourners came and the casket was lowered. No one would know young Poonam Kapoor had a sleeping companion.

Part of him wanted the body to be found before then, because a game of tag isn't much fun when played alone.

He looked up at that tree, at a smooth patch of wood barely noticeable behind a wrinkled shard of bark. Peeling off about six inches, he scratched the name *Mahtab* on the trunk with his knife.

Gabriel left the cemetery and drove east along Central Avenue and then north on Ash. Glancing up at the rearview mirror, he decided he looked tired and skinny. Actually he was tired and high. He did it to forget.

Parking near a small brown stucco house on Vassar Drive, he studied the road, the cars, the front door. The place of his next appointment.

There was slender tree to the right of that door still blinking with a solitary string of Christmas lights someone had forgotten to remove. A narrow alleyway separated the house from its neighbor, where tall blades of grass grew between the ruts, suggesting it was rarely used for cars.

Monday night, almost midnight. The sky was black, stars winking overhead and always in his favor. He was conscious of a crisp breeze that came in through the crack in the driver's window, felt the prickle in his cheeks. He'd missed the delicatessen car that always pulled up outside the small adobe house with an order of food. Seven o'clock every evening. Funny how thin, rich girls always seemed to eat a lot. Especially alone.

As far as Gabriel could make out, there were no security cameras, nothing that would announce the presence of an intruder. But he wasn't ready yet.

It would be three more days before he would kill again. Three more days before Demon told him what to do.

EIGHT

Despite the slow speed of the jeep on the way to Northwest Area Command, pitching and rolling on the narrow road that wound along Guadalupe Trail, Temeke almost fell asleep at the wheel. It wasn't until he swung out and overtook a jogger with a gym bag that he decided to close his mouth and quit snoring.

Probably one of those squatters in a house he often called *the ruin,* five houses down from his and on the other side of the street. The residents complained about comings and goings, loud voices and unsightly trash piled against the east wall. Temeke had called the homeowner, suggested he started gutting the property to make it safe again.

The clock showed seven forty-five on Tuesday morning when he finally arrived at the rear gate of the substation, opened his window and showed his card to the reader. Sod his usual three to eleven shift. It was all day, every day now.

A slate gray sky and a single ray of sunlight which turned the trees a bright shade of gold. Perhaps there's hope, he thought. Perhaps the police could still find Lily Delgado.

As the gate went up, there was sudden movement to the left of him. A flash of cameras, mics and booms, and Temeke instinctively held up one hand. He heard journalist Stan Stockard's voice from the shadows.

"Detective Temeke, there are rumors that you've found a young woman's body. Can you give us her name?"

"No comment," Temeke said, easing the car forward through a small group of photographers, half blinded by a burst of light. He had no idea if Stan was fishing for information on the disappearance of Lily Delgado or if it was a general probe for an update on where they were on the case.

Bloody nowhere was the correct answer, especially when Hackett was desperate enough to call in Knife Wing, the lying psychic.

"Will there be a press conference?" Stan asked, following the moving car and shoving a microphone under Temeke's nose.

"Do you lot always hide behind trees?" He saw the microphone drop, the flicker of a frown. "Seems like a sodding waste of time to me. I'd hate to be a journalist. Out in the freezing cold at, what, six o'clock in the morning? Coffee... protein bars. Tough life. And it's going to be tougher still when you have to hack your way through the wilderness to get to that swampy crime scene."

"Where... where is this place?" The microphone was back up now and Stan's eyes were like two big cups.

Buggered if I know, Temeke thought as he closed the window, turned the wheel and watched the gate go down behind him.

Made a fresh pot of coffee when he got to his office and sauntered over to the window, light fading and rain spattering against the glass in neat little dots. He could see the camera crew below, saw Stan Stockard taking pictures of him at the window and talking into that sodding microphone.

Temeke felt his gut tighten. Why did he always have to open his big, fat mouth?

He glanced at the table beneath him, littered with photographs and a detailed spreadsheet. Alice's face was the last thing he saw before he went to bed, the first thing he thought of when he woke up. He knew it was a trap to fall in. Pale skin like the inside of an oyster, amber eyes... or were they hazel? It didn't matter. The visions were endless, kept him awake ever since he'd seen that dreamy expression – and it was beginning to get under his skin.

Valerie Delgado had not answered the question of whether Alice had depression. In fact, she'd sidestepped it with claims about demons flapping about in the attic. Another case of denial, he thought. All parents had it.

Logging into his computer, he found an email from Malin. Four hang-up calls had been made to Valerie Delgado over the last two weeks. The department pinged the number and found it was registered to a pest control technician who had reported his cell phone missing three days prior to the calls having been made. The network provider compared the signal strength and time lag, and triangulated the phone's position to Gibson University's central library. It was found perched on top of a green banker's lamp and dusted for prints. The owner of the phone had never visited the library.

Subsequent calls to Valerie Delgado were also within range of at least two cell phone towers in the same area. Although the last call was handed off by two towers in southeast Albuquerque they were likely dropped rather than someone hanging up. There simply wasn't enough data to determine the caller's path of travel.

Temeke forced out a loud sigh and looked up the website for Los Poblanos Academy, a private school off Rio Grande. It appeared to be hidden behind an avenue of cottonwoods, a mission style building with courtyards and arches and an enfilade of rooms. Elaborate gardens and a senior students' parking lot on the south side, fifty-two gifted students lounged under wood beamed ceilings, listening to the splatter of a water fountain outside. Lucky sods, he thought. Since when did students start bringing their own ponies to school?

Temeke saw a list of celebrity boys and girls who graduated in 2012. It all blurred into a gray smudge and then slowly edged back into focus. He rubbed his eyes, wished he hadn't had that last cigarette before breakfast. It was a stupid thing to do and no amount of mouthwash and fluoride ever took away the taste. He only hoped it took away the smell.

South African, Korean, Greek and Saudi Arabian names. Odd, he thought, to have such a salubrious school in the forty-ninth poorest state in the US. Maybe that was the saving grace. There would be no paparazzi peering through the bushes. The school was bloody hard to find.

He scoured the home page for the number and called the admissions office. A Phoebe Baca said she would meet him at four o'clock and not a minute later. He already had a visual of the woman. Pearly tweeds and a rear end you could balance a plate on.

"How's it going?" Malin asked, lithe body slipping in through a half closed door.

"Could be better. You?"

"So, so." She took off her coat, dropped a protein bar and a wadded up tissue on her desk. "I had another bad dream last night."

"Oh, yeah."

"It's really dark and I'm in my car. Up ahead, there's a bend in the road and there's this girl out walking all by herself. All of a sudden she turns and stares at me like she wants to tell me something. So I wait and then I hear the words *solid ground, not sinking sands*. I woke up after that."

"Something on your mind?" He could see that there was, even though she shook her head and stared out of the window. "I would say the car signifies a safe place.

You're in control. But the girl… she's vulnerable, out in the open. Knows she's being followed. As for sinking sands—"

"Hard facts, not make-believe." Malin gave him a look as if she was letting her gut senses feel things out. "And talking of hard facts, Homicide are betting on how fast you can crack this case, sir. The stakes are at fifteen hundred bucks, so I thought I'd put a few dollars in myself."

The sound of Malin's rippling laughter made Temeke smile. It reminded him of the sound of a cowbell with a few extra snorts here and there. "Am I the only one working on this case or do you have anything worth sharing?" he said.

"Flossy's in court today but her assistant called. Said latent fingerprints on the cell phone found in the library belong to the account holder and two possible family members. Maggie's out collecting statements. Another thing," she said, sliding a photograph across the desk and stabbing a finger at a teenage boy standing in the crowd. "You always told me to look for variations… contradictions. I can't help feeling there's something here."

It was Alice Delgado's funeral and Temeke recognized Asha Samadi and another girl with a good singing voice whose name he'd forgotten.

"I've confirmed the names of all the attendees. His name's Paddy Brody," she said.

Temeke studied the boy in the dark suit, brown wavy hair and deep set blue eyes. He stood directly behind Lily and her mother, head turned slightly and staring right at the camera. "Anything different about him?"

"He's the only one not looking at the casket."

He was the only one with a small smile that played around the corner of his mouth, an odd expression at a funeral. Temeke swallowed hard, pulse throbbing in his neck. "It's probably nothing, just a boy who's noticed a journalist taking photos in the bushes and wants to make front page news."

Malin frowned, appearing unconvinced. "He could be a model in his spare time. Tall enough for runway."

Temeke took another look. He couldn't seem to tie down the face that floated like a dark blob behind Lily Delgado and he was suddenly struck by an intense feeling of protectiveness. What had Malin seen? What had she sensed? He stared at the girl on the far right, nondescript features, not that tall, a young man next to her, shoulder hiding behind the girl to his left. And then he saw it. The faint outline of a hand on Lily's shoulder and he wondered why he hadn't noticed it the first time around.

"Familiarity?" he murmured.

"Intimacy," she corrected. "I was thinking about Mrs. Delgado. Why would she use the word *kidnap*?"

"Her husband was a celebrity, famous racing driver, big fortune. Then her elder daughter commits suicide and the younger one buggers off. No witnesses, no known motive. Kidnap doesn't do it because if there was a kidnapper he would have left a ransom note."

"No known boyfriend, although Mrs. Delgado did say something about a man who's got her. That he'll let her go when he's ready."

Temeke took a sip of coffee, let the caffeine jumpstart his brain. He grabbed the first photograph Malin had shown him and pulled the car keys out of his jacket pocket. "Call that rep from Midas Mutual. Find out exactly how much Lily Delgado inherited. Where it was deposited and the date of the last withdrawal. I'll go to that posh school and see what I can dig up."

NINE

Temeke turned off Rio Grande into an avenue of cottonwoods, finding a parking space outside the school granary between a Ferrari and a tradesman's van. He walked to the main entrance which exuded the sweet smell of honeysuckle and where a peacock sauntered over the peristyle roof of a small courtyard, train shimmering in blues and greens.

He could smell furniture polish as soon as he walked into the foyer of Los Poblanos Academy; the realm of the privileged. It reminded him of the dining table Serena's father had given them for their wedding. It was gone now, along with the family he no longer saw and he dismissed the thick wave of gloominess as soon as he met the principal. Phoebe Baca, middle-aged with deep set eyes and a blast of perfume.

"Come in," she said, holding out a hand and scrutinizing the badge he offered. "Miss Baca. You must be Detective Temakay."

"Temeke," he offered. "As in Entebbe."

"It's about Lily Delgado, isn't it? Yes. I thought so. Coffee?"

"No thank you, ma'am."

She pecked her way over hardwood floors in high heeled shoes, hair locked with some kind of industrial strength foam that even a high wind couldn't shift.

"We're dealing here with a girl who is missing,

ma'am."

"I'm sorry to hear that." She gave a half smile and led him into an unoccupied study and closed the door.

"Are males segregated from the females at night, ma'am?"

Miss Baca cast a glance in his direction and squeezed herself into a narrow chair. "The boys occupy Sisneros House, the girls are in Quartermaine. Classes are taken together."

"Tell me about Lily?"

"Quiet girl. Rather introvert as I recall. She was one of the few resident students I had. The rest are usually overseas or out-of-state. When Alice committed suicide, Lily blamed herself. We all tried to tell her it wasn't her fault and so did the police. Quite frankly, it didn't help that her mother thought it was foul play. It wasn't of course. Anyone could see it was a suicide."

"Must have been bloody awkward finding her dead on your watch?"

"Awkward, detective? Hardly an appropriate word. It was frightening, actually. I expect you'll want to see the bathroom."

"If that's not too much trouble, ma'am."

He tried to piece together facts, analyzing different scenarios and formulating consequences, and he came to the not so startling conclusion that Miss Baca may have unwittingly left out a crucial piece.

"Do you smoke?" she asked, waving a hand in front of her nose.

"I do, ma'am."

"You won't be allowed to smoke in here."

He wasn't aware that cigarettes caused such a stench, except when Malin complained – which she did with maddening regularity.

Temeke followed Miss Baca into a well-lit room. There were twelve tables arranged on a hardwood floor and beneath the stone fireplace was a high table where the principal and administrators sat. Four French doors opened out onto a swimming pool and a lawn irrigated by an elaborate mist of water.

"Alice sat here next to Zarah Thai." Miss Baca approached a table and tapped one of the chairs with both hands. "Zarah was Korean, descended from Emperor Gwangmu and one of his concubines. Lily sat over there by Rosa. And on this side were Senator 'Lucky' Barnes' twin granddaughters. Both played a Stradivarius and—"

"Does the school have its full quota of students this year?"

Miss Baca raised an eyebrow. "Not quite."

"Why?"

"There were, shall we say, some cancellations. Let me show you around."

They entered the first classroom to the sound of scraping chairs as the students leapt to their feet and droned a greeting. Miss Baca allowed him a brief look before leading him down a narrow hallway where a grand piano was nestled in the crook of a sweeping staircase.

"Students and visitors are never allowed use the front stairs."

"I would take off my shoes, ma'am, but I haven't changed my socks in a couple of days."

"This piano was often played by Asha Samadi, especially in the evenings," she said, leading up the staircase. "Chopin's Prelude in D-flat major. No one has mastered it since. Lily shared a room with Rosa. She was an opera singer. Sang the national anthem at the Yankee stadium last year."

The one in the photograph, Temeke thought, whose name he had forgotten. The bedroom faced east and looked out on a wide expanse of lawn where a small gazebo stood at the northeast corner, capped with a dome and supported by four pillars. He squinted at the weathered stone, gray and silent as if there was no life in it. His thoughts were interrupted by hers.

"We call it the Pepper Pot," Miss Baca said, following his gaze. "Lily was clever though, you could see it in her eyes. Then her father died. It was like a dark cloud across the sun. All teenagers have it. A black hole between fourteen and eighteen. They want to write gloomy poetry and hang themselves in the bathrooms. In some cases, I wish they would. You're not taping this are you?"

"No ma'am. Wouldn't dream of it."

Ms. Baca clacked along the corridor to the bathroom, a white tiled room with French doors leading to a small balcony and a fire escape.

Temeke felt a stab of sadness when he saw the tub and its lion's paw feet, shower attachment sitting on a silver cradle. The nozzle pointed to the left, suggesting a right handed user.

"This is where I found her."

Her voice trailed off then and her eyes seemed to follow a dust mote as it settled against a double-hung window five feet to the right of the French doors.

"Do the girls also take showers?"

"Our foreign cousins prefer to bathe, detective. We provide both."

It was a free-standing tub, white, elegant, the type you could fall asleep in. He recalled how Alice was found that night, head thrown sideways, water crimson with blood.

He walked to the French doors, each fitted with a security bar. Looking through the metal girders of the fire escape, he saw the parking lot, the lawns and the Pepper Pot. He checked the door. Locked.

"Everything's to code, detective. All fire escapes are fixed, two on each side. The window used to stick a little. It's secure now."

"Any burglaries?" He wished he had been the reporting officer that night, wished he could have checked the locks then.

"None." She seemed absolutely certain. "There is something I would like you to have."

She led him back down to the study and unlocked the top drawer of her desk. It was a thin leather bound book engraved with the words, *The Lilin Esoterica*.

"Demonic nonsense." She drew out the last word as if it was the most terrible of felonies and half smiled at the same time. "It belonged to Alice. I found it behind the bookcase in her bedroom."

"Did she smoke?"

"They all did. We found cigarettes in bird houses, toilet cisterns, pianos. And vodka in shampoo bottles."

"Teenagers can be quite enterprising."

"Not quite. They were all in love with the same boy. Silly business. Alice confided with one of the younger teachers that someone had been flirting with her boyfriend. Of course, we never encourage intimacy with our students."

"The boy's name?"

"Patrick Brody. He not only hung out with Alice, but there was another girl he took a shine to. Adel Martinez. And then he migrated rather rapidly to Kenzie Voorhees. The air was thick."

Temeke pulled the photograph of Alice's funeral from his pocket and handed it to her.

"That's him," she said. "Do you understand now?"

Temeke wasn't sure he did. He wasn't even sure he'd heard all of it in those tight twenty minutes.

The four o'clock bell rang and she handed him the book. "Naturally I would offer you tea but tongues would wag. I don't want your lot all over the place again. There are limits."

Temeke made his way to the parking lot and lit up a cigarette. Snooty-ass cow, he thought, taking seven long drags before crushing the rest of it out under his heel. It left white shreds of paper and tobacco on the gravel.

He looked at the pale stucco walls and a coil of ivy that had snaked its way almost as far as the base of the fire escape. Wind whistled through the metal frame, and somewhere up there was a delicate ring, a wind chime whose terminals butted up against the girders. He hadn't heard it from inside.

Turning his back to the building, he stood there for five long minutes, staring at the curve of a small path, cutting through the lawn and leading to the Pepper Pot. If he tried hard enough he could imagine a shadow behind a float of drapes, eyes set in a tight gaze, red hair tousled in the wind.

He looked back at the bathroom window, the horizontal platform and a fixed staircase below. The boys would have had no access to Quartermain house, at least not from the inside. He wondered how many had attempted that lofty climb just for a quick peek? Perhaps someone else stood in this very spot the night Alice died. Someone who might have seen Alice with Paddy Brody. Someone who sneaked off again, only to come back later and pay her back in kind. The Martinez girl certainly had a motive. It wasn't one of those surefire hunches, just a hypothesis born out of jealousy.

Hugging the book to his chest, he sensed the scrutiny of a workman in the parking lot, someone in a gray van parked next to his jeep. He lifted a hand and walked toward it, heard the engine turn over a few times before roaring into life. Saw the rear end fishtail as it hurtled up the drive toward the street.

Dumbass, he thought, clearing his mind and jumping into his car.

So what have we got? A slender, dignified redhead and a sister entrenched in witchcraft. There was nothing extraordinary about a redhead. It was the witchcraft that bothered him.

TEN

Gabriel waited in the darkness, all for the sake of that book. He had a feeling it was here and he could smell it like the stench of wet dog. Counting the minutes, he studied the cars that came and went. Two dark colored sedans, a white Bronco, three light colored trucks and a sports car. Vassar Drive had never been busier on a Wednesday night.

It had been this time last year when Mackenzie Voorhees applied for a job with Élus Models. She wanted to shake up the industry, win an exclusive contract with *Rogue's Bazaar* and bring in more dollars than a supermodel. They accepted her, of course, because she had the genetic coding for stardom.

Kenzie... that's what they called her at school. But beautiful was not how Gabriel remembered her. Uglier than a pug and with half the brain. Pity he couldn't bring his camera this time, too heavy, too loud. He'd have to use a cell phone instead.

There was a smell in the van, a musty odor in the fabric seats that reminded him of the locker rooms during his senior year. He cast his mind back to the memory, when he had been standing on the soccer field and Kenzie had whispered those awful words in an Afrikaans accent.

What are you now, ninety pounds? You're a puke and a disgrace.

Gabriel remembered running to his safe place, arms

curled around the stone pillars as if they would embrace him in return. Patrick Brody had been groping Adel Martinez in the bushes, walked over when he heard him sobbing, offered him a tissue. It was all so humiliating.

The rhythmic sound of his heart and the strumming of snowflakes against the window brought him back to the present. He couldn't relax. Far too nervous for that.

The delicatessen car pulled up outside the adobe house. Nine o'clock. A man with spiked hair took a bag of steaming food to the front door.

Gabriel pulled on a thick woolen beanie. He was darker than a shadow tonight, screwdriver tucked into his pocket and a black mind to go with it. Zipping the jacket up to his chin to cover his protective clothing, he reached a single-hung window on the west side of the house, studied the frame, rotten and peeling just as he thought. Although the bottom sash was in place it was slightly crooked in the frame, suggesting the latch had not been fully engaged.

The bug screen was hardly substantial and inserting the screwdriver blade along the bottom edge of the wire mesh, he felt the spring pop as the frame jumped from the grove. He pushed the frame upwards, barely letting in a sigh of wind and it gave him enough time to crawl over the frame and close it before a blast of cold air announced an open window.

Loud music. A pure-toned contralto voice singing about heartbreak on the TV. Gabriel liked the song.

It was a sparsely furnished sitting room, one couch and an easy chair. The skin of an African deer had been stretched tightly across one window, letting in only a thin bar of light, and a galley kitchen lay beyond the open door. There was a bottle of wine and a romance novel spread-eagled on the table.

Kenzie was still talking to the delivery boy, voice fading in and out over the music. It gave Gabriel time to have a look around, time to search for a brown leatherbound book.

During those precious seconds a pack of cigarettes caught his eye, a gold monogramed lighter and the stove with its five silent gas burners. It was as if someone had thrown a railroad switch in his head and he began to speed on a diverging track, onward and downward into that black tunnel.

The front door thudded loudly and when he felt the vibrations of a heavy tread against the wooden floor, he slipped behind the living room door. His breaths came in quick, short spurts now as he watched Kenzie swing a plastic bag onto the kitchen counter, reach for a plate and pour herself a large glass of wine. She seemed to hesitate when the phone rang across the hall, waited for one more ring before changing her mind.

As she sauntered toward the phone, Gabriel darted for the stove, smelling a strong whiff of garlic and parmesan. He pushed the dials and heard each ignition stutter, not enough to spark into life, but enough that a simple breath of gas would be masked beneath the sounds of that soulful voice.

"Asha?" Kenzie's tone was surprised, then relieved. "No, she's not here. Probably with Sarah Hughes... African American Sarah."

Gabriel sensed a burning sensation in the pit of his stomach. It was Paddy that Kenzie was talking to. Had to be. Paddy didn't know Asha was covered by a thin layer of topsoil and packed into the New Mexico dirt. He didn't know this was the last time he would ever speak to Kenzie Voorhees either.

Gabriel's heart was thumping like a jack hammer as he made his way toward the back door, breath steaming against a pane of glass. He took a black sharpie from his pocket and wrote the name *Kohinoor* in large letters on the underside of the doorframe. She wouldn't see it immediately. She might not see it at all.

The door knob was stiff, creaking slightly beneath a shaking hand and the slight rustle of his hooded coveralls. How long would it take to fill such a small house with gas? How long before Kenzie lit a cigarette and was engulfed in a tidal wave of flames?

So much cleaner than leaving blood spatters all over the floor, so much easier than carting a stinking body around in the back of a van. It was like a science experiment, only not as trivial. This was blistering hatred, the type that gripped and squeezed until you grabbed whatever object you could find and pounded until it was all gone.

Your parents should have used birth control. Retard. . . look at you, bag of bones. Be-Atch.

Gabriel was out of the house in the count of three, careful not to let in too much of that cold air. It would only spoil the fun.

Making his way to a young cherry tree in the front yard, he watched the lighted window between the fulcrum of two branches and snapped a picture with his cell phone. There was no flash and he realized it would be blurred. But it was the memory that mattered.

Kenzie sat at the kitchen table, plump lips pursed around a fork and fingers gripping the stem of a wine glass. Her eyes were fastened on that book, turning pages with the flick of a finger and taking a sip of the wine now and then. She was already drunk and Gabriel wanted to laugh. If ignorance was bliss, Kenzie must have been the happiest person alive.

But Kenzie had a few dirty little secrets. She'd kissed Paddy Brody in the back of her Mercedes G-Wagon, steamed up those windows for a good two hours. Gabriel was the only one who knew, the only one who saw.

And Kenzie was anorexic. A face-stuffer. Threw up each meal to stay thin. No chance she'd throw up this one.

There wouldn't be time.

Gabriel shivered, feet trampling the grass just to stay warm. Ten minutes... fifteen minutes and Kenzie was sitting back against that chair, book in hand.

"Go!" Demon whispered.

Gabriel took short steps, still keeping his eye on that window. It was the sudden clap of a screen door that made him turn, the patter of feet on the neighbor's driveway. Shoulder length hair, and the mystique and charisma any girl would die for. The man's lips began to move.

"Are you looking for someone?" he said, face sullen.

Gabriel shook his head and began to smile. He shouldn't have been so flippant, not when they stood so close to a gas leak.

"Haven't I seen you before?" the man asked, not waiting for a reply. "Name's Tom, by the way."

"Gabe."

Tom snapped his fingers. "I remember you. Same class as my sister. You must know her. Miriam Lahaye?"

Gabriel shook his head. He hadn't heard of her.

"Who are you looking for?"

"Phoebe Baca." It was the only name Gabriel could think of.

Tom looked up and down the street and took a deep breath. He was taking his time, too much time. "Doesn't sound familiar. Most of these are student houses. You could try Donnington. Number three four eight, house with the red door. There are four girls living there, I think."

Gabriel took a few steps back and tentatively looked at the house Tom was pointing at, keeping Kenzie in the periphery of his vision. He thanked him, turned on his heel and didn't look back.

He heard the sound of a car ignition turning over a few times before it caught, then a rattling along the pavement behind him.

Come on, he thought, walking faster and seeing a flash of white cruising along the road beside him. The Bronco caught up, passenger window lowered. "Hey Gabe, wanna lift?" Tom shouted.

Gabriel waved him on, smelling a thick trail of exhaust as the car sped down the street. His mind was tumbling now, visions blurring in and out with the thrill of the moment.

He ran back to the van, fumbled for the keys and turned on the ignition.

Dead.

He tried it again, this time rocking in his seat and pumping the gas as if it would help. Again and again until the thing sputtered into life.

"Easy does it," Demon said, "or you'll flood the engine."

Gabriel sat there rubbing his hands and taking deep breaths. "The thing's dying," he said. "It just wants to die."

"It's just old," Demon whispered. "I'll keep it turning over. You'll see."

The nausea came in waves and so did the memories. Gabriel kept zoning in and out; an incident in the school grounds, jeering, taunting, as they pushed a girl against the wall, soaking her blouse with water so her bra showed through. They left her there to cry.

You might be beautiful on the outside, Mackenzie Voorhees, but not on the inside.

Gabriel drove to a space five houses down, didn't want to part with Kenzie yet. It was forty-five minutes before a sports car pulled out from a neighboring house, gave a full-throated treble roar as it hurried down the street.

Then came the explosion, shattering glass and flames rippling from what was once the living room window. The noise fractured the sleepy street, detonating car alarms and hurling roofing tiles at least forty feet into the air.

Houses left standing were dusted in orange shadows from the dying flames and dust and debris flitted down the street, leaving a caul of white on the pavement.

Gabriel took his fingers from his ears, watched the house come down like a deck of cards, a cap of gray hovering above it like the mushroom cloud of the atom bomb. He knew the police would spend hours agonizing over the blast pattern, thinking it was some kind of homemade incendiary device.

The only thing Gabriel would agonize over was the proof. Was Kenzie finally dead? Had that patronizing, rubber-lipped mouth finally been silenced? He had to admit… a tiny part of him took pleasure in her suffering. He was even a little smug.

Because if that bitch wasn't dead, no amount of cosmetic surgery could replace the face she once had.

ELEVEN

West Albuquerque was a somber pallet of adobe and sandstone, and the sky was beginning to redden between the houses.

Malin inserted the key into the door of her second floor apartment at Puerta de Corrales. Her head was buzzing with modeling agencies and collaged headshots, all with intense, confident gazes she couldn't hope to copy. The reflection that stared back at her in the bathroom mirror only came off as sour and defiant, and she gave up pretending.

Pouring herself a shot of wine, she slumped on the couch, glad to put her feet up after the shift had ended. There was nothing on the TV, thumb tapping the remote control until she settled on the Channel 4 news. A spool of old photographs, house fires where the narrator warned of the dangers of smoking in bed and leaving gas burners unattended.

The phone stuttered in her pocket and she instinctively fumbled for it.

"Isaac Estrada from Midas Mutual," the voice said. "Sorry to call you so late. It's been one hell of a day."

Malin cleared her throat and muttered a cool thanks. It must have been the search warrant that added to that hell-of-a-day and she assumed Mr. Estrada had called Northwest Area Command to verify her credentials. But this late?

"As far as I can make out, Ms. Delgado has received all her monthly payments since September 2008. Paid into Wells Fargo," he said, rattling off a ten digit account number. "They would also know the date of her last withdrawal. I can only tell you the amount the Mutual transfers each month."

"Which is?"

"This is off the record, isn't it?"

That's why he called so late. "Of course."

"$10,000. Is there anything else I can help you with?"

Ten thousand . Malin nearly choked on that bit of news. "No... no, thank you. I think that'll do it."

Listening to the dialing tone for a few seconds, she hung up knowing she would be meeting the manager of Wells Fargo Bank tomorrow morning if she could swing it.

She cracked open the sliding doors to the balcony and breathed in the cool night air. There was a small trickle of water over a palisade of rocks at the front entrance and an owl sitting in the cottonwood, eyes caught in the headlights of a passing car. The road was wet and shiny, reflecting the light from the gas station at the end of the street and Malin could hear the wet hiss of car tires on tarmac. She wondered where Lily was, whether she was missing because she wanted to be, whether she was chained to a wall and crying her eyes out.

The clouds had rolled in during the evening and behind them was a full moon. She refocused on a scatter of rain drops on the glass, closed the sliding door and checked the lock.

Old Man Topper, a neighbor downstairs, had given her the remains of his newspaper. Most of it had been used to dab up an oily mess on his countertop and the salvaged part showed a gutted house on the southeast side of town, leveled in what was originally thought to be a terrorist attack.

Even anchorman, Stan Stockard, pointed to the wreckage on the late night news, saying that no terrorist in his right mind would be interested in a student house off Smith Street, unless he had somehow overshot Kirtland Airforce Base. It was an accidental gas explosion where a young woman had been killed and several residents injured.

A sudden thought gave Malin a jolt. What if Old Man Topper left his gas on? Hopefully, someone would smell it even if he didn't, because he smoked all kinds of things in his bedroom, some of which were still in his mouth when he woke up in the morning.

The cell phone was pinging again. Wingman, the man she had met in a chatroom a few months ago, had sent her a message. No longer willing to risk using email, he had elected to send text messages instead.

Wingman: According to the weather reports it's going to be one humdinger of a January. So I'm going away, my little bird. Going south. How will you manage without me?

Malin shook her head and typed: Better than you think. What in hell's name did he look like? He had to be an old judge according to his vocabulary. Wouldn't want to tell me your real name before you leave?

Wingman: No, I wouldn't. Besides, you'd only despise me and I rather like this anonymity. If you're smart, you'll find out all by yourself. That's the mark of a good detective. Now, if anything should come up, I'll be checking my messages from time to time.

That was comforting, she thought. He'd be checking them late at night when his wife, if he had one, was out of mind. Malin determined he lived in a large house, definitely had three children and a Mexican cook.

She had already tried two options. To open the command console on the computer and run a who-is check on the emails he'd sent and second, to run an internet lookup, both of which resulted in no data available. A cell phone would be easy to trace. The only person she was willing to confide in was Temeke, only he would chastise her for not telling him sooner.

Malin: Would you like to meet?

Why not? What kind of detective wouldn't ask to meet a faceless stranger on the internet. One who had been so helpful with their last case.

Wingman: Nice try, Malin. But we are meeting, in a way. Isn't virtual the thing these days?

Malin: Not very original, is it?

Not very personal either. It was getting boring tapping out texts. So much quicker on the phone. So much more revealing in person. And why not get a court order and get it over with? The back of her neck felt clammy despite the chill and her fingers lingered on the keys.

Wingman: I'll get straight to the point. The man you're looking for has an unnatural interest in Temeke.

Malin felt her throat tighten, stretched her fingers and then began to type: Unnatural?

Wingman: I knew you'd hang onto that word. Use your talent, dear heart. It's all in the details. You're just starting to get the hang of this caper. Starting to get that fire in your belly. Our perp is in for a treat.

Our was a word they commonly used when a case pulled at the heart strings, Malin thought. Putting it before a name meant only one thing. Wingman was associated with law enforcement.

He was quiet then, waiting for her next move. She decided to change tack. Do you know the perp?

Wingman: I never really know them. It's always guesswork.

Name? she asked.

Wingman: Tut, tut. We've been over this before.

Malin: Height, weight. Why not arrest him yourself?

Wingman: He wasn't doing anything wrong.

Malin: Then why worry?

Wingman: Because he will, Malin. This one's a little green-eyed, tipped right over the edge. Dangerous place to be. Would you like to be Unit Commander one day? Supervising Northwest Area Command and representing the police department on various committees and boards.

Malin: No.

Wingman: How about a pay increase? Let's consider doubling that $58,000 you currently earn.

How the heck did he know that! I've done the money thing. It's not all it's cracked up to be. Captain Fowler's looking for a break. Why not give it to him?

Wingman: You wouldn't want that. And anyway, there's no shortage of volunteers, but I need someone with good discernment, intellect. Someone who has a passion for the job. Nice office, leather chair, your own admin.

Malin felt her eyes stinging from the strain of it all and wanted to sign off. I don't have the experience. Bottom of the food chain.

Wingman: That's not what I said, Malin.

Malin: So you'd push me in the deep end and expect me to swim?

Wingman: The alternative is pushing paper until you're sixty-seven and that's only if you last that long.

She didn't care for a nice office or a leather chair, or someone to type her reports. She looked around the small apartment and rather enjoyed the fact that the entire complex was run by an office manager and all she had to do was pick up the phone.

To pull all this off, Wingman had to be the Chief of Police, Governor Bendish, the Attorney General, the Mayor… She wasn't going to beg him for information, because by then it would be too late to rebuild her usual poised image and she was determined to have the last word.

Malin: Guesswork. You're in your late fifties, early sixties. Wear a suit and a tie, probably earn around $80,000. Can't be Commander Hackett because he's got a soft spot for Temeke. But you could be the DA.

She signed off giving him no time to protest. There was something in his manner, the speech pattern, which led her to believe she had met him in court. Not Hackett, since his notoriously bad spelling was bound to emerge in a message.

The DA. Because he disliked Temeke enough to remove him from the state and he was high up enough to swing it.

TWELVE

Temeke was glad to be home, shrugged off his coat and dumped the book on the couch. There was a strong smell of ammonia in the air and something told him it was likely to linger for days.

The cat lay on its belly on an easy chair, paws curled inwards and tail flicking from side to side. He seemed to be staring intently at the floor, where his bowl had not been filled since morning.

There were clumps of dirt on the carpet and shredded cigarette papers, and Temeke followed the trail to the potted plant where a large hole had been dug in the soil. He sniffed repeatedly. The cat wasn't about to let him use the plant as an ashtray without covering the hole with half a pound of excrement.

"Just my bloody luck," he muttered, looking around for an antiseptic wipe.

Thursday afternoon had been spent in the admissions office at Gibson. A Mr. Fiennes had been evasive until he was acquainted with Temeke's badge. He smiled a little too much after that, said Lily Delgado was a bright young woman with a bright young future.

Temeke stripped the clear film from a fresh pack of cigarettes, lit up and lay back against the couch with a sigh. He glanced at the book shelf, at the reading lamp that hovered like a decorative shower attachment over a reading chair, at the binoculars on the window sill and the book on the seat next to him. Then he filled his lungs with smoke, held it for a few seconds before releasing. His mouth was coated with a sour nicotine flavor and he was convinced his tongue was coated in fur. All he could hear was the dry wheeze of the boiler and a dog barking outside. And he couldn't think straight.

Strange how clear the moon was, how bright. It reminded him of a bleak 1922 silent movie where a young man, who was about to go on a long journey to help a count find a house in a fictitious German city, was told *what matter if it costs you some pain – or even a little blood?*

He couldn't stand the silence, pulled the cell phone out of his pocket and decided to call Malin.

"These killings weren't done by a bunch of thugs out on a Saturday night ramble, Marl. And as for the Syndicato de Gato Negro, they wouldn't waste time with such elaborate crimes."

"The SGN have a pattern, sir, certain procedures that don't fit in this case."

Like a smear of peanut butter over a corpse for wild animals to scent, Temeke thought. The perps were fools if they thought a partly devoured body could never be identified.

"Which leaves only one possibility," he said. "A contract killing."

"I have a question. Do you remember the Pardoe case?"

Temeke blew out a jet of smoke as he sorted through his thoughts. "The perpetrator who was so distraught after losing his wife to cancer he killed the doctor who diagnosed the symptoms?"

"Yeah, that one."

"As I remember it, he claimed a mysterious woman drove to his house and offered him magical powers to get over his sorrow. He also said he was possessed by a *familiar*. The house in question stood in the heart of a dense wood surrounded by a high wall, gates secured with padlocks. It could only be accessed by a footpath, which meant the man received few callers and was lying through his bloody teeth."

"But you can't deny the demon theory isn't a possibility in the Delgado case," she said.

"I never thought it was a shaft of lightning up his ass if that's what you mean."

"The thing is, if our killer has a *familiar* then he's arguing with the devil. And maybe he's had years of practice. Mix that with drugs and you've got a legal combination."

"I'll read the sodding book tonight and get back to you in the morning."

The room went quiet after he ended the call and he stared at the book on the couch, thinking of every excuse not to open it.

There was enough mystery in the Delgado case, enough lies and deception to keep the police guessing. But whatever had gone wrong all those years ago started when Alice bought that damned book.

Everything's a racket, he told himself, relishing the feel of soft leather and wondering if the girls swore a bond on the book. He might have known he'd have to delve into folklore and magic at some point in his career. After all, crime was full of nutcases who claimed they had been possessed by a demon and then admitted afterwards it was all a bad joke.

It was a fine looking book, pages musty and stale after their long entombment in Baca's top drawer. Seven endorsements from local publications in the front matter and an author's note in the back.

Dr. Fatima Gupta (1901-1997) founded the Lilin in 1934, a sisterhood dedicated to the world's oldest traditions and symbolic disciplines, an organization that exalted Satan.

In her long career, Dr. Gupta's knowledge in the fields of philosophy, spiritualism and psychology have earned her fifty-seven awards worldwide and a doctorate in philosophy at Gibson University. The Lilin Esoterica represents a lifetime of research into symbolism, demonology and mythology.

Dr. Gupta's hope was to dispel the myth that women were the weaker sex in society. To educate them on how to ignite the divine spark and become conquerors of the universe.

Temeke poked the cigarette between his lips and turned the page. The prologue gave a brief description of a demon who was said to be a teacher of astronomy and liberal arts, and whose sigil was a wolf vomiting fire. He was also a psychic and a spell caster, and with credentials like these Temeke half wondered if the demon could solve the case for him.

He turned to chapter one.

There is a place high up in the mountains where the snow meets the sun and a woman can touch the moon. This is where her familiar lives.

To become a sister of the Lilin, a woman must summon a familiar and make herself mistress of everything in the world, evil as well as good, pain as well as pleasure, cruelty as well as mercy. Only then will she be in perfect balance to the power of infinity.

A blackened log stirred in the fireplace and crashed onto the hearth. It gave Temeke a jolt, took him a while to adjust his breathing as he flicked the remainder of the cigarette into the hearth. In his mind, he could hear his own voice asking if the book had any link to these killings. Because if it did, it threw a huge wrench into the "contract" theory.

The cat was scratching the paint off the front door, meowing and making a racket. Temeke remembered seeing a miniature dog jacket in the hall closet, one that had once belonged to Serena's toy poodle. It would keep the bugger warm.

He wrapped the Velcro bindings around the cat's belly, opened the front door and watched a blaze of red shoot down the driveway and shimmy up a tree. Temeke stood there shivering for a time, then closed the front door and poured himself a large whisky.

How much of this witchy malarkey did Valerie Delgado believe? Poor old cow, he thought. Just when she was getting over her eldest, the youngest had gone and done a runner.

He lay back on the couch, picked up the book and paged through the table of contents. Six short chapters named for each the sisterhood.

Longed For, Light of the Moon, The Bright One, Garden of Roses, Mountain of Light, and Like A Star.

Leafing to the final chapter entitled *Destiny of a Servant,* he was interrupted suddenly by a continual barking. Not a greeting sound when a dog senses the arrival of family, or a cat up a tree, but a warning signal.

Crooking the book under one arm, he walked over to the window and glanced at next door's dog. It was tied to a long leash, nose pointing at the ground.

He caught sight of a figure beneath a tree and if he wasn't mistaken, the person appeared to be examining his front door through a wide angle lens. Swapping the book for a pair of binoculars, Temeke fiddled with the focusing wheel and found he was mistaken. The man was staring right at him, and no sooner had Temeke focused both barrels simultaneously than the figure darted into the shadows.

Bloody teenagers.

He berated himself for not closing the blinds and for reading the stupid book in the first place. He should have taken the sodding thing to forensics.

His cell phone vibrated against the coffee table and he clamped it to his ear. "Go ahead, Luis."

"Two things. Hackett's pissed about the article in the *Journal* this morning. It leads the public to believe there's a body in the mountains. Why can't you keep your mouth shut, bro?"

Why not indeed. "Don't tell me, the bloody Peak Tram's being going up and down like a pimp's zipper."

"Listen. I just had a call from Southeast Area Command. Student on Cornell Drive sounded worried. Her roommate's gone missing. Said it wasn't like her to leave without telling someone."

"When did her roommate go missing?"

"Two days ago."

"South*east* Area Command, you say? Why us?"

"Ms. Martinez received an email from her roommate this morning—"

"So she's not missing?"

"…Saying if Ms. Martinez wanted to find her, she was to call Detective Temeke. Looks like you're being spread a little wider this time, bud."

Temeke raised his eyebrows and checked his watch. "On my way."

THIRTEEN

214 Cornell Drive was a standard ranch home, long and squat and overlooked Loma Linda Park on the southeast side of town. There were two cars parked outside, a Toyota 4Runner and an Audi two-door coupe. Both dark gray, both fairly new. Temeke walked to the front door, ground the remains of a cigarette under his shoe and rang the bell.

He drifted back to a time early in his training when he had been sent to a workshop to learn new interrogation techniques. Back in 1986, three FBI agents had drawn up a nine-step approach to an effective interrogation. It had been latterly thought unreliable and responsible for false confessions. It was the fifth step Temeke rather liked. Physically touching a suspect got their attention, but maintaining eye contact and using a first name invariably got results.

He heard the squeak of a raw hinge and showed his badge to a tiny crack of light. "Detective Temeke," he said.

A young woman with long disheveled hair stood in the hallway, reading glasses perched on the end of a thin nose. He shot one hand out to shake hers, estimated about five feet eight inches and one hundred and thirty pounds under black yoga pants and a sweater. She introduced herself as Adel Martinez, make-up slightly smudged beneath one eye.

A dead ball of mistletoe brushed the top of his head as he followed her into the first reception room, larger than he expected with a fireplace on one side and a small grand piano on the other. Both the brown leather couch and the easy chair were covered with fleece blankets, likely hiding a few holes if student housing was anything to go by.

"It's just not like her," Adel said, heaving a sigh and looking at him with those pale, gray eyes. "She missed a piano recital on Tuesday night."

"What's her name?" Temeke partially unzipped his jacket but didn't take it off.

Adel sat on the couch, legs tightly together. She offered him the chair and a recent photograph. "Asha... Asha Samadi."

Temeke didn't need the photograph. He could still picture the stage, the piano, the girl, and he could still hear the piece if he thought about it. What he needed was a stiff drink and he was suddenly having trouble breathing. The name was on every tongue, every billboard, and the last place he heard it was in Los Poblanos Academy archives.

"When did you last see her?"

"Saturday morning."

"Any idea where she might have gone?"

"There's this guy she likes... Paddy Brody. He sent her flowers on Friday." Adel's eyebrows jumped a little when she mentioned the flowers.

"Was there a card?" he asked.

"There were two. I don't have the first one. It said *you light my life* or something like that, all typewritten with handwriting on the back. I didn't recognize it."

Just like any florists card, thought Temeke. The only difference was the handwriting which would signify the order was made in the store rather than over the phone.

"Was it signed?"

"With the letter *P*. That's what made me think it was

Paddy." There was a gleam in her eyes, cold and dark. "Said he wanted to see Asha around eight o'clock."

"How well do you know Mr. Brody?"

He watched the twitch in her bottom lip and she seemed to limit herself to a nod. He'd ask for the second card later.

"He's my ex."

"And you were OK with him dating your roommate?"

"I'm over him."

Her voice sounded so serious Temeke had to smile. He needed a moment to digest each feature and to understand why Paddy Brody had ditched her in favor of Asha. Here was a slim young woman with eyes that tapered out to the sides, beauty of which many women could only dream. She was elegant and in a class of her own.

"Where were you on Saturday night?"

"Staying with a girlfriend."

Why not a boyfriend? he thought, watching the direction of her gaze which seemed to scoot up and down his chest. "Your friend's name?"

"Sarah Hughes."

"Description?"

"Heavy set. Black... mixed parentage."

"Nothing's ever black or white." Temeke got a smile then and forced himself back into focus. "Address?"

"She lives a few streets away. Columbia Drive. But I wanted to give Asha some time alone."

"How long have you known Sarah?" Temeke took a small pad of paper from his jacket pocket, wrote a couple of words and pretended to write a few more. She was still looking at him.

"I met her at Gibson. So... four months."

Not long enough to form a strong bond, Temeke thought, and to voice any suspicions now would be premature. "And Asha?"

"We were at school together."

Temeke felt a sudden rush as she said it, felt the nudge of a few questions burning in his mind. How well had she known the Delgado sisters? How jealous was she of Asha? Instead he settled on, "You didn't think of calling the police sooner?"

"It was this," she said, pulling the second card out of the waistband of her pants. "I found it on the mantel the next day... in place of the other one. I thought they were pulling my leg. Run off, you know. Then Paddy called. Asked me if I'd seen Asha. That's what made me worry."

"Anyone else you know with the initial *P*?" he said, turning the warm card over in his hand.

"No."

"Any signs of a struggle when you came home? Overturned furniture, that kind of thing?"

"No, it was the same as when I left."

Temeke read the card. It was a vulgar rendition of the William Tell Overture – typewritten – only this time larger than the standard and without a florist's logo.

A possible scenario shot through his mind. Worst case, the first card had been left to bait Asha into believing she had a date. The second card was a ploy to keep Adel from calling the police. It would certainly buy the kidnapper a few more days.

"Mind if I have this?" He waited for her to say yes, would have taken it anyway even if she hadn't.

He pulled out an evidence bag from a stack of several in his jacket pocket, logged the chain of possession, name and description and then bagged the card.

"Did you call her. Text her?"

"She left her phone in her room. So I emailed. Haven't heard anything. Called her dad too and now he's worried."

"Anything missing?"

"Her laptop, a hand towel and the shower curtain. We didn't bring much. So I'd notice if there was anything else. These houses are so run down. Old neighborhoods, you know," she said, as if that explained everything. "I was hoping she'd be back in time for the funeral. She doesn't even know."

"Funeral?"

"A school friend of ours died in an accident. The funeral's this weekend."

Temeke was about to give his condolences when she got up abruptly and disappeared into the kitchen. She came back with an iPad, placed it on the coffee table and swiveled it toward him.

"She sent this email yesterday."

Temeke gave the message a cursory glance.

Hey Dello, just wanted you to be the first to know. I'm in heaven. Love's a dream. Lost my key so took the spare. Can you pay the rent until I get back?

"Does she always call you Dello?" He saw the quick nod.

"I told her I was worried about the recital and I asked her when she was coming back."

"You also told her she was a bitch. That's what it says here." He pointed at the one word response before the second email about the recital.

"What am I supposed to do? Pay for everything until she gets back? It's a scam."

Temeke saw the frown, the sudden flinch. He continued to check the most recent incoming and outgoing emails. Two one-liners from Asha asking Adel not to forget to put out the trash and to keep an eye on her car.

He wanted to shrug it off as a young woman's desire to be alone, to escape the humdrum of everyday life, but it was the final email that made his skin prickle.

If you need anything, ask Detective Temeke.

Temeke wondered why Asha would have singled him out and he began to pant slightly through a half-open mouth. They had never met.

"Taking her laptop's a good thing though, isn't it?" Adel said. "It means she knew she was going away for a while?"

Temeke felt his head bouncing on the stem of his neck, if only to reassure her. Said he'd have to take the iPad so they could monitor the emails.

"Music's her life." Adel stared at her feet, hands tucked under both thighs. "There's no way she would have missed that recital, not with a scholarship."

"So you're saying this email isn't from her?"

"It just doesn't sound like her."

All Temeke could do was read it again, sensing a faint nudge of unease. Unless Adel could come up with anything else, he wasn't entirely convinced. "Sometimes people want to be alone."

"She left her car. You can't be serious?"

As a heart attack, Temeke wanted to say, but glanced instead at the email. He was aware she was studying him from head to toe and assessing if he was going to linger too long or leave abruptly. He decided on the latter.

"Just one more thing. Can I look at her room?"

Adel nodded and showed him to a small room with a queen sized bed, a single sash window to the front street and another window that looked out on the east side.

A black cell phone lay on the desk, red light blinking from two incoming texts.

"Those are from me," Adel said. "That's how I knew she'd left her phone."

Asha's purse was on the chair, music stand by the wall, a closet full of clothes. Evening dresses mostly. No signs of a struggle, nothing extraordinary except for a hint of jasmine that hung in the air as if she had only just left.

"Music scores," he said. "Where does she keep

those?"

"In here." Adel retrieved an open leather case from behind the door bulging with sheet music.

Temeke gave a curt nod and peered out of the east window at the house next door. "Clothes, make-up... money?"

"I don't think there's anything missing."

He glanced into the Jack-and-Jill bathroom, saw the medicine cabinet and an empty blister pack of pills in the trash can. "Couldn't get me a glass of water, could you?"

When Adel sauntered into the kitchen Temeke took a photo of that blister pack with his cell phone. He then opened the medicine cabinet. Makeup, toothpaste, floss, skin cream, Omeprazole, 20 milligram capsule, yellow and white. Name, Adel Martinez. Eleven refills before 9/9/12.

Out of date, he thought, popping off the cap and pocketing a few. He heard the light thud of Adel's footsteps and stepped back into Asha's bedroom.

"Your room untouched?" he asked, taking the glass she offered him. Two sips of tepid water and he left the rest on the dressing table.

"Yes. Everything looks the same."

Temeke took her word for it. He wasn't about to go rooting around in the girl's drawers, but he advised a female officer would come back later and that's what she'd do.

"Let me know if Asha contacts you," he said, making a point of looking at his watch. He handed her his card and took the iPad. "The school you attended. Was it here in Albuquerque?"

"Los Poblanos Academy. It's on Rio Grande."

Temeke turned his back on her, zipped the jacket up to his chin and headed for the front door. He began digging around in the various compartments of his brain for a motive for Asha's disappearance. Ditching a piano recital was hardly the most efficient way to raise a grade and Asha didn't seem like the quitting kind.

The spongy rise beneath his feet caused him to look down at a Persian rug, a plush pattern of red, white and black. "Nice carpet."

"It's a prayer mat," Adel corrected. "Asha's father bought it for her."

"Does she use it?"

"No," Adel shook her head and gave a half laugh.

His eyes followed the weave where he noticed a slight fault in one of the florals on the short axis. It was red instead of white.

Stopping in the narrow hallway, he examined pale eyes behind square rimmed glasses. "You might remember the Delgado sisters at school. Alice and Lily."

Adel grimaced it seemed with sad recollection. "You know Alice died?"

Temeke nodded, said that he did. He told her Lily was missing, had been for weeks.

Adel's frown was sudden, eyes wide. "But I only saw her last week. In the library on Wednesday night, I think. And then the Frontier for lunch the next day. We didn't speak. We never do."

Temeke felt the goosebumps prickle. "Any idea where she might have gone? Who she hangs out with?"

"No. She's always alone."

Temeke's mind began to race, blood pumping in his ears. Bloody hell, was this possible? A missing girl eating lunch and reading books in a public place? He gathered his senses as he opened the front door, realizing he didn't have anything yet. Nothing concrete at least.

"I'll send officer Watts over in the morning. She'll need a list of all the items missing." He turned back to face her. "Ever heard of a book called *The Lilin Esoterica*?"

The eyes were no longer heavy-lidded, quite the

opposite. They were alert and the comment had ignited a spark.

"A book that empowers women," she said.

"Where did you get it?"

"Alice bought it. Said we should try it."

Temeke wanted to ask her if she believed in it, but he decided to leave it for another day. Wanted to see if she would be quite as accommodating the next time he called.

"If you think of anything else, you'll let me know?"

Her eyes suddenly widened and she snapped her fingers. "I forgot! The poker... the one by the fireplace. It's missing."

FOURTEEN

Gabriel shrugged on his jacket and snapped the fasteners of his black leather gloves. Cradling an oblong object wrapped in a plastic bag, he walked toward the back entrance of the café on Fourth Street.

The Fat Mule was his usual haunt and it would do as long as the ape hangers didn't give him sideways looks, mouthing obscenities and squeezing empty beer cans with one hand. He threw the object in the flatbed of a nearby truck and grinned as he did it.

Collapsing with a big sigh on a hard bench, he couldn't feel his legs and all he could hear was a drone of conversation on the far side of the room. Looking around, his senses began to soak up every atom. Five aging bikers at a corner table, two of them stroking handlebar moustaches and staring at him as if he had no clothes on.

Gabriel continued to look out of the restaurant window at a cornfield with rolling ruts and red dirt. He could hardly see it in the dark, only as far as the light from the windows would allow. But he could imagine the endless rows of brittle stalks and the secret trails that ran between them. A meeting place. A hiding place.

He almost smiled at the attention he received, watching the old men from the corner of his eye, knowing with half a chance they'd beat him up in the bathrooms. He combed a hand through his hair, black and shiny and almost down to his shoulder. Except for light brown eyes, he could easily pass for Hispanic.

He saw the detective three days ago in the school parking lot. Studied him from the confines of his van. The same man who caused a lump in Gabriel's throat and a heart that threatened to stop beating. Saw him on TV a few times, and then followed him to a white house bordered with cottonwoods on Guadalupe Trail. Found a derelict house nearby so he could breathe in the same air. There wasn't much Gabriel could determine from under that tree in the darkness and he assumed the detective lived alone like he did.

"You can't be loved by everyone," Demon whispered.

Gabriel took no notice. Instead, he couldn't stop thinking about the detective framed behind that window, a dark silhouette in front of a reading lamp. He wanted to take a photograph to keep the memory locked on paper, but there hadn't been enough light. The house was wired for movement, two strobe lights flashing on the closer he got, not to mention the incessant barking from next door's dog.

There would be other times, other ways to get the book. And besides, Demon had wings. Why couldn't he just fly in there and get it himself?

"Don't be stupid. The Hierarchy don't have wings," Demon muttered.

No, the Hierarchy had bodies like humans, spoke like them too. You could pass one in the street, sit next to one on an airplane and never know it. It was the Inferus, the lesser kind, that fluttered about over rooftops and perched in trees.

A sudden prick of sadness when Gabriel remembered Los Poblanos Academy and the familiar scents of a place he once called home. Alice Delgado, suicide girl, was still there, somewhere. Her spirit wandered along those trails where trees arched overhead like a series of spiny tunnels and where crickets pulsed in the summertime. It would have been green and fragrant with honeysuckle then. But it was winter now and everything was dead.

"Coffee?"

Gabriel bit the inside of his cheek as he looked up at the waitress. Late fifties, blonde hair tied up in a messy do, flabby cheeks and a little too much makeup. He mumbled a yes.

"Looks like you're in love," the waitress said, leaning forward a little and flashing those deep brown eyes. "It's one thing when they're good to you. It's another when the world's full of trash like mine."

She didn't wait for a response. Just shuffled off to the other tables, smiled, poured more coffee and then brought him a cup. The air in the room suddenly turned gray and it was difficult to breathe.

Gabriel wiped his hands on his jeans, wrapped them around the coffee mug and leaned back against a vinyl bench. It was nicest thing anyone had said to him in a long while. The waitress was right. The world was full of trash. Except the detective. Simply put, he was magic.

"Take your time," Demon said, interrupting his thoughts. "Watch for signs."

"What signs?" Gabriel whispered, eyes restlessly wandering over the heads of the people in the coffee shop.

"See those men? Who do you think they're staring at?"

The floor seemed to open up and Gabriel felt he was falling, spinning, heat rising in his face. He jerked back against the bench, unconsciously shaking his head as if trying to dismiss the stares.

He began to enjoy that bitter tasting coffee, wondering if it was worth asking the heavily jowled lady behind the counter to give him a fresh cup. Only he'd have to stand then, walk in front of the gawking bikers and watch them size him up out of the corner of his eye.

He was fit, but he wasn't overly muscular. No matter how many weights he lifted, how many sets, how many repetitions, his body would never be like theirs, stocky and well fed. He hadn't the stomach for it.

He fumbled through his pockets and retrieved a wad of crumpled toilet paper, gave his nose a loud blow and coughed a few times. The two staring bikers resumed their friendly chatter, hands instinctively covering their mouths.

"Can you believe it," Demon said. "Men always stare. Size each other up. They even stare at women as if they're the last goal in a football match."

Gabriel studied his coffee. He couldn't remember what he was doing there, couldn't remember where his car was parked either.

It was Demon that made him forget. In hindsight, he knew he shouldn't have opened his mind in the first place, shouldn't have caved in to the fear.

Demon had turned him into someone he no longer recognized and, like a drug, he had chemically reprogramed Gabriel's brain, his loyalties, his interests, even his loved ones. Memories faded away into the past and all that mattered was the next high. He craved Demon more and more, and he knew if he had a few days without him his mind came back in flashes, if it ever came back at all.

I can't go on, he thought, can't keep killing. Weren't two deaths enough?

"Two down, three to go." Demon reminded, nails clacking on the table top. "Remember what they did to you. Remember how it was. Onwards and upwards."

"What if I get caught?" Gabriel whispered.

"Then you'll be incarcerated in one of New Mexico's finest correctional facilities and you wouldn't like that, would you? Wouldn't like all the—"

"No, no, don't say it!" Gabriel begged. The images were bad enough.

The bikers fell into silence, fingers raking their

nicotine stained beards. They were all looking at him now, wondering why he was talking to himself, wondering why his hand was suddenly in front of his face, head lowered.

"Get away from me!" Gabriel whispered to the seat next to him.

He could feel warm breath on the inside of his hand, feel the vibration of his voice. If Demon didn't go away he'd threaten him with a name. The pastor on 19th, the one who had counseled him at school.

"Remember the rules," Demon reminded. "No pastors, no prayers. Or there'll be no peace."

Demon was always full of rage and fire, and the pastor's name always seemed to whet down the kindling. Gabriel was beginning to feel like an actor in a poorly directed film, where he was standing on an empty street without a bullet proof vest. For some reason Demon had been voted in all those years ago and he'd been a dictator ever since.

Gabriel was halfway out of his chair when the whole room began to lurch. He waited, felt the ground harden beneath his feet and tried again. This time he made it to the door, stepped out onto the low concrete step and didn't look back. He knew they were watching, stroking those long gray beards and wondering what he was all about. That was the trouble. They'd remember him if they were asked.

Pulling out of the parking lot, he veered sharply onto Alameda, headed west along a familiar stretch of road that would have led to a familiar house. All he could think about was Asha's laptop, tucked away in his bedroom and wrapped with an extension cord.

He wanted to see how many emails there were because he'd already replied to a few of them. Kept the momentum going, kept up the pretense.

Too many deaths in one week would only arouse suspicion and the girls would be missed in a day or two.

Better take a break and breathe in some good fresh air. Better rethink the whole thing, because the detective had been asking questions at the school. And that could only mean one thing.

"Number three," Demon said with a melodic giggle. "A car drowning I think. Poor little *chinless*. She's there every Friday night."

"Where?" Gabriel's mind was scrabbling for a reason to slow down. He could read Demon's face without turning. It was like a sunny spot in a cloudy sky, lips set, cheeks dimpled. Everything was a game to him, the more intricate the better.

"The cycling path under Alameda Bridge," Demon said. "Nice and quiet."

"You can't get a car anywhere close to the river."

"There is a place. On the bank. No concrete wheel stop. Clean drop all the way to the water."

"I need time."

"Time for what? For the detective? Looks like you'll have to kill him too."

Gabriel took one hand off the steering wheel so he could flip a finger. "You're actually jealous."

"I'm actually worried."

Gabriel had his own theory but he said nothing. Demon had been by his side since school, cold limbs clutching and cleaving like ivy to brick. "You wouldn't like it if I found another friend, would you?"

There was no reply from the passenger seat, not even a whimper as they turned right into the parking lot.

Damn him for showing up as someone familiar. All dark ones do that. Nothing new. But Demon had to be handsome, had to be the legend plastered in everyone's subconscious, the one you couldn't ignore. And now he sat there in silence for once, all because he couldn't think of anything to say.

"I could lock myself in a room," Gabriel blurted.

"Course you'd try to get in. But you wouldn't have much luck if I renounced you."

"You're being flippant now."

"You don't exist."

Gabriel tried to rationalize how it all happened. How a bond was sworn over a secret book and how that same bond could so easily be broken.

I renounce and forsake the master demon and his false claims of allegiance.

That night, six women dismissed reason, sense and sanity for a touch of the absurd. Just to see if it worked. To see if it was real.

I renounce the spirit that has made me a slave to drugs and destruction.

The pendulum swung from hard right to hard left. Their lives would never be normal again because Demon had the power to kill them. Hadn't he proved it with the first three?

I renounce the evil one who has filled me with hatred. The one who manipulates and controls.

Alice, Asha and Kenzie were dead. Rosa, Zarah and Adel were almost. In these six women Gabriel had created family, a distant memory he kept in his head. But he had been the victim, the one they hated, the brilliant one they didn't understand. The pain still stung sharp just as it had at school.

Drowning? Rosa? It suddenly made no sense. She was an opera singer. Got lungs larger than a blue whale.

I renounce the fear that has held me captive.

Like a fever, the nightmare broke and Gabriel began to feel a strange sense of control, if only for a moment.

"Rosa Belmonte," he whispered, pushing his foot hard on the gas. "Let's hear you sing."

FIFTEEN

Malin studied the Los Poblanos Year Book and stared at a row of smiling heads. Her skin prickled as she focused on Asha, the young woman they had not yet found.

Adel's email yielded one message from Asha in the last twenty-four hours. She had been asking about her car. Malin typed out a response on that iPad, told her everything was good and asked when she was coming home. There had been no reply since.

Mass alerts had been issued to the media and the New Mexico Department of Transportation had distributed a picture of Asha on all the state highway billboards. Someone must have seen her.

Malin sensed a rush of apprehension as she plugged search criteria for similar homicides into a computer VICAP form – the Violent Criminal Apprehension Program and the FBI's database of crimes countrywide. The NCIC database yielded a list of missing persons, twenty-one females between the ages of fifteen and twenty-five reported missing in Bernalillo and Sandoval Counties. She added the list to the file.

Taking a deep breath, she felt a prick of pain under her ribs. *Need to get out in the fresh air and start exercising again.* "Need to find Asha first," she muttered.

Tucking the photographs of the Delgado girls under one arm, along with a copy of *Glamor* magazine, she walked down the corridor and knocked on the frame of

Luis' open door.

It was one forty-five on Friday afternoon and her eyes were sore. What with Temeke calling her last night about his interview with Adel Martinez she'd had little sleep. Temeke had advised Adel to stay with a friend on Columbia Drive and Malin hoped she was OK.

She studied the lieutenant as his voice rose one minute and fell the next, telephone crooked against his shoulder. He played a toothpick between his fingers and heaved a weary sigh.

"We're not that nosy down here, you know. Not like Homicide," Luis said to the person on the other end of the phone.

Malin slid into the vacant chair without being asked, crossed her legs and suppressed a yawn. On the desk was a file labeled *Performance Evaluations* and another labeled *Leave Requests*. Otherwise, the desk was tidy so he could keep a clear head and only a computer and a large bowl of fruit told you someone actually worked there. A healthy somebody who kept a vegetable garden in his spare time.

"Offensive? What part of the article was offensive?" Luis began to laugh. "Well, that's as maybe, but he's a cracker under fire and we haven't had a detective quite like him... Yeah, yeah, yeah, so it was a little unconventional, but he knows what aspects mark a serial killer, sir, what methods."

Luis rolled his eyes at Malin and mouthed the name of an old case they'd put to bed before Christmas.

"Those victims weren't selected at random, sir. Temeke always said the murder was motive enough... Cornell Drive's blocked with what?" Luis covered the phone and jutted his chin at Malin. "Criminalistics motorhome." He listened some more and nodded. "Yeah, well brains run in his family, sir. You should have met his mother... Doesn't trust you? Must be your suit, Chief...

How much did you say? Three grand!"

Malin felt the giggle in her gut and grinned at Luis as he put the phone down. He held his breath and then let it out in one long hiss. "That's one big sweepstake they've got going on. He'll never do it."

"I bet he does. He never misses a trick."

Luis waved a hand and looked down at the file on his desk. "Ms. Samadi's car is with forensics, an Audi coupe. Nice ride. Nice and clean. Temeke found a few pills in Adel's medicine cabinet. Adderall. Not the medication the doctor had given her. Any new messages on that iPad?"

"One from Asha asking Adel where her car had gone."

"Which means whoever's got Asha's laptop is keeping an eye on her house."

"Which also means they know *we're* keeping an eye on the place, sir."

"Suggesting if they're playing a dangerous game with law enforcement they might want to pack it in." Luis dropped a search warrant on the desk. "This is for you. Ask for Mr. Hanlon when you get to the bank. Heavy set, balding. He's expecting you."

Malin wasn't looking forward to spending her afternoon at Wells Fargo, but she knew if she stared at the photograph of Alice and Lily one more time, she'd wear her eyes out. There was something in Alice's expression that bothered her, a stirring in that age-old memory that refused to rise to the surface.

She placed the photographs and the magazine on Luis' desk and tapped them with two fingers.

"You recognize the older girl." She waited for him to nod. "This is the younger sister. Also featured on the front cover of this magazine."

Luis frowned and rubbed the sides of an open mouth with thumb and forefinger, eyes narrowed as if he was mentally computing the face in a bank of many.

Malin flicked through the pages and showed him three full length photographs submitted by Orion Modeling. "A private show in Beverly Hills. Here, she's dressed in a pant suit and in these two, she's in a Sorrento evening gown. Her hair's longer and blonde at the ends. It's called an Ombré."

Luis leaned forward a little. He stared at the magazine silently for a moment and then looked up and frowned. "So, she plays dress up and sells clothes."

"Your sister was a model with Orion," Malin said, reluctant to say the name of Temeke's ex-wife. "How often did she do catwalk?"

"Started when she was fourteen, dresses with splits up the back and down the front. Mom threw a fit and made her go to college. Then she met you-know-who and that was that."

Malin caught a glimpse of something in her memory, a face, a pose, someone she had run into recently but couldn't recall. The cell phone buzzed in her pocket and whatever it was that clicked inside her head shattered at the sound. It was Temeke.

"Lieutenant Alvarez is looking for you," she said.

"Tell that crafty old buzzard I'll be back in ten minutes," Temeke barked over a car horn. "Oh, and tell him I'll get my report to him this afternoon."

Malin gave Luis a tight nod to convey the message and then turned her attention back to Temeke. "I've got an appointment this afternoon with the manager of Wells Fargo, sir. About Lily Delgado's account."

"Oh, not that fat, balding man with shifty eyes. Make sure you get a flaming statement," chopped in Temeke. "And make sure you take some breath mints. It can get bloody rank in there."

Malin ended the call, wishing she hadn't pressed the speaker button. She lost her train of thought and caught Luis cackling.

"Chief wants to can him," Luis whispered. "Asked me to give a *below average* on his performance evaluation. Truth is he exceeds expectations. You both do."

"Thank you, sir."

"So, I'm asking you to talk to him. In confidence. Ask him to tone down the sarcasm, because people here don't understand it. And ask him to give a little appreciation to where he's working."

"He's just teasing, sir."

"I know that. You know that. But everyone else finds it offensive. Might want to take him the HR manual. Give him a refresher."

"Talking of offensive, sir." Malin played Luis the tape of Fowler. Watched two eyes narrow to slits and a heavily knitted brow.

"It's time Hackett made a few decisions about him he should have made a long time ago."

"You and I both know that'll never happen."

"Keep it between us," Luis whispered, "but Hackett received a complaint from Mrs. Delgado yesterday. He was mad alright."

All the way to the parking lot, Malin couldn't help feeling lightheaded. Fowler was in for a treat. She also wondered how Temeke had managed to stay employed for as long as he had, why even the hard nuts in Homicide turned a cold shoulder, snickered behind his back. They were jealous, that's all. He'd make a great chief of police, she thought, and then laughed out loud.

She nodded at Hackett and Fowler as they sauntered toward her, tried to force a smile at the takeout boxes from Marcello's Chop House. On the way to the bank, she picked up a microwaved pasta dish from Smiths and ate it in the car with a plastic spoon.

The front foyer was bright and empty, and a teller dressed in a black suit waved her over with a smile. Two girls stood behind, eyes glistening and hands covering a bout of snorting. Whatever the joke was, the teller lifted her chin and chose to ignore it.

"Bernard Hanlon," Malin said, sliding her badge under the window. "I'm a bit early, but he's expecting me."

She was ushered down a narrow corridor, eyes instinctively drawn to a Post-it note that had become stuck to the back of the teller's skirt. There was a question mark written in black sharpie and as to the meaning, Malin could only guess.

Bernard Hanlon interlaced his hands and rested them on his oversized paunch. A round face and three chins, Malin counted, with a fourth secreted behind a navy blue tie. His lips were thick and moist, and an occasional spray of spittle found its way to the blotter on his desk.

"Detective Santiago. Thank you for seeing me," she said, popping a Tic-Tac in her mouth.

"You must understand," he began, "this is all very unethical. Law enforcement or no law enforcement, I'm not in the habit of revealing the particulars of a customer's bank account."

"But you are in the habit of conforming to a search warrant," she said, dropping the envelope on the soggy blotter. "I would like hard copies of all her statements. My lieutenant called ahead. Said they'd be ready to pick up."

Malin hoped it would be quick. The office was slowly fogging up with halitosis and she wasn't sure how long she could stand it.

"She saved it all," he whispered, swiveling his chair to the credenza behind him and grabbing a large brown envelope. "If I had the privilege of half that money, I would have bought an Aston." He slapped the envelope down between them and pushed it toward her. "Instead, she bought a vehicle from Minerd's Scrap N' Haul. I saw the transaction. We send all the statements to a PO Box. Zip code 87114."

Rio Rancho, thought Malin. "You don't send them to

her mother?"

"We received a letter requesting they be forwarded after Ms. Delgado moved out."

"Moved out?"

"Yes, detective, moved out. It's all in there." He nodded at the envelope.

Malin pulled out the contents, found a letter clipped to a pile of statements and date stamped. The signature was said to be Lily Delgado's and approved against any previous checks she had signed. It was simple and straight to the point, asking for all correspondence to be forwarded to a four digit PO Box number in Rio Rancho, a sub-station near the Farmer's Market on Corrales Road.

"Have you heard from her?" Malin asked.

"The most recent phone call I had was a month ago, asking if she could withdraw $10,000."

Her monthly allowance, Malin thought. "Why such a large sum of money all at once.?"

"I didn't ask. She didn't say."

A flash of intuition worked its way through Malin's gut and into her head; she suddenly saw what was important.

Solid ground, not sinking sands.

There wasn't much she could glean from a post office, but there was a truck-load she could prize out of a junk yard.

SIXTEEN

Gabriel walked down the bicycle path until he reached the bridge, body strong, mind sharp. The air was strangely thin as the sun bled out along the western horizon and the lights in the parking lot pulsed on, piercing the dusk with a silver haze.

He lifted his chin at the honk of a goose, squinting at the v-shaped formation in the sky. Where were they going? What were they thinking? Could they see him down there, a small black speck stopping on an incline that led into the parking lot?

A bitter scent of rotting detritus among the cottonwoods and he could hear the bubbling river and the occasional rustle of a wood duck. There were remnants of footprints in his mind, those of family as they had walked along the Bosque Trail all those years ago. Sometimes riding bikes, sometimes horses. There had been no worries then.

He felt a stab of fresh air in his lungs as he inhaled, felt the joy of homecoming. Once, those rolling hills of sage and sand had been inhabited by coyotes and rabbits, and now they were layered with houses and dust covered streets, brightly colored playgrounds and manicured parks.

The houses behind Corrales Café were reserved for the cultural elite. Even businesses had evolved in his absence, fluorescent signs blinking in the approaching dusk and the steady sounds of traffic as cars rumbled across the bridge toward the crowded restaurants. Everyone ate out these days.

He wasn't here to reminisce. There would be plenty of time for that. It was then he noticed a metal flood gauge tacked to a wooden post at the river's edge. It was here he left his mark.

Gulshan.

Muscles tensed and relaxed, his feet met the pavement with the same old spring he remembered as a child.

A street lamp spread a weak yellow light around its base, bright enough to see three cars in the parking lot – two if he didn't count his van. A white Chevrolet Cavalier and a dark gray Mazda RX7, both facing the river and parked on the summit of a steep slope that curved down to the water's edge.

The latter interested him the most with its diamante framed plate and the words *Ms. Bling* emblazoned under the license lamp. Chinless Rosa… so fashionably tacky.

He cast a cursory glance through the rear window as he walked past, saw a young woman sucking Red Bull through a straw. He watched her from inside the van, studied those painted fingernails as they reached down to the passenger seat. She threw her head back and dropped something inside that large mouth. Two bites and whatever it was had been crunched into a pulp and swallowed.

She came here every Saturday night at six forty-five after eating salad with the other singers at Waterfall studios. Parked by the river to eat an addition to that healthy salad, a large portion of waffle fries and honey mustard from the Burger Giant drive thru. Left around seven ten.

The white Chevrolet reversed out of its space, headlights blinking into life as the tires crunched on pine needles and gravel. Just as the white cloud of exhaust tapered off into the night, Gabriel slipped a shoe lace and a small flashlight into his jacket pocket and scrunched an old blanket under one arm.

Never good to feed a habit. Never know who could be watching in the darkness, he thought, walking over to the black Mazda and reveling in the thought that Rosa's life was very much in his hands.

He dropped the blanket on the ground behind the left rear tire and tapped on the driver's window. There was a brief whoosh and a clunk before a slit of light appeared at the top of the frame. She turned off a loud belting of classical music and turned to study him.

"Sorry to bother you," he said, conscious of the salty aroma of French fries. "I hope I didn't frighten you."

"No… no, that's fine," Rosa said, with a sigh. "What is it?"

"It looks like you ran over a dog. I wouldn't normally worry, only this one has a collar."

Rosa glanced at her wing mirror, saw the crumpled heap by the rear tire and groaned. She tapped her forehead with the heel of one hand. "I didn't see anything."

"It was probably too dark when you drove in. Don't get out. I can handle it."

He backed away from the driver's door, scooped the blanket up in his arms and walked about ten feet toward a clump of foxtail barley. He knew she was watching, crying perhaps, as he laid it lovingly behind the grasses. She wouldn't want to look at a bloody pancake of matted fur, wouldn't want to see the collar and know the poor little thing once had a name.

He could hear Demon in the rustling leaves, hear him urging to hurry up and get on with it. Gabriel's chest grew thick and tight and he tried to catch his breath.

Click.

The car door opened behind him, gravel grinding under a pair of shoes. Training shoes, he imagined, because the sound was somehow deeper than the simple tap of high heels.

He waited for a few moments until she was clear of the car and then turned slowly, taking painful steps toward her. "You mustn't worry," he wheezed. "These things happen."

"Is it dead?"

"Quite dead."

She looked so forlorn, nose wrapped in a handkerchief and shoulders heavy with guilt. Gabriel almost wanted to call the whole thing off, give her a hug and just go home. But he had a job to do. And he was beginning to wonder if he felt well enough to do it.

Her breath almost mingled with his as they stood there in the parking lot. Brown hair slicked back behind her ears, roots boosted with mousse and ends flat-ironed to death. It was a popular style, better suited to a woman with a chin.

"Can I see it?" she said.

He wasn't expecting that. "No, don't. You'll only make yourself sick."

She stared at the foxtail barley tufts stooping in the breeze. Took a few steps forward and then stopped with her back to him. "I didn't mean to. Really, I didn't. Did he have a name?"

"Otto," he said, taking a brief look around the parking lot before taking the shoe lace from his pocket, curling it around both hands as he crept up behind her.

"We should call the number. The owners will be worried."

Gabriel was tired of the charade and rolled his eyes. The ligature caught her by surprise, tightening around her neck until it was so tight she could no longer breathe.

He half-carried, half-dragged the dead weight back to the car and arranged her in the driver's seat, clicking the seat belt into place.

Once the driver's door and window were closed, he walked around to the front of the car and crouched beside the front bumper. Sure enough, no concrete wheel stop, good clearance between the underside and the ground, nothing to stop that car hurtling to the bottom of the river.

He inched around to the passenger side and turned on the ignition. Shifting the gear lever into drive, he pushed the passenger door closed, never heard it click as the car inched forward slowly at first, before tipping over the verge and picking up speed down the slope.

As the car bounded over the bicycle path, the passenger door swung open. Gabriel could do nothing but watch as it hurtled over the sandy verge, rushing toward the deepest part of the river.

It hovered there for a time, front end slowly dipping beneath the waves like an old gray submarine.

SEVENTEEN

Temeke arrived at Northwest Area Command at seven fifteen on Monday morning. He looked around the parking lot hoping to see the reassuring sight of Malin's black SUV, but no sodding luck.

He recalled waking up in the night to a feeling of panic. The cat had been missing since last Thursday. Never made it home after racing up the nearest tree and for all he knew, Dodger was still up there, looking down on the world from his leafy perch and not as stuck as Temeke believed.

And then there was a crackling sound like gravel being hurled against a window. He checked the glass for cracks, or better still, no teenagers skulking about in his driveway, giggling and carrying on.

It reminded him of the figure he'd seen under the tree that night, left knee turned sideways and shoulders back as if he was in the military. Certainly not Paddy Brody. He was too stocky for that. But Temeke had mapped the posture in his head and he would remember it if he saw him again.

The road had been darker than freshly brewed coffee and he'd sucked down a few jugs at three forty-five in the morning. Couldn't stop wondering about the Persian rug in Adel's house, whether it was blood that had disfigured the pattern when he'd last seen it. So he called Matt Black, resident crime scene specialist, and asked him to take a look.

He yawned loudly as he tugged at the front door of the sub-station, book wrapped in an evidence bag and tucked under one arm. There was no sign of the impact sergeant in the lobby and Sandra was the only admin behind the front desk.

She placed a flat hand against the corner of her mouth and whispered, "Fowler's in the boardroom with Hackett. They were supposed to be going through bonuses."

"Blimey, love, that's like luring a child into your car with candy."

"Remember the woman who died in a gas leak on the southeast side? Commander Roach called. Might not be an accident. And there was a witness, a student who thought he saw a stranger about an hour before it happened."

"Names?"

Sandra tapped the keyboard and peered at the computer screen. "The gas leak victim was a Mackenzie Voorhees. She was a student at Gibson. Witness; a Mr. Tom Lahaye, also a student at Gibson. I'll write his number down."

A toilet flushed somewhere in the building and Temeke was aware of the gentle blast of hot air on top of his bald head. The heater came on and it wasn't the only thing. Like a light bulb, he recalled what Adel had said about a funeral at the weekend. She knew the deceased, Mackenzie Voorhees.

"We've got a couple of visitors coming today," Sandra whispered, handing him the number on a yellow sticky note. "Hackett wants us to be sure to say hello."

"We'll give them our detective's welcome. Pat them down, throw them to the floor—"

"They're ladies, sir. Interns from Cibola High."

Temeke nodded, relieved it wasn't the Chief of Police. "Do me a favor, will you? Run a search on Mackenzie

Voorhees."

"Righto, sir. Anything else?"

"Could you check a Patrick Brody? Also goes to Gibson."

"I gave that information to Detective Santiago."

"She was here this morning?

"Yes, sir. Left around seven. Something about a scrap yard. She'll be back in a couple of hours."

What an efficient girl Malin was, Temeke thought.

"Do me a favor, love. Fowler's been looking a bit down in the dumps, you know, lovesick. Get him a number fourteen from the Heaving Dragon, will you?"

He swiped his card in the reader and took the grinding elevator to the first floor. There was a tremor in his belly about those crime figures and he tried to chase it away with thoughts of coffee and a good nap. Calling Mr. Lahaye was his top priority.

He shrugged off his coat and locked the book in his top drawer. The smell of freshly brewed espresso and toasted bagels wafted along the corridor, a breakfast perhaps for the Cibola girls. He was a few feet from the boardroom when he heard whispering and saw the back of Fowler's big, fat head through the crack in the jamb. Hackett stood next to him, tall and bay-windowed from decades of food on the go.

"Over three thousand bucks... Temeke?" Fowler said, slapping a generous portion of cream cheese on his bagel. "You gotta be kidding. He's been deviating from every procedure since he arrived here. He's a foreigner. And foreigners suck."

"Lieutenant Alvarez speaks very highly of him. He's the only one who can get the job done."

"He's not the only one. What about Suzi Cornwell from Southeast Area Command?"

"I'll think about it."

"And Santiago? I mean... c'mon. There's nothing

between the ears. I've been watching her, sir. Someone was talking to her on the internet, sending snippets of confidential information. I know what she's up to and I'll make sure she never hears the pop of a Champagne cork on my watch."

Temeke heard Hackett clear his throat. "She's more resourceful than you think. Luis gave me a tape this morning. A tape of your voice."

"Mine?"

"You asked Santiago out. Said something about a tranquilized carthorse. You also said something about black people. Couldn't make up my mind if it was sexual harassment or racism. I just happen to think it's both."

"Sir, it was—"

"I think it's offensive when top brass can harass innocent people and get away with it. You'll write a statement of apology. To both of them. And, while you're at it, one to Mrs. Delgado and all. I can't have all these complaints." Hackett straightened his back. "Who is it... this man she's talking to?"

"He was piggy-backing on unsecured wireless networks. Squatting, sir. Connecting through her wireless router."

"Was?"

"Must have known he was being monitored. Mr. W. Ingman or something. Haven't seen him since."

It was the footsteps and the chink of crockery that caused Temeke to abandon his short recce for a cup of the good stuff. He looked over the banisters, saw Hackett's admin tripping up the stairs with a plate of cookies.

Lucky sods.

He loped back to his office with black visions of nailing Fowler's ass. But a three thousand dollar sweepstake wasn't half bad. Temeke had to prove himself, that's all. Had to get a result and urgently. Or that three thousand dollars might as well be a rumor.

He could no longer afford to worry about Malin's downtime and he needed to quit worrying about department intrigues. Maybe it was force of habit from all those years in Homicide where you prairie dogged the guy in the next cubicle to make sure he wasn't stealing your promotion.

According to Fowler, Temeke would never receive a promotion. Although he might have met the health and physical criteria, he didn't have the necessary references from civil servants or senior executives, least of all the DA.

On the rare occasion detectives fraternized with prosecutors, Temeke had been invited to lunch with the DA. On the way out of the restaurant the bloody wind only had to change direction and ash from a lighted cigarette found its way to the upper side of DA Meyer's fly. The smell of charred wool attracted a nearby firefighter and it was lucky he had a bottle of iced water handy.

"Adel Martinez," he whispered out loud, as if he could erase corporate politics with a name.

She had been all alone in that house when a few things went missing. A metal poker which, according to the statement Maggie Watts took, had a loop handle and a peg hook. And then there was a blue vinyl shower curtain and a green hand towel for when things got messy. Lucky Adel had been out that night. And damn lucky she wasn't living there anymore.

He lit the first cigarette of the day while the computer booted up, heard thunder roaring in his stomach reminding him that a tablespoon of Greek yoghurt was hardly breakfast.

There was a copy of the *Duke City Journal* on his desk. Malin must have left it there, folded neatly where the article began and another fold where the article ended.

Detective Leaks Information On Delgado Girl.
By Jennifer Danes
Journal Staff Writer

Law Enforcement front-runner, Detective David Temeke reacted to a question about Lily Delgado. When asked if he knew anything about a young girl's remains found in the mountains Temeke spilled the beans about a nasty hacking in a swampy area of Cibola National Forest.

This comment goes against the police department's mantra of "conserving" information that might be upsetting to the general public and discards a long-standing tradition of respecting victim's families for no good reason.

Further, for observant readers who are affiliated with the Duke City Journal, Commander Hackett urges people to disregard the flippant comment made by Detective Temeke in a time of considerable stress for the public and law enforcement alike. The report on 'leaking information' was found to be false.

We asked a neighbor, Mr. Fitz Riley, to comment on why Detective Temeke was voted this month's Worst Law Enforcement Officer in the Albuquerque Echo.

Mr. Riley said: "When you think of Detective Temeke, you've got to think one thing. His love of pets, particularly his cuddly cat. Heck, no one knows Temeke better than me, how he jogs down his driveway at five o'clock every morning, barks at my dog, brings the paper to my doorstep when it rains and isn't afraid of being assertive and aggressive when his friends are threatened. If that's not a good neighbor, I don't know what is."

Temeke mashed the newspaper and threw it in the bin. It was Stan Stockard he had spoken to not Jennifer Danes and how she had got hold of any snippets of information he would never know.

He was about to stub out his cigarette when he noticed another *No Smoking* sign on the wall, only this one was much larger than the last. A circle had been drawn around the dot above the 'i' with the words, *this is a covert camera and we are watching you.*

He found his gaze straying furtively to that dot, falling right smack into the trap. Gritting his teeth, he ripped the sign down with one hand and hurled it into the bin to join that equally asinine article in the *Journal*.

"Mr. Lahaye?" he asked, after dialing the witness' number.

The young man needed no reminding of the terrors of Wednesday night and he'd clearly been waiting for Temeke's call.

"I saw a guy hanging around outside," he said, "kind of between my house and the neighbor. He said he was looking for Phoebe someone. Forgot the last name."

"Could you describe him?"

"About my height."

"Which is?"

"Five feet ten. Had a thick jacket on, couldn't tell you the weight. Said his name was Gabe. Might have been a little lighter than me. One thirty, somewhere in there. Wore a black beanie, white hoodie... and pants."

"What color pants?"

"White, like a painter. Looked familiar. Thought he was someone in one of my sister's classes. But he didn't seem to know her."

"Notice anything unusual?"

"He looked kinda lost to be honest. So I asked him if he needed a ride. He said no. I watched him in my rearview mirror. Drove an old van."

"Did you see the color?"

"Dark blue or gray."

"What time was this?"

"About ten fifteen. I drove to a friend's house after

that."

Temeke invited him to come in to see the composite artist as soon as he could, ended the call and ransacked his memory about the van.

He had a detective's memory, never forgot faces, dates, the sound of a person's voice, car models, license numbers, case numbers, all filed away in his brain never to be erased. A gray van had been parked next to his car at Los Poblanos Academy. High-tailed it out of the parking lot when Temeke saw him. It was a long shot, but what if it was the same van?

There was a telephone message from Malin. Adel Martinez had been prescribed Omeprazole for a peptic ulcer about a year ago, but the capsules Temeke took from Adel's house were Adderall, usually prescribed for ADHD. Explained the empty blister packs in the trash, he thought.

There were no messages from Hackett or Luis and he began to wonder if he had been purposely excluded from another secret meeting.

He balanced a fresh cigarette on the top of his computer. Googled the word *witchcraft* and got a number of hits; Wicca, spells, ancient history, a definition by Merriam-Webster and an article from the *New York Post* about spiritual deception – most of which seemed to focus on making a person richer, stronger, smarter. But this didn't appear to resemble any of these.

He paused at the last paragraph, wiping his hands down his trousers as if something hideous had leeched into his skin.

If a girl is excluded from the sisterhood she will experience rejection and isolation, and she will come to believe she is truly possessed.

EIGHTEEN

While the rest of the department and their guests were sucking down the dregs of stewed coffee and chewing on the last of the bagels in the boardroom, Temeke was debating on reading that sodding awful book. It was so cold in the office and every time the rotten door opened a blast of air gave him the shivers.

New Mexico. Sand and wind, where nothing grows. He'd begun to hate it almost as much as he loved it.

His finger absentmindedly caressed the grip of the desk drawer. The book was in there, had to be read, had to be examined, and his mind was shouting obscenities if he didn't hurry up and get on with it.

It's like a novel, for crying out loud. A thriller. You like those.

Temeke slipped the book out of the evidence bag and opened it, frantic to sidestep the yawning pit of nightmares that threatened to suck him in if he let it. There was an elusive scent, not sweet, rather salty like brine on the ocean bed and the pages had turned a nicotine yellow. Beneath the title on the first page was a logo of a lion holding a sword with the sun behind it, reminiscent of the ancient Persian symbol of royalty. The publisher name was obscured by a date stamp where the ink had turned green with age.

Verron's Bookstore, it said. November 11, 2007.

Temeke googled the book and found eighty-two mixed

reviews since publication. He then called the bookstore in Old Town Plaza, heard three rings before a voice with a Slovakian accent answered.

Romanian, the man assured him. "I'm a citizen, detective. Been here for fifty years."

"It's not about your citizenship, Mr. Verron." Temeke cleared his throat, hoping the thick accent hadn't seeped into his response. "I have a book you sold several years ago. *The Lilin Esoterica.* I wonder if you remember it?"

"Brown leather. Yes... I remember the book. Hard to shift something like that. I told all my customers it came from Transylvania. To make a sale, you understand. Cash buyer."

A good hearty laugh and the phone vibrated against Temeke's ear. He wasn't keen to listen to the rantings of an old man or a bleeding vampire story from another century. He could easily have lunch with Hackett for that.

"Any chance you kept a record of who you sold it to?"

"So long ago."

"Yet you remember the person paid cash."

"A young woman. That's all I remember."

Just like Adel Martinez had said, Temeke thought and ended the call.

He had one of those bad feelings, the same damn feeling that had him spooked. He'd been a detective long enough to read the subtle warning signs and the words *so long ago* triggered all kinds of possibilities and sadly, no leads. It also triggered a sense of time. Mr. Verron knew roughly when it was sold, even if he didn't have a name.

The mysterious book lay open on his desk, ancient and tired, like an old man you wanted to help across a busy street. A man who wandered home alone, if he even had a home.

A gray twist of ash landed on the keyboard and Temeke brushed it away with a hand, stubbed the cigarette out on the corner of his desk and threw it in the trash. He read the first chapter.

In women, there is a powerful drive which emerges in the instinct to survive, to procreate, even in grueling and desperate conditions.

There are impulses which move women – love, lust, hate, and the urge of marriage and motherhood. This is the destiny of a sister.

Temeke sensed a sudden rush of wind, the sound of breath against his ear, forging past him as if born on cloven hoofs. He slapped the side of his head and began to mutter the word *hogwash*, as if by repeating it he could encase himself in a tall hedge nothing could penetrate.

If any sister does not obey she must be cut out from the Lilin and left to perish.

For it is said the first shall be buried alive, the second shall have her limbs severed, the third shall be cast into a fire, the fourth shall be drowned, the fifth shall be poisoned and the sixth shall be starved of air.

For woman is cracked and tarnished, just as the last light on a dying world.

If Alice had held séances in the school attic, brewed belladonna, and started a cult, she might also have been coerced into a spiritual marriage with a few of her friends.

Just as a nun enters a religious order, a Lilin must take a new name. This name will reveal her character and her destiny and it will also signify a new beginning and a new end. It will transform the woman who acquires it by making her a sharer in the sisterhood.

Temeke's thoughts seemed to have run their course, ebbing into gray bars as his eyes narrowed and he saw only the faint outline of his eyelashes. He sank deep into his chair and tried to ward off an unexpected surge of nausea.

There were only two options in his opinion. The shrewd one, which was to talk to Malin about the occult, only he'd be forced to listen to a rant on the evils of witchcraft. Or the reckless one, which was to go it alone.

The phone rattled on his desk and a voice introduced himself as Matt Black. It was the initial report on the Samadi house Teneke had been waiting for.

"There were blood spatters on the carpet and on the piano, namely the key slip and bed," Matt said. "The keys were old and yellowed with age and some chipped at the corners. Looks like they had been wiped with a cloth, but not enough to clean the side grain. Basswood. Very porous. Same blood type as on the carpet. We'll let you know when we have a name."

"Fingerprints?"

"Whoever it was wore gloves."

"Consistent bastard."

"But there was a strand of hair. Scale patterns indicate it's human not animal, very coarse and bone straight, possibly Asian. The follicular tag was intact meaning it could have been pulled out in a struggle, but we'll run nuclear DNA on the root pulp. Another thing, there were traces of skin and bone inside the piano. Dr. Vasillion said they belonged to the third and fourth right distal phalange."

"A what?"

"Two fingertips."

NINETEEN

Temeke couldn't help thinking the *Esoterica* had some association to the deaths in the Albuquerque area and he certainly couldn't rule out the possibility that the killer was copying the format.

As for Cornell Drive, it was riddled with K-9s tracking scents through clumps of tumbleweed in the back yard, handlers going through rubble and trash in the alleyways. So far, the small tract of land had yielded nothing.

A photograph of Asha Samadi had gone out to all law enforcement agencies and the surrounding states, and a hefty $350,000 reward had been offered by her father. Unfortunately, the same photo had ended up on Jennifer Danes' desk at the *Duke City Journal* promising an exaggerated and highly erroneous article.

It was the next call that unnerved Temeke as he sat there trying to understand the phalange nonsense. Luis had a car he wanted Temeke to look at. A gray Mazda RX7 found bobbing like a champagne cork under Alameda Bridge.

"When it rains, it bloody well pours," Temeke said into the phone.

"Jarvis called it in. Said there was a woman inside."

"I'll be there. Seen Malin this morning?"

"She's at Minerd's Scrap N' Haul. Told me to tell you she'll be back before lunch."

"Thanks," Temeke muttered before ending the call.

He would have liked to have gone with her, but she was doing everything she could to keep up with the case, watching tapes of the late Alan Delgado, interviews, phone calls, reporting. He was proud of her.

Ten minutes later, he swung the jeep into the Alameda Bridge parking lot, choosing a spot away from the secured scene, the ambulance and the fire truck. It was a crying shame there was no video cam fixed to the only light fixture in situ. He gave the river a long, hard stare, higher than usual due to all the recent rain and swirling with red mud.

One Field Investigator was taking photographs of the front of the car, another was drawing sketches of the river and embankment, and Matt Black was tagging, logging and packaging. It must have been their third walk-through.

A videographer was shadowing Stan Stockard from Channel 4 News to get in on the best of the pictures, until Stan swatted him with a hand and took his camera crew down to the river. It was funny enough for a few loud cackles.

Officer Jarvis stood beside the ambulance, drenched to his waist. He walked toward Temeke, wiping his hands on a fluffy white towel someone had given him.

"Found the car after seven this morning. Driver's dead, sir."

Temeke could see that. One of the men in the medical response team that he recognized as Lauren De Paul, assistant to Dr. Vasilion, gave him a terse nod and pointed at the body bag. Temeke held up three fingers and nodded back. He turned back to Jarvis.

"When you got here, what was the first thing you saw?"

They both stared at the car which stood in the parking lot now, dripping water and sediment through the open passenger door, windows intact.

"When I drove over the bridge," Jarvis said, "I could see a woman down there in the driver's seat. She had her seat belt on, looked like she'd overshot the slope. I waded in and tried to open the driver's door, but it was locked. The passenger door was open slightly. She could have got out if she wanted to, sir. Might have been a suicide."

"We'll leave all the science to forensics, shall we? Automatic or stick?"

"Automatic."

"Was the car in drive?"

Jarvis' eyes swept from side to side as if the question was obvious. "Yes, sir."

"When you drove into the parking lot, which way was the car pointing?"

"The hood was down, front side facing the trees. All I could see was the underside, sir."

Sounded exactly like a straight shot from the parking lot, thought Temeke, judging by the tire marks in the grass leading down to the water. Although he would have liked to have seen it for himself. There was another set nearer the bridge where the car had been pulled out, but it was the open passenger door that bothered him.

The victim could have climbed out unless she was intoxicated or rendered incapable before the car went under. Heart attacks could do that to a person, so could drugs. But a passenger door couldn't have opened by itself. It meant only one thing. The passenger had jumped clear just as the car went in and if that someone hadn't been found, it left another option, one Temeke wasn't willing to consider yet.

"Purse? Cell phone?"

Jarvis jutted his chin at the crime scene specialists. "All bagged, sir. They also found a blanket and a shoelace with some hair on it. Probably nothing."

"Everything's *something* at a crime scene, son."

Temeke reckoned the slope was roughly a twenty-five

percent grade and there was no knowing how fast the vehicle had been going. Probably fifteen at a stretch, he imagined. Might have raced in from the road, only a sharp left-hand turn would have prevented any antics of that nature, unless she was being chased.

The temperatures had been in the low thirties at night and it made sense the car windows were closed. The sun had already burned through the dampness that had settled overnight and there was an eerie orange light through the trees.

He walked over to Lauren and stared down at the head of a young woman, hair matted against her cheeks and almost unrecognizable.

"Name?"

"Rosa Belmonte. Twenty-one, five feet, six inches tall, one hundred and twenty-eight pounds. All there on her driver's license. Take a look at this," Lauren said, unzipping the bag a little further and pointing at a prominent deep mark around her neck. "There are abrasions along the ligature furrow, pattern overlapping. Means she may have struggled a bit."

Temeke curled his toes in his boots, felt his mind swim in cyberspace for a second without sound or color. "She was strangled?"

"Looks that way." Lauren seemed to sense the question on Temeke's face. "She was probably taken by surprise. Lost consciousness fairly quickly."

"Any other marks, cuts, tattoos?"

"Didn't see any."

"Was she wearing shoes?"

"Training shoes. They're badly scuffed at the heel and sole." Lauren handed Temeke the bag and let him take a look.

"Bloody waste."

Temeke saw the shoes were a mixture of white leather and mesh, but a series of deep scores along the heel revealed Rosa had been dragged, possibly across the parking lot. He noted both shoelaces were intact and handed the bag back.

"Officer Jarvis said someone found a shoelace. Could it have been used on the victim?"

"It's possible," Lauren said. "The doc will have a better handle on it when we get her to OMI."

The last time Temeke had visited the office of the medical investigator he had asked Vasillion what he thought the victim might have seen or felt in those final hours. The doctor responded, "I've often imagined it. I think they beg internally for someone to come and rescue them, and then their minds scream, *my God, I don't want to die*."

The bland-faced doc took pride in his work, tidying up the remains other people had destroyed. He cut and sliced, sometimes humming a tune. And all this time, Temeke assumed Vasillion was hardened by it, no longer able to feel like he once had.

What Temeke couldn't stomach in this case was the demonic component which had crept in through a sodding witch book. Someone thought they had an unholy mandate to snuff out innocent lives *and* take precious resources away from other investigations.

"Anyone else in the car?" he asked.

"Didn't look like it. But there's frogmen north of here, following the current."

Temeke studied the open space where the teams were beginning to pull out, leaving a tow truck for the deceased's car. He noticed one light on the south side of the parking lot, a metal halide fixture with a rectangular head. It would have shed some light on the area but certainly not enough to alert a passing car on the main road. Most drivers clocked fifty-five over Alamada bridge when no one was looking.

Temeke gave Lauren a slight wave of his hand and

walked back towards the river. He heard the conclusive rasp of the zipper as he reached the summit of the slope, an eerie sound he had come to terms with over the years.

He crouched and squinted sideways at the wide imprint of tire tracks along the embankment. There were no scuff marks on the asphalt below, nothing to indicate the victim had been dragged in any direction. All he could hear was the breeze and voices bubbling from the emergency teams, and his gaze was briefly locked by a dragonfly caught in a strip of sunlight on the surface of the water, wings a twilight blue as it hovered over a wooden post. It was lucky to be alive.

Temeke stood, reached in his pocket for his cell phone to call Malin… and then paused. He was jarred from his thoughts by a scrawl of graffiti on that wooden post and the closer he got he could make out a word.

Gulshan.

As to its meaning he had no idea, but words near a crime scene deserved to be photographed. He took a picture with his cell phone for good measure and flicked his fingers at the videographer.

"Better snag that before the water level rises."

TWENTY

Minerd's Scrap N' Haul was on Broadway, a large lot with tier-upon-tier of rusted out car parts without a gap of light between them. A few old sedans graced that dismal graveyard and the only thing that brightened the parking lot was a pimped out Chevrolet Caprice with forty inch chrome rims parked outside the office door.

Malin studied the manager, unable to determine the gender even as he came closer.

"Like your sunglasses," he said. "Aviators, right?"

"Yeah."

"You look like a pilot."

"That's the idea."

"Name's Charlie Miller," he said, holding out a hand. "I was *Charlotte* in the old days. Course, the state assumed I was sex starved and picking up women in bars."

"Were you?" Malin showed her badge, feeling the phone vibrate in her pocket. She chose to ignore it.

"Yeah, I was actually. But what I do in my spare time's got nothing to do with applying for a business license, has it?"

"No it hasn't, sir."

There wasn't a vestige of femininity in that body now, arms etched with tattoos and chest flattened by a snug button-down shirt.

Charlie began pacing in a wide circle, probably felt a tad uncomfortable after dishing out a whole pile of redundant info Malin couldn't care less about. Unless he was running a closet drug business, which would explain the pursed lips and a foot that quickly pressed a half-smoked joint into the sand, he expressed the typical behavior of a person confronted by uniform.

"So, how can I help?" he asked.

Malin frowned a little behind her dark glasses. "Sold any used cars recently?"

"How recent?"

"Last two months?"

Charlie rubbed his chin with oil stained fingers and nodded. "Three sedans and two vans."

"Thriving business."

"You could say, only the vans don't sell too well."

"Remember who you sold them to?"

"The vans? I'll have to check inside. Some old guy bought the white 1972 Chevrolet C10. A young guy bought the gray Chevy van, same year, I think."

It was the latter that sparked Malin's interest and the mention that the man was young. "What did the young guy look like?"

"Pale skin, black hair, brown eyes."

"Pitch black?"

"Huh?"

"His hair?"

"Oh, yeah. Darker than yours, so black it was blue." He seemed to laugh at that.

Malin appreciated Charlie's feminine side. It sure helped to give her a vivid picture and the young man clearly wasn't wearing sunglasses if Charlie could tell the color of his eyes. "Anything unusual. Accent... walking stick?"

"Accent? Came from round here, I think. Black

clothes, if that helps."

It didn't really, but Malin forced her worries to one side and refrained from pushing it.

"He was carrying scissors," Charlie said, as an aside.

"Scissors?"

"I don't think he was clipping his nails over there by the sedans. You can start a Camry with a pair if you can unlock the door first. Wrote a check for the deposit, then paid the rest in cash, wads of it. I'm not complaining. Always nice to have cash."

"Always nice to keep the books in order."

Charlie's eyes seemed to wander a bit, sometimes up, sometimes down. "I bet when you were at the police academy you were one of those muscular gels, you know, pumping iron to outshine the men."

"I don't know what you're talking about." Malin looked around the yard, taking in a stack of brand new tires by a blue porta potty and a mangy dog that hobbled on three legs between the cars. "Got an address for that young man?"

A nod and Charlie mopped his face on the back of his sleeve. He swaggered toward the RV, a Great Dane of a rig, fully loaded and painted silver.

Malin followed him in, saw a bunch of papers on a table, noticed how easily Charlie dug beneath the pile and found exactly what he was looking for. He turned, eyes wide as cups when he saw her standing on the top step.

"Here," he said, pressing a few sheets of paper against his belly and smoothing them down with a hand. He held them out, wrist twitching slightly.

"Not fiddling your taxes, are you?" It was a stupid question, but one Malin couldn't resist.

"Naw, I don't do taxes."

Malin grinned. There was something about Charlie she rather liked. A raw strength, a couldn't-care-less attitude and heck, look at the monster RV. He must have been doing well for himself.

Malin skimmed the paperwork silently for a moment, blinked, read it again, noted the address and the date of sale. Sure enough, the van was bought a month ago by a Mr. Gabriel Mann, address off Bridge Boulevard near Central Avenue.

"How much did you sell it for?"

"Three grand. It was worth more than that, but the kid had a frowny look like he could really use it."

"Kid? I thought you said he was a young man."

"He was. Green, you know how they are when they're first starting out. Felt sorry for him."

Malin checked her watch and gave Charlie the paperwork. "I appreciate you showing me this," she said.

She sauntered back toward her car, moving one foot in front of the other, feeling the thudding of her heart. She had no reason to suspect Charlie of anything and it was hardly his fault if he took cash from a young man who made every effort to remain anonymous.

The number was no longer in service when she tried it and she suspected the address was false too. The truth was, she had nothing to go on.

She wanted to find answers before Temeke did, a man so skillful in tracking a felon, he put all his peers to shame. A man who was everything she would never be. She shrugged off the thought the same way she shrugged off bad dreams because she had a choice. It was a matter of making the right decision and forgetting Wingman ever existed. He was a distraction, just when things between her and Temeke were going so well.

Tapping into the computer, she checked the wanted status of *Gabriel Mann*. No felony warrants, no misdemeanor warrants, nothing state wide or county wide. Two things struck her as possibilities. If Temeke was being followed as Wingman had suggested, the in-car video camera system would prove invaluable. Since a prisoner sitting in the back seat could be monitored by live feed sent back to the 911 call center, so too could a car following a few feet behind. Provided the windshield of the following car wasn't tinted, the driver could be made out by video enhancement and latterly matched with a criminal suspect.

Unless Temeke had been driving his jeep. No video camera in a 1962 Hotchkiss.

Malin turned on the ignition and planted her foot firmly on the gas. The back wheels stirred up a shower of gravel and dust as she accelerated back onto Broadway. Stretching her back, she forced herself to breathe slowly while she drove to Northwest Area Command with one question churning around in her head. How was she going to find Gabriel Mann?

Fear seemed to gust toward her, rolling off the road like curls of smoke and poison gas. Fear was the one thing she hated and the one trick she refused to fall for.

Opening the window a slit, the wind blew into her eyes, making them water. She breathed in a cloud of diesel as she pulled onto I-40, heading west into a long line of traffic and slowing down behind a black BMW.

The metallic paint seemed to give off a flash of blue and she peered over her tinted lenses to confirm what she saw. A dance of color in the sunlight reminded her what Charlie had said about the young man's hair.

So black it was blue.

TWENTY-ONE

Light seeped in under the steel blinds and Temeke curled his hands around a warm mug with the words *Up Yours* written on the outward side. The office was bigger than the one he had in Homicide, if you could call a cubicle an office. Gray paint, gray filing cabinets, bleak and basic, a room that demanded productivity so at the end of the day you didn't mind getting the hell out of it.

He and Malin were what Hackett proudly referred to as the inner core of the investigative unit. It was his way of pumping steroids into the smallest department of law enforcement Albuquerque had. The place where castoffs were given compassionate smiles in passing and a pat on the back; the place where soaks just kept on soaking.

There was that bottle of whisky...

He stared up at the white board, a collage of crime scene photographs – long range, mid-range, short range – *Journal* articles, dates, an exhaustive record of events since Asha Samadi had disappeared. On the top left was a photograph of Alice Delgado, the face he couldn't forget. And a new face. A composite sketch of Charlie Miller's version of the man he saw. Temeke wasn't ready to put the sketch out to the public yet and alert the perp to a countrywide manhunt.

His mind went back to the interview with Valerie Delgado and he wondered what type of people lived on Bazan Loop, backgrounds, occupations, how big the houses were, how he could get an 'inside' look at the floor plans.

He searched for a realtor who served the area, a Bart Stein who had two houses for sale on the same street.

"Number two seven five, a single family house. Four thousand square feet," Bart boasted. "Four bedrooms, three full, one partial bathrooms, lot size... one acre. Been with Steins for about thirty days. Would you like to take a look?"

"Any other unique features?" Temeke asked.

"Some have turret rooms, lots of light. Nice views. Skylights in the kitchens. I understand from my colleague there are two houses in the neighborhood that have boot rooms, basements, back shops, space for antique cars, that kind of thing. But not the ones on our inventory, I'm afraid."

The sudden jolt of the office door against the wall startled Temeke. He slid his feet off the desk and ended the call. Fowler stood in the doorway, wiped his brow and began pumping antiseptic gel on his hands from the green plastic bottle on Malin's desk. His nostrils were twitching as if he had somehow managed to trace a residue of cigarette smoke.

"Morning," Temeke said, marveling at the sanity of any man who dedicated so much time to his wardrobe. "You look like crap."

"Don't raise your hopes." Fowler pressed his lips together for a second and winced. He tried to smooth back his hair and straighten his uniform. "Sandra brought me a take-out from Heaven's Dragon. A number fourteen. I was doubled over with the worst pain I've ever had in my life."

"A number fourteen? That's German Shepherd isn't it?"

Fowler slumped in Malin's chair, tapped a fist against his mouth and began puffing out his cheeks. "I was alright until I got as far as my car and then I got cramps and gas."

"There's a reason why we call it the *Heaving Dragon*," Temeke said, resisting a roll of the eyes. "Lucky you weren't in the emergency room."

It was the mushrooms – tiny gray rubbery things that always made Temeke hurl. Something about them, made you see bright colors if you kept them down long enough.

"Sarge had a call from a builder this morning. Found a plastic bag in the back of his truck, a metal poker and a towel, both covered in blood and hair. Matt Black went over to pick them up. Fat Mule parking lot on Fourth."

Only three bloody minutes from home, Temeke thought, feeling his stomach lurch. He rubbed his shoes together to get the circulation going. No mention of the shower curtain, but then he half expected that. "Anyone see anything? Security cameras?"

Fowler cussed loudly and shook his head. "Place is as run down as a homeless shelter. Listen... Mr. Lahaye is downstairs with the artist. Just wanted to let you know."

"Very good."

"And that girl you went to see. Adel Martinez? Think she knows anything?"

Temeke felt he was suddenly in free fall, floating weightless until he gripped the sides of his chair. He was tired, that's all. "Ms. Martinez was under the impression Asha Samadi had left the country with a boyfriend. When I spoke to Miss Samadi's father that wasn't the case. He keeps her passports in his safe, arranges all overseas trips. His daughter isn't as independent as some."

"Passports?"

"She was born in Riyadh. Family was plastered over the front page recently for having a winner at the Kentucky Derby. Desert Rum it was called. She rarely goes home to the Kingdom now. Mother's name was Salwa Bint Saud. Hefty price tag if we don't find her. There's some movement in her credit card account, gas stations, hardware stores, clothing stores. All of them here in Albuquerque. According to Luis, someone sent a message on Asha's laptop. I'd like to email them back and tell them to pack it in."

"What about her lifestyle? Money?"

"Gobs of it. Father's a prince, remember?"

"What's to say she didn't drive to Miami and set sail for the Bahamas."

"Not likely, is it?" Temeke gusted through the information he had on his computer. "And while we're on the subject of women, keep your sniffer away from Detective Santiago. One touch, and I'll have a harassment report on Hackett's desk."

Fowler looked pained, but only for a second. He clearly played a dominant role in his own castle and the rest of the time he was a toady for Hackett. It provided the only excitement in his artificial, mendacious lifestyle.

"Do you have any leads yet?" Fowler asked, which in Temeke's opinion, was another way of asking if the case was in a rut.

"Not yet."

He suddenly saw the word *loser* on the walls. He saw a few other words too, *failure, letdown, FIASCO* growing larger and larger until they all hit the ceiling. He began to wonder if he had a bunch of fairies in his head.

"Must be hard living on your own now," Fowler said, pushing his chin forward, nostrils wider now. "Got any pets?"

Temeke didn't know how to take the pet comment. It could have been some sexually suggestive reference to females, or it could have been code for *we're replacing you at the end of the month whether you like it or not*.

"Dogs are the best," Fowler continued, "only you've got to walk them. But they're good company. We had a cat once, only it got stuck down a hole …"

Temeke couldn't bear thinking about Dodger in his

little red coat stuck down a hole. It was time to put a few flyers around the neighborhood, an article in the newspaper. He'd already called the animal shelter, the pound and the veterinary clinic in case someone had taken him there. The scd hadn't been microchipped, but he did have tags. Someone must have seen him.

"My head hurts." Fowler finally muttered, forcing himself to a stand. "I feel terrible."

Not wanting to contribute to a conversation on the worst foods that gave a man Delhi belly, Temeke carried on typing his report. "See you tomorrow," he offered.

Temeke's fingers couldn't help tapping out a rallying tattoo on the keyboard as he entertained a suspicion. It struck him as odd that Fowler was talking to him in the first place and in a mature manner that promised to end with a handshake rather than a few rude gestures he could name. They rarely agreed on anything.

The bugger was fishing, that's what. Seeing if he could squeeze another desk into that small office for Suzi bloody Cornwell. He liked her. Could have passed for a young Randolf Scott if the right movie role came up.

Temeke's jaw began to hurt from all that thinking because when he thought too much, he invented destructive scenarios that often gave him whiplash. Like the time when Fowler stole his jeep and rushed back to Serena for a round of heavy petting.

It never happened, of course, and how such filth found its way into Temeke's head in the first place, he never knew. He had beaten the imaginary Fowler to death with a baseball bat, blcod and brain matter all over the wall before the vision disintegrated into the drab room he now called his office.

Another knock cn his door. Luis this time and for some reason Temeke's throat seemed to contract and the room began to sway.

"I got your photograph of the water gauge. *Gulshan*?

You might be interested to note that Matt's boys found a word scratched in the kitchen doorframe of Cornell Drive. *Mahtab*. Mean anything?"

Temeke shook his head. "Sounds bloody foreign to me."

"Not only did our victims go to Gibson," Luis said, reading from a slip of paper in his hand, "but they also went to Los Poblanos Academy on Rio Grande. I took the liberty of calling the principal, a Ms. Baca. She recalled six girls in that group. Including Alice, there was Asha Samadi, Adel Martinez, Kenzie Voorhees, Rosa Belmonte and Zarah Thai."

"Zarah Thai, you say?" Temeke felt his eyebrows arch, took a deep breath. "Do we have an address?"

"5507 San Rafael Avenue, Victory Hills. And yes, there's a unit outside her house as we speak."

TWENTY-TWO

The look in his eyes was bright and intelligent and Malin was conscious the young man was nervous. He must have been all of twenty-two years old, six feet tall and about one hundred and sixty pounds of brute muscle.

"I was hoping you'd come," he said.

"What made you call me?"

"Well, it's all over the News, isn't it? Lily Delgado missing, Asha Samadi missing, a hotline number, your name... officer Santiago."

"Detective," she corrected. "If you have any information you can use the hotline number."

"I prefer meeting in person. More intimate this way."

It was the same voice she'd heard on the phone, the one that asked her to meet him at Maloof Air Park on 81st Street. The one that made her shudder enough to use a lapel cam to keep the facts straight and an officer in a backup car to follow Paddy Brody home.

"Do you know where the girls are?" Malin said.

"The last time I saw Asha was in the library about two weeks ago. Just to nod to, not to speak."

"And Lily?"

"At least four weeks ago outside the Frontier restaurant. I waved, but she didn't wave back. She can be like that sometimes."

He stood in the middle of the paved runway, hair tousled by the wind and haloed amber by the sun. There was no sign of the frown Charlie had spoken of, or any hint of blue in that dark brown hair. And there was no way you could call Paddy a kid.

"Why did you want to meet here?" she asked.

"So I wouldn't be followed." Paddy stared across the runway at the parking lot, eyes wavering between Malin's SUV and a white truck. Eyes so blue they made you blink.

"Someone following you?"

"I was driving downtown last Thursday night," he said. "Just cruising down Alcazar when I saw him. Nearly stepped off the sidewalk in front of me."

"Who?"

"Gray hoodie over his head, black hair, sunglasses... long middle finger. Don't know his name." Paddy's shoulders were hunched inside that ski jacket, breath misting in the cold. "Guilt's a terrible thing, detective. Makes a person want to crawl into a hole and die."

"Whereabouts was this?"

Paddy sent her a sideways glance. "Near Talin Market."

Better known as the International District, Malin thought, as she recalled the drug dealers who used to frequent the area. They had latterly moved to the alleyway behind the Old Bernalillo Courthouse. Who said law enforcement was stupid?

"You said black hair?" she asked.

"Shoulder length."

"You'd recognize him if you saw him again?'

Malin saw the smile was replaced by a concerned expression, more fitting for someone with something to hide. Paddy Brody knew the guy. He just wasn't saying.

"He owes me money. So, yeah. I'd recognize him."

"How much?"

"Fifteen hundred. Didn't have it so he disappeared into thin air. Not a good place to be."

Malin homed in on a thought, a recent message from

Wingman. *This one's a little green-eyed, tipped right over the edge. Dangerous place to be.* There could have been a connection, slim chance, but it was worth a try.

"Does the name Gabriel Mann mean anything to you?" she asked, trying to read his face.

"No." His toned implied why would it? "I wanted to talk about Alice, if that's OK with you."

Malin nodded. It was the reason he'd called her. She couldn't help wondering how far away he lived. Whether it was one of those new houses she saw in the distance with terracotta pitched roofs and matching block walls. Or whether he lived rough under a tarpaulin in the trees behind the runway. It would be easy to find out. "How did you meet… you and Alice?"

"It was a Saturday afternoon and some of us were tanning by the pool." Those same watery eyes seemed to roam over some inner landscape, losing himself in the memory. "She heard me say I was reading *The Portrait of Dorian Gray*. Wanted to talk about it. I was flattered."

"Was she beautiful?"

"I thought so. I liked her mouth, the way it curled around every word, the way she spoke, the things she talked about."

"What things did she talk about?"

"Astrology. Demonology mostly."

Malin caught a whiff of cologne. "Did she believe in it?"

"Oh, yeah. She thought she could talk to her dead father better that way. I think it comforted her."

"How did that make you feel?"

"I was raised Catholic. We weren't allowed to do séances or anything like that."

Malin waited for Paddy to go on, but when nothing came she asked him again if he was scared.

He went very quiet then, eyes holding her in a viselike grip, and the smell of cologne was suddenly very noticeable.

"We started seeing each other. So I couldn't tell her what I really thought. I took her to a bookstore in Old Town, found a book that taught us how to trap a demon. She collected ash from the fireplace downstairs, spread it around her bed at night. Said she'd catch one soon enough. When she woke the next morning, there were demon tracks. You could tell because they have bird talons for feet." Paddy saw Malin's raised eyebrow and grinned. "Adel did it when Alice was asleep. Scared the crap out of the others."

"Was Alice afraid?"

"No. She said the more informed we were, the weaker the threat."

"And you?"

"I went along with it. Thought she'd like me better if I did."

"And that was important to you?"

"She had a way of drawing you in."

Malin started suddenly and then ran a hand through her hair to hide it. "How?"

"Some kind of magic, I suppose."

"What about Lily?"

If Paddy hadn't been staring off into the distance with narrowed eyes, Malin would have thought he hadn't heard her.

"She was in and out. Too many shadows in her life, I guess."

"Explain."

"She was private. Didn't let anyone in. The girls... they were a little harsh sometimes. Not that Lily didn't deserve it. She did. Needed to get a grip, you know?" He gave an uneven sigh, voice trembling as he spoke. "She was beautiful once. Had long hair like Alice. Reminded me of a painting by John Collier. Lilith... do you know it?"

Malin pressed her lips together and shook her head. Paintings weren't her thing and if he was about to give her a pompous lesson on art she'd throw up.

"It's a painting of a nude wrapped in a snake. White skin and a body so perfect you can't stop looking at it. The way she stands, the backward tilt of her head. And all that red hair... down to her waist." Paddy motioned with one hand. "The queen of the night."

Malin nodded mutely; no one was queen of the night. A pulse throbbed hard in her neck as she listened to the deep, whispering voice, unable to understand how it could hover somewhere between both extremes at the same time. "Did you sleep with her?"

"Not saying I didn't try. Wasn't her type. She preferred the dark ones," he said, pointing to his skin.

Malin gave him a look that would have been interpreted as surprise. Paddy had a well-honed physique, strong jawline, intelligent eyes. Certainly someone you'd look at twice in the street. "Would you say Alice and Lily were close?"

"They argued sometimes. Alice was upset when Lily cut all her hair off. Said she was rebelling against her mom."

Malin followed his gaze, fixed briefly on a row of trees. Sunlight slipped between the trunks, making long shadows on the runway, some jumping in a sudden gust of wind.

"Were you surprised when Alice died?"

"You keep looking at my eyes, my nose. Think I'm high on something?"

"You do a little weed now and again." Malin could smell that cologne even stronger now.

"I dabble in this and that." Paddy looked away for a moment and then back again. "I know you think I'm nuts."

Malin didn't think he was nuts and she told him so.

Just a little disturbed by the books he must have read at school, most of which were probably still fresh in his mind. She wondered when he would lose all that literary pretentiousness. If at all.

He smiled. Said he liked her honesty. "Anyone tell you you're beautiful?"

"It's not important to me."

"Of course it is. All women want to be told they're beautiful." He brushed a strand of hair from her forehead and she took a step back. His hand dropped then, but not his smile. "Do you believe in the occult?"

"Do you?"

"Let me put it this way. Do you believe in demons?"

Malin shielded her eyes from the pale desert and a deep blue sky. "I believe there's a battle going on above us, a battle for souls. So, yes, I believe in demons."

"Do you think they can make us do anything they want?"

"Depends which side you're on."

"Let's not pretend you know your enemy as well as he knows you. All that sidestepping... all that armor. It won't help you. He knows exactly what goes on in that head of yours. He knows what you want, what you're afraid of... all your little mistakes."

Malin's heart pounded loud in her ears and her blood seemed to ice over at his words. Her own voice was like a child's in her mind. *Go away, go away, go away.*

"I can tell you the thing that haunts you the most, the thing you dread. Aloneness. I can tell you what you want more than anything. Family." He ignored her raised hand, the shake of her head. "You have to hear me out. Aloneness is all I've known these past few years. My father said I wouldn't amount to much. Real men go to university and do a masters in politics, he said. They become marines, serve the country, die for it. I chose art history. Haven't spoken to him in years. Then along came

Alice. She offered me a gift, a rare gift. So I took it."

"You didn't have to do that."

"She made me whole again."

Malin began to sweat in her jacket, gloved hands clenching in her pockets and she had to struggle to breathe normally. They likely bonded over absent fathers. "Did you love her?"

"Would you think less of me if I said no?"

Malin shook her head. He must have been so young then. So utterly convinced this was the right thing to do. "But you liked her."

"She had a way with people, had them eating out of her hand. Should have been a stand-up comedienne… should have been class president."

"Did she love you?"

"In her way. Not head-over-heels. That wasn't her style. Kept it all on the inside."

"So, what stopped you from loving her?"

"Alice got bored of the parties. Wanted to expand the alumni, take it more serious. But that wasn't my thing. I started sleeping with Adel. It was the drugs, the guilt."

"Guilt?"

"Alice said I was like a locust in a cornfield, only worse because I could never be satisfied. She said I'd corrupted them."

Malin knew Paddy just wanted the fun and excitement, but he had grazed his way through that meadow until there was nothing left.

He shook his head as if berating himself and then recoiled slightly as if someone had thrown a spider at him. "Do you know how demons are made? Sunlight and smoke. And sickness."

"Who told you that?"

"Alice."

"It was *The Lilin Esoterica*, wasn't it? I've seen the book." She saw the unblinking gaze and the way he suddenly looked down at his hands.

"There were pictures in it," he said. "When I close my eyes at night, I see ice, miles of it. And when the wind blows, there are shards in the air cutting like knives. Demon is always a gray silhouette on the horizon, cloak swaying from side to side as he comes closer. There's a mallet in his hand and it's bloody. He never gets close enough to reach me, not if I run... He can break you into a thousand pieces and you'll never find them again."

Malin felt a sharp wind against her cheeks and shivered. "Who is he? This Demon."

Paddy stared hard at her. "Cruelty, hatred, shame. He's all of it. The night Alice died she tried to get rid of him."

Malin felt her eyebrows shoot up, felt the color drain from her face. Her feet were stuck there on the runway as if she had been cemented to it. She wanted to reach out and touch him, see if he was warm. But something told her he was as cold as she was.

"She was in the attic burning candles and sage... reciting incantations. Baca found her and confiscated the lot. Three days later Alice was dead."

"Did you know she was going to kill herself?"

Paddy's face went white and he seemed almost on the point of fainting. He rubbed his eyes with the heels of both hands. "No."

"Did you know she had a knife?"

Paddy shook his head and then stiffened. "I would have taken it from her if I had known."

For one panicky moment, Malin wondered if Paddy Brody was telling the truth. Or would he stab her in the back and drag her body through the trees to a shallow grave he had already carved out of the sandy loam before she arrived? She took two steps toward the parking lot and then looked back.

"Know anything about Rosa Belmonte?"

"Saw it on the news. But that's not the answer you

wanted, was it? I was taking a late class, Native American Art II. Didn't get out until eight."

Malin all but rolled her eyes. He clearly kept up with current affairs. "And Kenzie Voorhees?"

He blinked a few times, struggled to swallow, and she could see the tears in his eyes. "We were all friends at school."

Malin tried to fit all the pieces together in her mind but failed. "Where were you on the night of February 10."

"Hosting a reception at an art gallery with Adel. And no, I don't love her either."

It was both brutal and honest, and triggered something inside that made Malin angry. And then he said what her intuition warned her he would say.

"I'm not going to pretend I'm loyal. Not wired that way."

"Well, then, I can see you've obviously got all your instincts under control." She handed him her card, told him to keep in touch. "Let me know if you remember anything else. Oh, just one more thing. Did you send Asha Samadi some flowers recently?"

"No."

"Write her a note?"

"No. Why are you asking?"

"I'm not going to give away a confidence. Not wired that way."

Paddy gave a cheeky grin, eyes flicking down the length of her body and up to her face again. "We have our chains of command, detective. We're all answerable to someone. Alice tried to cut the umbilical cord, tried to burn the book before it became a curse. The others… I don't know why they died."

"Is Lily dead?"

Paddy blinked a few times as if the cold air was hurting his eyes. "She is to me."

TWENTY-THREE

Temeke cleared his throat and turned off the tape recording. "I'd like to smack that smug bastard in the mouth. It's the work of a sick mind."

"Sick mind or not, sir, I think Paddy's mad at Lily." Malin tapped the cover of Alice Delgado's investigative file. "Lily told Baca and Baca confiscated the book. She did what she had to do."

"Right," Temeke said, swaying slightly. He was already dead on his feet and was in no mind to disagree with her. "Why didn't Baca hand the book over to the police after Alice died?"

"Probably didn't think it was important... didn't want a scandal to taint the school. Loss of funds and all that."

"Yet she handed it over when Lily went missing."

"By then it was serious. By then it was evidence."

Temeke heaved out a loud sigh. "Didn't Paddy say he was with Adel Martinez on the night Kenzie Voorhees died?"

"His story checks out. The Roadrunner Art Gallery on Central had a reception from seven o'clock to eleven. Paddy and Adel volunteered as sales consultants. At least five people confirmed seeing them, including the owner. Paddy was in a class when Rosa Belmonte died. The lecturer's a female. She remembered him."

"So... Mr. Brody is Albuquerque's answer to *The Bachelor*. Only, some jealous cow got busy and hired someone to narrow the playing field."

Temeke could almost see smears of blood in the flatbed of the builder's truck on Fourth Street. The samples from Cornell Drive had been confirmed to be those of Asha Samadi, elevating the missing report to a possible homicide. It was the worst night of the year.

The composite sketch lay face-up on his desk – Tom Lahaye's interpretation of the man he saw. Temeke pinned it to the board beside the Charlie Miller sketch and marveled at the similarity. Lahaye had even asked for a first name. Gabe.

"Did you call Admissions at Gibson about the name *Gabriel*?"

"No listing, sir," Malin said. "Not in his sister's class."

Yet Lahaye thought he saw someone he knew.

Temeke rubbed his eyes and stared at the clock. It said eleven forty-eight at night and every so often it would start wigging out, minute hand shuddering as if the battery was nearly flat. He stifled a yawn, wishing someone would come in and tell him to go home.

"I called Dr. Vasillion about two different hair samples they found," Malin said, rubbing one eye. "The ones tangled in the hook of the poker belong to Asha Samadi. He also mentioned hair fibers on the carpet which are commonly made from poly-silk mesh. Likely a lace wig. Oh, and the time of death for Rosa Belmonte was Saturday night between six and seven in the evening."

Temeke let out a long sigh and wondered what Paddy meant when he said Lily was dead to him. Had he killed her for tattling on her sister? Surely, there were better ways to get even?

"When you watched the tapes on Alan Delgado, what did you see?" he asked.

"Saw the interview he had at Laguna Seca when he lost to Claude Chaboud. Struck me as a quiet man, rather humble, actually."

Despite Delgado's irrefutable charm and ability to persuade the public to dance to his tune, Temeke wasn't buying it. How a driver could finish second and display such enthusiasm over his competitor was, in his opinion, suspicious. Nobody in their right mind behaved like that. Least of all him.

Hit him where it hurts the most were the unspoken words in Temeke's last evaluation. He was grateful to Hackett because it renewed his focus, made him work harder to prove them wrong. But it didn't stop him from punching the wall out in the bathrooms.

What would coming second have done to Alan Delgado? With all that pent up frustration, how would he have behaved when he got home that night?

Temeke rubbed his temples and every so often he thought he heard a squeaky rendering of a well-known song coming from somewhere down the corridor. "What the hell is that?"

Malin exhaled a loud breath that seemed to have been held for a good minute. "Someone fastened a singing toilet seat to Hackett's private bathroom."

"Poor old sod." Temeke lit a cigarette. "Four plush rolls of his favorite toilet paper went missing last week. Now he's using standard issue tissue. I bet that wiped the smile off his face."

"Hackett wants a face and a name on a Wanted List by the end of the week, and bulletins sent out to all US agencies. We're gonna have to use those sketches, sir."

"Nothing like tipping our hand." Temeke rubbed his forehead, feeling dark clouds pressing in a second time. "We could give Hackett a sketch of a man in a gray hoodie. Can you draw?"

Malin grinned. "As long as its confined to law enforcement agencies and not the public."

"Keep on at those stolen car reports. You never know what might turn up."

"I bet this perp's got a pack of fake IDs," she said. "Might have plenty of money if he's been chipping away at Lily Delgado's savings. He's safe. He's hiding."

"Where's he hiding?"

"New houses, old houses, warehouses. No one keeps track of those. And as far away from his hunting grounds as he can get."

"What is it with these villains? They're getting too sodding good these days." Temeke let his eyes wander over the office which smelled of stale cigarettes and coffee, and then huffed out another cloud of smoke to add to the flavor. "Might not be a *he*? Could be a *they*. Maybe it's a hierarchical group like Chicago's Temple of Set."

"Doesn't feel like it," Malin muttered. "Feels more like an individual, self-styled, or a pseudo-Satanist. Someone who rebelled against a controlling parent and then became seduced by a satanic cult. Someone who used the knowledge they gained from a rule book to justify a fantasy."

Temeke recalled what a criminal profiler at the FBI's Behavioral Science Unit once said. That elements of the occult were present in the psyche of many serial killers. Illegal drugs such as crank, speed, meth, crystal and psilocybin, an hallucinogenic drug similar to LSD, were often part of their modus operandi. This individual could be a youth sub-culture Satanist, belonging to a group that had a leader, a goal and a set of rules. But what if the individual had latterly become disillusioned and broken off by themselves?

He thought of that Persian carpet laid out on a table in Matt Black's lab, rusted with gouts of dried blood and a light powdering of human bone. He'd already called Asha Samadi's father, listened to him sob and howl like a baby. It was the nightmare he didn't need at nearly ten minutes before midnight.

"My head's buzzing, Marl. There's too much work. I

wonder if we can handle it all."

"I've already interviewed the bank manager about Lily's accounts. Looks like she drew out ten thousand in cash on Thursday, January 17. I thought we could tie her to something with her bank records, but no plastic, no paper trail since then. And Minerd's sold a van to a Gabriel Mann. Number's no longer in service and the address is invalid. The report's on your desk."

She pointed at a stack of typewritten pages in his in-tray and then looked sourly at his cigarette. "I've applied for a search warrant for Paddy Brody's residence."

"If he has one—"

"Actually, sir, I asked Maggie Watts to drive behind me this afternoon. She followed Mr. Brody home and I confirmed the address with Adel Martinez."

Thoughts ricocheted around Temeke's head and he felt the adrenalin pumping. Malin was good at creeping about in the shadows, rather like a reporter he knew at the *Journal*. "What was Paddy's state of mind?"

"Stressed. Jumpy. Kept looking around like he was expecting someone. He's dabbling in things he shouldn't be dabbling in. The occult's dangerous. It can get you all weirded out and start playing with your mind. He seems normal on the outside, it's the inside that bothers me. Like a bunch of wires that have got all tangled up and don't work right. I'm guessing he was too far in, had a thing for Alice. There's always jealousy if the girls liked the same guy. Isn't that what the principal of Los Poblanos told you…"

Temeke listened to the words, hardly able to take it all in. He chewed it over and stared through the window at a gray-clouded sky. Cult leaders had a way of manipulating their members with emotion-laden tactics and mind control. But who would have coerced an intelligent young woman to take her own life?

Over Malin's voice he thought he heard Fowler

thudding up the stairs to Hackett's office, took a final drag of his cigarette and flicked it in the trash can.

"... what's the betting someone did something and forgot they'd done it? It could have happened if they were high."

Temeke felt himself stiffen. "How can anyone forget committing a murder?"

"Paddy said he dabbled in this and that. Probably did more than weed if he could get it. And don't forget the amphetamines and partially digested belladonna the lab found in Alice's stomach. Dr. Vasillion's report mentioned an empty shampoo bottle with traces of vodka. It was on the floor when they found her. Toxicology said her blood alcohol level was twice the legal limit. What if they all had a little stab at it, sir... kind of like what happened to Julius Caesar?"

"Then she wouldn't be covered in self-inflicted wounds, would she?"

"What if they weren't self-inflicted?"

"Listen, I've had it up to here." Temeke indicated a point well above his head. "Haven't had a sodding wink of sleep since this whole thing started. You know what I think? I think Paddy Brody hasn't got anything better to do but waste police time."

"Two dead bodies isn't a waste of time," Malin said, tapping the headline section of the *Journal* on her desk. "They're claiming Ms. Voorhees and Ms. Belmonte are the victims of a serial killer. And there's another article underneath titled, *Asha Samadi puts distinct stamp on Chopin. Will the pieces of this cryptic puzzle ever be found?*"

Temeke began pacing around the office, blowing out a chain of deep sighs and wondering why it was so bleeding difficult to keep anything from the Press. "Who's been talking to them?"

"The articles are all written by staff writer Jennifer

Danes. She must have spoken to the faculty heads, students... parents. Clues are pouring in thick and fast."

Temeke could only see the top of Malin's ponytail over the newspaper, head turning from left to right as she scanned the articles.

"Tried to call Paddy Brody this morning. Never picks up." She turned a few more pages. "Looks like those electronic cigarettes are becoming popular. It's called vaping."

"Put that damn paper away." Temeke had no intention of swapping nicotine for steam and it was the second time she'd suggested it.

"Let's talk about appearance, Marl, because it's important. These victims had no physical characteristics in common. The first was a redhead, well-toned, physically fit." He wanted to say beautiful but the word stuck in his mouth. "The second was Arabic, dark and slender, and the third was tall and blonde. Different academic fields and disciplines, and apart from Alice they lived within five miles of each other."

"They all went to Los Poblanos Academy and Gibson Uni, sir. Oh, and I checked in with Zarah Thai. Everything's good."

Something had changed in Malin, Temeke thought. It wasn't like he was indulging a novice, a simpering girl too wet behind the ears to deal with the horrors of Violent Crimes. By ignoring her emotions, she found a rotting corpse stinking like old vomit in the undergrowth more manageable. No, she'd done some growing up since then. Gone out on a limb and made her own decisions. And they were good decisions.

Temeke almost jumped when the phone on the desk gave a piercing squeal.

Malin hooked the receiver onto her shoulder and for a brief few seconds she just listened. "5025 Watercress Drive. Off Jefferson, you say? Yes... I'm on my way.

Thanks, Maggie."

Malin tapped something into the computer and gave him a wide-eyed look. "Paddy Brody's car is registered to that address, a white Honda Accord with a damaged passenger wing mirror and out of date tags. I'd like to follow him."

"I need to pack it in, love. Get a few hours' kip. You ladies be careful." He looked at her a beat too long, saw her eyes drop.

Temeke walked out into the parking lot, felt a stab of fresh air in his lungs as he blinked the moisture out of his eyes. He half walked, half ran toward his jeep, breath drifting like clouds as he unlocked the door.

He was half way up Guadalupe Trail and about to turn into his driveway when he saw the figure. A young man standing in the middle of the road, dark hair gusting across his face and jutting cheekbones that made you think he needed a good meal. It was what he was holding that made Temeke screech to a halt.

A gray cat with a little red coat.

TWENTY-FOUR

Temeke turned the wheel as hard as he could, veering sideways to avoid hitting the man. He pulled over and lowered the window, pushing his head out into the cool night air.

"Where did you find him?" he shouted.

"Under that tree," the man said, jingling the identity disk with one finger. "Caught a bird and ate it."

"Cheeky sod. The cat, I mean."

Temeke tried to make out pale features in the shadows, thought he saw the flicker of a smile and then a pair of anxious, melancholy eyes. Young, early twenties at a guess, hair partly covered by a woolen hat.

"You live around here?" Temeke asked.

"Just passing through. Here."

A ball of gray fur was suddenly posted through the window, claws clacking on the dashboard as the cat settled into the passenger seat with a disgruntled meow. Temeke noticed his rearview mirror was filling with the headlights of a passing truck and he motioned to the young man to step further back onto the grass curb to let it pass.

A loud honk from the driver indicated Temeke was too far out in the road, so he put the car in gear and rolled forward a few feet into his driveway. Holding his breath, he counted to three as the truck sped away leaving behind a thick spray of leaves.

His eyes swung back to the grass curb. There was no sign of the man, not until Temeke caught a slither of movement in his wing mirror. A figure jogged down the middle of the road through a cloud of exhaust, turning sharply to the left and stooping beneath the branch of a tree.

Temeke closed the car window, fumbled with the key fob and locked the car with a bleep. He wasn't about to lose sight of someone whose comment of *passing through* gave the bell in his brain a small tinkle.

The identity disk was engraved with his last name and address, and since Temeke was pulling into the driveway the young man would have naturally assumed he was the owner. But how long had he been waiting?

It looked as if he had bolted in the direction of the small adobe ruin. Temeke called it the *ruin* because the owner had done nothing in the past ten years to make the rental look habitable. Cracked stucco walls and weeds reaching almost as high as the nearest utility pole. It was the dope hut of the neighborhood.

He started walking away from the car, blinked a few times and wiped a stream of moisture from his eyes. It was bloody freezing and he thought he felt the first brush of snow on his bald head. Two street lamps spread a circle of light on the pavement below, not enough to give him an inkling of what lay beyond the trees.

Jogging down a small slope into an overgrown front yard, his boots crunched on brown balls of sycamore fruit and tapped against loose gravel. He studied every bush and shadow, hoping to see something moving near the perimeter. It was darker than a coal shed and he tensed and took a few steps forward.

To the right was a barrier of saplings and a rotting trellis. To his left a culvert of slurry and ice that swung sharply around one side of the old house. He'd seen the homeowner, what... twice? Spoke to him about the renovations, told him about the squatters. The City had recently dug a trench for the cabling, anything that might bring the place forward into the twenty-first century.

Temeke shouldered his way through a narrow gap in the trellis, cupped his hands around his face to peer in through a small side window. Couldn't see a whole lot through wooden boards and tattered curtains, and the back door was locked. He was glad. Didn't want to find two people in there having a shag like last time.

Locked?

So someone was looking after the place.

He had a sense the man had run along the gravel track behind the house. Couldn't hear shoes pumping against rock and there was no sign of movement. Picking up speed, he jogged for several minutes beneath a full moon that had risen above the trees, blue and brooding against a wintry sky. The path was well worn and level, leading through clumps of sage to a cornfield and a stand of cottonwoods beyond.

Right where the field ended and where the trees began was a dark colored van parked on a narrow road that tapered round to Guadalupe Trail. He couldn't recall the name of the road, but he reckoned it was a minor artery that fed into Fourth Street. One the farmers used. He had a moment of distraction, couldn't decide if the towering stalks were maize or corn, and judging by the musty smell, the farmer had left the field to dry out too long.

The sound of whispering made him stop, made him peer between brittle husks, eyes swinging up and down the rows watching for movement. He couldn't make out the words, only a slight swell in pitch before it was accompanied by a female voice.

He cast a glance behind him so he could get his bearings. Taking two careful steps at a time, he paused and listened to a rise in the wind. The voices grew louder, leaves rattling as if they had taken off toward the far corner of the field.

"It's not working," the female voice said.

"You're just scared." The second voice was deeper, certainly male.

"Well, maybe I am. I'll get caught. The bad guys always do."

"Down like flies. One by one. Dead and buried. You can do it."

"I can't do it," the woman whined. "They always come back from the dead."

"Then we'll just kill them again."

Temeke could see a cloud of breath above the corn as if the woman had thrown her head back in frustration.

There was nothing unusual about two lovers debating the course of their relationship. It was the reference to killing someone that made the hairs on the back of his neck itch, made him wonder if they were dealing in more than just morbid repartee.

Gang activity had become massive over the last ten years, bringing a whole new meaning to the slogan *united states*. Heroin and cocaine trafficking were only the top layer of the onion; the internet being the most powerful medium for key players rather than meeting in basements like they used to do.

He felt like a sodding stalker and without a good visual he had no idea if he was following the cat-man or two drugged-up lodgers from the old ruin.

He heard a sneeze and then an angry word. The man was playing her.

"Don't even think about it. I know how your squalid little mind works. But then again, what makes me think you even have a mind?"

"Why me?" she said. "Wait, let me guess – it's because you're too chicken."

There was silence for a moment before stalks began bending and swaying as the couple broke into a walk.

"You'll be free of them. Just think." The man drew out the last word, said it like it would make a difference. "You have to do it. And you're already half way through. Can't stop now."

The wind tugged at the stalks and the whole field seemed to rattle from the sudden gust. Temeke never heard her response, only the sound of the man's voice when the wind died down.

"How I love this time of night. Porcelain and pristine. So very pretty."

Temeke had to force himself not to run, feet moving carefully through the crunching detritus in time with their footfalls. He stood still for a few seconds, thought he saw movement through a thicket of corn about ten feet ahead. Snapping sheaves and swaying tassels told him the couple had circled back around, heading this time toward the very place he was standing.

Backing up in a narrow aisle, Temeke held his breath and listened. He parted two branches with both hands and watched a figure step out onto the moonlit track. The same man he had seen on Guadalupe Trail, the man who likely had a molt of cat hairs on that jacket of his.

"I'll get the pizza." He paced from side to side and seemed to be staring at someone in the shadows. He couldn't have been more than ten feet away. A rustling sound and he stepped off the path and back into the darkness. "We'll leave it outside the door with a note. She likes pizza and she likes cheese. Don't you remember?"

"I can't—"

"Oh, but you can. You can go to Keller's and get a bone. And don't forget to cancel that dinner order."

"There must be another way."

Temeke noted the change in the woman's voice, frightened now and trembling. He couldn't see her, couldn't identify her, and that made him nervous.

"There's always another way." The man paused for a

moment. "Wait… I heard something."

Temeke's breath came hard and fast, adrenalin racing through his veins, and he covered his mouth to hide the vapor. The other hand hovered over the Glock in his belt.

A brief silence before leaves snapped and the two of them thundered in a southeasterly direction. It wasn't as if the man assumed Temeke's footfalls were those of a grouse. He knew he was being followed.

Temeke ran as close as he could, breaking out at the edge of the cornfield behind the van. He heard a door slam, engine revs, and then the thing swerved from side to side along the narrow road without any headlights.

Lurching onto the main road toward Corrales, it disappeared into the cold gray night.

TWENTY-FIVE

Gabriel approached Victory Hills around eight thirty on Friday night. He parked on Girard and removed the magnetic pizza delivery banners from both passenger doors.

Then he walked the rest of the way, smelling the metallic scent of a butcher's bone in his backpack and the rush of a cold breeze. It was a close call.

He'd been playing that detective like a fish on a line, wanted to see how far he could go without being caught. There was a fifty-fifty chance those sharp black eyes had the license number of the van.

"You better hope it was too dark," Demon said.

Gabriel stood at the west end of San Rafael Avenue, looking east toward a glazed hump of a mountain range, peaks capped in snow. It was the police unit parked halfway up the street that caught his eye, the only thing that marred his sense of peace.

"Always a cop when you don't need one," Demon muttered.

Gabriel stood beside a one-level home, white brick with a gray tiled roof. A corner lot with a five foot wall that faced Girard and curled around to San Rafael. Hauling himself over the wall, he scanned the back yard and the lots beyond. Judging by the block walls between each property, Gabriel only needed to scale about four of them to get to the back of number 5507 without being seen.

It was easier than he imagined. The homeowners who hadn't drawn their blinds were glued to the TV, never saw him bolting across their yards.

When he arrived at the house, Gabriel saw the dog before it saw him, lips drawn back to receive a shank bone he'd bought from Keller's meats. It was like a big spotted Labrador with a wagging tail, didn't take much to coax it to the back corner of the lot where the thing had dug a crater-sized hole out of boredom.

The back door was locked, Gabriel could see the shadow of a bolt between the frame and the latch. The doggie door was his best bet, a large white frame that took up nearly half the bottom panel. He removed his backpack, pushed through a wide vinyl flap and crawled into the kitchen.

The remains of a medium-sized pizza box lay on the kitchen table with sprinkles of parmesan on the floor. She had staggered into the living room where he found her sitting on a wheel-back chair, groaning and hunched over a desk.

He unzipped the top pocket of his backpack and took out what he needed. If Zarah heard the rustle of cord as the ball hit the floor, she wasn't quick enough. Arms and torso already bound to the chair, there was barely a scream out of her open mouth before it was silenced with a strip of packing tape. Two legs thrashed under the desk, but only for a moment.

Gabriel saw the frown, read the expression on her face and twisted the chair around to face him. "That doggie door's way too big. The wood's as rotten as your heart. May I?"

He sat on a blue floral easy chair and smiled. "You're probably wondering where we've met before."

Zarah blinked a couple of times, chin sinking to her chest. Her head was inclined slightly, ear pressed against one shoulder.

"Remember the time you won Miss Coronado?" He emphasized the word with two index fingers. "It was raining... hailstones, I think. Pinged off the cars and made dents in the paintwork. You were so happy. You and your crown, and your long mermaid dress all covered in sparkles. I complimented you, said you were beautiful. Only, you said I was stick thin. No, wait... you said I was a scraggy pile of bones. Then you threw pizza at me. You and all of them."

Gabriel saw the hint of recognition and then it was gone behind narrowed eyes. "I know what you're thinking. You're thinking, it can't be. Didn't think I could look like this."

Zarah shook her head. It was all she could manage.

"I should be dead by now." Gabriel dredged up that same nudge of pain from somewhere deep inside and his eyes began to water. "Do you know what it's like to be laughed at... hated for something you can't help? Do you?"

Zarah shook her head again, eyes glistening. There was a look on her face that scared Gabriel for a second. At first he thought it was terror, and then he realized what it was. Resignation. Zarah Thai knew she was going to die.

"Asha's already dead. And buried," Gabriel whispered, watching a pair of eyes that darted back and forth. Maybe Zarah was looking for a weapon, wondering how it would end. "She didn't suffer. Died with all the dignity of a concert pianist, only without a couple of fingers. Can't have her playing up there when I die. Drive me nuts."

Gabriel finished off a glass of wine that had been sitting on the coffee table and poured himself another.

"The way I see it is this. Each time I rid this town of a demon, I get a little credit. And you are a demon with your cold, cruel heart and your fake smile. I know what you did out there in the parking lot. Oh, it was just a quick fondle, nothing to worry about. As long as Alice Delgado didn't find out. As long as she didn't know how many of you had the hots for her boyfriend."

The coughing started then, the panting, the puckered face. "Not so pretty now, are you Zarah? If you really want to know I cancelled your order and brought something better. Homemade with a dash of rat poison. And you're so careful with your food. Stomach's probably lost its lining from all that throwing up to stay thin. It won't take long, a few seizures... I mean, you've got to die of something. Might as well die like a rat." Gabriel leaned forward a little. "Think I'm joking, don't you?"

That seemed to make Zarah whimper and fret, tears leaving glossy trails down her cheeks. She couldn't scream, couldn't run, just sat there jerking for a time until her eyes became glazed and her head rolled forward. As the minutes turned to hours, the coughing behind the tape grew still and so did her body.

Unless she was faking it.

Gabriel poked her a few times. Definitely out cold. "Probably regretting the day you spat on me. Said I was evil... I'll show you evil."

Gabriel left her there, didn't want to lose the last traces of a such a memory, the scents, the sounds, the flavor. It was all in his mind, all in his past, and he refused to leave it all behind.

The bedroom barely had room for a queen-sized bed and on the dressing table was a large tub of moisturizer. He opened the lid, poked a gloved finger in the center and scooped enough cream to smear all over his face. Then he carved another name in the kitchen door frame, one inch below the hinge.

Estheri.

He climbed out the same way he had climbed in; the dog flap was large enough for a slender man. Peering through the garden gate at the road, he saw the cop on the phone eyeing the front of the house with a yawn.

Probably thought everything was OK, like the pizza delivery van that had eased up to the curb a few hours ago and left a tasty treat on the doorstep.

Gabriel kept to the back of the house, scaled a block wall and dropped into next door's yard. He counted four more yards until he found the main road and that faithful old van. It was getting harder to start now, barely turning over in the cold weather. On the way home, he thought he saw a little Honda Accord in the rearview mirror, but all white cars looked the same and who in New Mexico didn't favor a white car to keep the sun off?

There was a puddle of oil on the narrow lane where he always parked. The van might not start at all tomorrow, he thought, feeling a twinge of grief in his gut. Might not live to see another sunrise.

He walked through the cornfield to the back of the house, unlocked the door and took a deep breath. He peeled off his clothes in the kitchen, rammed them into a trash bag and stood naked in front of the mirror. Gray skin shimmered under the fluorescent lighting, belly speckled with sweat. He was uglier than he had ever been.

"I am evil," he reminded himself as he peeled off the wig. "I am dead."

He would have turned away then, only today he stared at that reflection, repulsed by what he saw. Filthy. Dirty. Rags.

Gabriel had seen it in a dream. The growth, a tumor, an ugly sore getting bigger and bigger, fusing to bone and brain, a gradual death from the burden of his pain. He almost laughed because he imagined he had put it there himself.

Then he cried, because he knew he had.

The name of the growth was *Demon*. Everyone had one. Some came and went, some just got bigger and bigger. And then there were those who took their own lives before that growth ever had a chance to reveal itself.

He stared at his body one last time, knew what changes had to be made, what colors he would choose. He'd had enough of being held captive in a prison he didn't want, praying for harmony that never came. Sometimes it was better to be what God made you than changing it all for the sake of perfection. Or, in his case, for the sake of shame.

Why aren't you like her? Not even an atom of likeness. You did it, didn't you? It had to be you. Shame… shame… shame.

The memories. The whip. He could imagine it high over his head now, the long gray tail falling… falling. He tried to call out. "No… please!" But the whip struck him on the back and the pain made him gasp.

Those marks were still there, all the way down the back of his legs if he cared to look. They were there all those years ago when he was undressing at school. Gabriel had no idea what to say, how to tell all those enquiring mouths that life had been hell.

He was struck by the one dizzying notion that the only person he had ever trusted had been himself. And when *himself* was gone, there would be no one.

"There is a way," Demon murmured.

Gabriel took shallow breaths of warm air as he stood under the shower, scrubbed his body and head until they were both raw. Watched trails of muddy water slinking toward the drain like a trickle of tree roots.

He remembered the detective's face, the clenched jaw, the evasive black eyes. He was observant and cautious, and yet there was a profound calm about him Gabriel rather liked. A handsome man, shrugging on a coat over solid shoulders and arms corded with muscle. Gabriel had seen stronger men, but nothing quite like this.

He toweled himself dry, wiped a fist over a cloudy mirror and paused half a second. The face was the one he remembered, pink skin and eyes whiter in the corners than a fried egg.

He propped open the door with a small antique iron, watched the steam as it drifted toward the kitchen, felt the chilled air against his naked flesh.

He was excited, longing to make that call. Not just for the Smarts, but because he knew the dealer wanted to get high together.

On the mattress were jeans, shirt, boots and a brown leather belt with a single pronged buckle engraved with the first letter of his name; a memorable detail. Athletic, clean-cut, sparkling... no sense in calling too much attention to himself.

He smiled in his in-between world, marveling at how his brain had suddenly re-wired itself, how it enhanced the senses he had. He inhaled slightly, refocused his mind on the sudden stir of air under his nose, and listened.

TWENTY-SIX

Malin leaned back in the chair of her second floor office. The sky was black and her eyes were locked in the glare of two area lights in the parking lot. Stars blinked through the skeletal limbs of a sycamore and the moon shone down on a row of black and white units. She was waiting for Maggie Watts to call.

Turning her mind to Paddy Brody, she replayed the mental video recording in her head, brooded over it as if there was something she must have missed. His tone had been impossible to read and that made her tense. When she'd asked him if Lily Delgado was dead he simply replied, *she is to me.* There had been no edge to his voice, no reason to suspect he knew anything about her disappearance. Just four simple words.

There's always more to a killer than meets the eye, she thought. Some worked for an employer, some were gang related, most were thugs and only a few were independently contracted. This one targeted young, healthy females between the ages of twenty-one and twenty-three, no physical commonalities and each murder more elaborate than a bullet to the head. She wondered if it boiled down to timing since these deaths galloped ahead without restraint, as if there was significant ground the killer had to cover.

There was more than a thin thread that connected them, more than just a high school group of friends. A cult, money, and one shared lover. Comparisons and statistics on a case like this were slim to none and she hadn't a hope in hell of building an accurate profile if none of these deaths were related.

There was a more frightening category of killer; a loner. They weren't paid by an employer to kill, weren't expecting to collect insurance. The act wasn't spontaneous – an idea dredged out of a confused mind – it just didn't compute. But each victim had been put in a vulnerable situation, they were alone at the time of death.

This left another possibility. Revenge.

Malin paused to think about that for a moment, jumping to the natural conclusion that it was a love relationship gone bad and as for timing, it might have had something to do with the killer's cover being compromised.

She rubbed her eyes and peered at the computer screen. Asha Samadi had been reported missing sixteen days ago and according to the amount of blood found on the carpet, was regrettably dead. The papers said Kenzie Voorhees was found without vital signs and pronounced dead at the scene of an hellacious south side gas blast. The house had been leveled and debris scattered over hundreds of yards, some of it hanging on trees and neighboring houses. And then there was Rosa Belmonte, drowned in the Rio Grande river in her car.

Paddy was a solid witness – and let's face it, intimacy with more than one woman could make a man some interesting enemies. She wondered if Wingman could offer any clues. He was on vacation, so he said, only all sociable souls could text and his had gone eerily quiet.

Sixteen minutes past ten on Saturday night and Malin checked her phone. One private message. One text. She listened to the message first, wondering why she hadn't heard the phone ring.

It's Paddy. You asked me to call you if I thought of anything. Gray hoodie. Very transparent. I thought I'd seen him before.

Malin felt a wave of disgust, listened to thin air for a second before calling him back. No answer.

She scanned Maggie's text. A simple 'can you bring me some coffee?' Time to relieve her from a night of surveillance outside Paddy's house.

Malin switched off the computer, shrugged on her coat and padded downstairs. Sergeant Moran was reading a copy of *Time* Magazine and sipping a can of Coke. One of the graveyard shift officers was playing a game of solitaire on his computer; the lenses of his glasses recklessly mirroring a deck of cards.

She tried to slip past Sarge without saying hello, but his eyes were quicker than a snake.

"Being cordial is not just for cherries," he muttered.

"I'm going to meet Maggie, Sarge."

"She said she's freezing her butt off out there."

"She called you?" Malin saw him nod. "Tell her I'm on my way."

Malin raised one hand, uttered a tired goodbye and fled through the front door. It was Sunday tomorrow and the thought of a peaceful day gave her a little more energy. She headed for the twenty-four hour BadA$$ coffee stop on Fourth and Alameda, bought two cups of dark roast and a couple of blueberry muffins at the drive-thru.

Watercress Drive was a quiet neighborhood off Jefferson, looping around into Goldenthread Drive where four handy exits brought you back to Alameda. She pulled up by the curb about twenty-five yards down from Maggie's truck, couldn't see Paddy's residence since it was too far up the street and partially covered by a box hedge.

But Maggie could, and with a good pair of binoculars she could probably see as far as the clock on the mantel if he had one.

Malin's phone vibrated, felt the warning before she heard Maggie's voice. "Done some checking. He has a roommate, Burmese guy called Maun Tung. Got his phone number if you need it. Paddy was looking out of the window about twenty minutes ago."

"Any interest in your truck?"

"Nope. There are two others on the other side of the street, same color, same model."

It wouldn't have made any difference, Malin thought. If Paddy was alert, knew all the cars in his street, he would sense a variation in traffic. "Bought you some coffee."

"I'll be darned..." Maggie said slowly. "Subject's opening the garage door. Most activity I've seen all evening."

"What's he wearing?"

"Black jacket, khaki pants. Putting a gym bag in the trunk."

"How big's that gym bag?"

"Weekend sized. About twenty-one inches."

"Bit late to be traveling," Malin murmured.

"Might be meeting someone."

"What sort of meeting would make a man leave his house at ten thirty at night?"

"A sick relative... a girlfriend. He's on his way. Shall I follow him?"

"I'll go," Malin said, and ended the call.

The smell of coffee and muffins reminded her Maggie would have to do without. Passing food across to another undercover squad car was as foolish as following a suspected killer.

She rubbed her forehead, felt a sudden ache creeping up the small of her back and settling into the base of her neck. She lowered her jaw to relieve the pain, pulled out into the middle of the street and nodded at Maggie on her way past.

Malin hung back as the white Honda Accord backed down the driveway and out into the street. She wasn't close enough to blind his vision in the rearview mirror with her headlights and, staring at a mud spattered back window, realized he likely couldn't see her at all. Her fingers began to tingle against the steering wheel as she kept about a hundred yards behind.

He turned west all the way to Camino Vega Verde and just before the turn off she decided it was time to get closer. He didn't drive to the Delgado House on Bazan Loop, but turned left at the fork and stopped before a white house with plantation shutters and palm trees which towered above an acre of lush grounds on the west side of the street.

Malin chose the right turn, drove anticlockwise around the loop until she was about thirty feet in front of him, pulled over to the curb and parked under a weeping willow with the headlights off. She slumped down in her seat and studied him, the direction of his eyes, the slant of his body, the general demeanor.

He didn't look up. Seemed in a hurry to take the gym bag from the trunk and lock the car. Six seconds later, he turned along a narrow path huddled in the shadows of two properties and bordered by a high wall. Wherever he was going, he didn't want company.

Malin checked her weapon and swung the driver's door open without taking her eyes off the white car. She stepped out into the darkness, locked the door from the inside, heard a faint click.

She blinked a few times to ward off a bitter breeze that swung from the northwest and sent a skitter of leaves along the same path Paddy had taken. A few stars twinkled overhead and the street lights gave off a pinky-yellow blush.

Narrowing her eyes, she peered around the corner of the block wall, advancing slowly at first before breaking into a jog. She was looking at every shadow, every clump of grass that led toward a faint rumble of traffic, stopping to catch her breath at the edge of a wide dirt track. Beyond it lay an arroyo and an empty parking lot that bordered Corrales Road, and to the right, a sandy track that meandered to the north.

There were no footprints, no sign of movement, and she closed her eyes for a moment to listen to the echo of silence and the emptiness in her head. Then voices drifted from a clump of cottonwoods behind the Café and to the left of where she was standing. Although she couldn't make out the words, it was a male and female arguing.

She passed silently under overhanging tree limbs, jogging over a wooden bridge that led to the floodlit restaurant patio. As the voices grew louder, she saw a man standing beside a table, head down and face illuminated by the glowing blue rectangle of his cell phone.

Pausing at the foot of a large tree, she held her breath for a few seconds and peered through the branches.

"I don't see any messages," he said. "When did you call?"

"This morning." Her voice was shrill with a whine to it.

A scraping sound as he drew a chair out from under a metal table, set the bag down between them. "Did anyone see you leave?"

"There's a cop car outside every night and one assigned to me during the day." She shrugged, lips widening a little. "They won't know I'm gone."

Malin could see the girl now. Long hair, black sweats, about a hundred and thirty pounds at a guess. She might have been tall judging by the length of one coltish thigh crossed neatly over the other and a foot that kept bouncing in the air as if she was nervous. Malin recognized her from the photographs as Adel Martinez, recognized her voice too.

He reached over and dropped a small zippy into the palm of her hand. "It's all I have."

Adel's head fell back for a few seconds and she gave a tentative sigh. "That's it?"

"I'm not a freaking pill mill. It'll keep you going for a while." He leaned forward and brushed a drift of hair from Adel's heart-shaped face, finger tracing her cheekbones and lingering on the pouty curve of her upper lip. "I want to tell you something."

Adel's face was stony. It gave Malin a jolt, made her feel nauseous standing under the cover of the trees, waiting for the inevitable.

"I did some bad things. Things I regret. You remember the time when you found me with Kenzie… in the Lion's Mouth? Well, I did sleep with her."

Adel hugged her stomach, chin quivering under the weight of that blow and there was something dark and mysterious swimming about her eyes. "You two-timing low-life—"

"I made one mistake. I know it was wrong. But after Alice died… it changed me. I tried to fight it. But it got worse."

Adel seemed to fill her lungs greedily, chin raised. There was nothing flexible or negotiable about her; she was simply looking for a way to snare him. "This isn't you, Paddy."

"OK, so maybe I deluded myself into thinking I was something special. Maybe I took things too far. I'm sorry."

There was several seconds of silence and Malin felt an inexplicable chill running down her spine, a dizzy sense of certainty. Paddy was milking the moment for all it was worth.

"You did something terrible, Paddy."

"Doesn't everyone?"

"You cheated. You stole, lied, hated. All because of

these." She slipped the pills into her jacket pocket. "All because you never had the guts to stand up to her. Does that make you happy?"

Paddy's face was impassive, but there was an underlying tension Malin sensed, a suspended moment when his mood could have shifted either way.

"We all got what we wanted. What's wrong with that?"

"You got what you wanted. All I see is black now. And I can't sleep."

"It'll all be over soon. Asha will come home."

"She's not coming home. She said there was this guy following her weeks before she disappeared. Some guy dressed in black. Had eyes like—"

"She was hallucinating. It happens to me all the time."

"What about Rosa and Kenzie? Don't you think it's because of what we did? And now there's only two of us. There's nothing you can do."

"There is something." Using his foot, he pushed the bag on the ground toward her.

"You think a few wigs and a girl playing dress-up is going to fool anyone?"

"You've done it before."

"You want me to disappear, is that it? Surely you're going to come with me?"

"I'm not going anywhere. Except to the police."

"Go ahead. Because you know what? You don't have one ounce of credibility. You're finished. I might go down with you, Paddy, but you're going to fall a hell of a lot harder."

"You're bluffing."

"You're facing twenty years." Her voice drifted now and then, and when she spoke, her words seemed distant, as if she was going back to her past if only to torture herself. "You want to make it all better, don't you? But it's too late."

"I don't think I can do that."

Thoughts swirled in Malin's head, spinning and dancing. What was too late? The silence grew thick and heavy and she gulped audibly.

Adel stared into Paddy's eyes as if she was trying to find an explanation. "You're not talking to anyone about this, OK?"

"That's not my problem."

"No, it's not your problem, Paddy. It was never *your* problem. Even when it destroyed her." A tear ran down the side of Adel's nose, chin bouncing with every sob. "Don't you care?"

Malin noticed a twitch at the corner of Paddy's eye, as if he had received some invisible communication right on cue. He leapt to his feet, kicked back the chair and started walking toward the tree Malin was standing under.

"Where are you going?" Adel said.

Paddy turned, long enough for Malin to creep back into the shadows behind the east wall of the restaurant.

"I'm going to find Lily. I think I know where she is."

TWENTY-SEVEN

He felt it even through the coveralls, hands braced, cheek inches from a hole in the drywall. Gabriel couldn't see through the bones of the house, it was too dark for that, but he could hear the sudden intake of breath, the snap of a twig outside the back door.

A presence. It was earlier than the appointed time. Couldn't have been the dealer. Must have been someone else.

Demon began cackling and saying how much fun it would be to watch, how the blood was already pumping through Gabriel's thick, mortal veins. "You are a brilliant host," he said. "And I am a patient witness."

"It's a novelty to you," Gabriel whispered, trying to focus on the threat. "A world teeming with life you want to destroy."

"Not destroy. Educate. I want them to know how powerful they can be. Lords of their own manors. *Imagine!*"

Gabriel had imagined. That's what had lured him away from a stifled existence in the first place, the in-your-face philosophies of how to be and what to say. He wanted to be king in his own world, wanted full control. It would be so much easier, wouldn't it?

Focus. He pressed a fingertip against the wall between him and the intruder, gauging the quiet but heavy sound of a boot, shuffling now to cover his approach. It had to be a male, Gabriel thought, and that made him mad.

He wasn't aware he was being followed, should have been more careful, should have doused the single candle on the floor. It was the detective and he didn't want to do it. Pulling the hood up over his head, he waited, senses prickling as he held his breath. He knew exactly when the curtain would go up before the show, because it was more dangerous inside the house than out, and whoever it was stood no chance at all.

"You'll cut him," Demon said. "And cut him good."

"He might have a gun."

"He doesn't."

What cop doesn't carry a gun?

Gabriel took the knife from the kitchen countertop, an antique slider his father once used for hunting. Thumb hovering over the button on the sheath, he estimated the detective was right outside the back door now, feet noiseless in the dirt and crouched behind the lower panel, eyes level with the keyhole.

Demon chuckled and the sound was flat. "Now, unlock the door and let him in."

Gabriel twisted the lock silently, hearing only the continual chunter of Demon's voice.

"By all accounts my kind should have been miserable when we were cast out. But we weren't. Not at the beginning. Now I just watch, wonder what it's like to be filled with hunger and desire. Man is one lucky—"

Shut up! Gabriel thought, flattening himself against the wall behind the back door. He realized the knife wasn't enough. He would need something to bring the man down, knock him out. He looked around blindly and that's when he saw the antique iron on the bathroom floor, metal, heavy, and leaning up against the baseboard. He padded only a few feet and lunged for it.

A scuffling sound. He enjoyed the mounting fear the detective must have felt as he saw a flicker of amber through that key-filled cavity. Even so Gabriel stiffened and bit the inside of his cheek, anticipated the drop of the door lever, the thin shriek of metal hinges as the door eased open no more than a hand's width.

The ice on the wind made Gabriel blink a few times and there was an odor of cologne, sickly, invasive. He waited, visualized the size of the man by the sound of his tread. Could only see one side of his face as he walked toward the center of the room.

Gabriel was behind him now. Saw a cloud of breath snaking through thin lips, sensed the detective was taking in the small space in front of him through an unfocused eye, the mattress, the black leather gym bag.

How foolish to enter a house without a weapon, no reason to be there in the first place. Unless he was looking for cash.

Detectives always carry weapons, fool! And they don't steal cash.

The detective must have smelled shampoo and a faint residue of steam, but he never felt the terrible weight against the back of his head. Knees slammed into the floor and perhaps… just perhaps he felt Gabriel's gloved hand at his cheek, the sudden jerk of his head and a cold blade that sliced through the large artery at his throat.

Blood arced as far as the mattress, a warm spray against Gabriel's cheek and the taste of it on his lips made him retch. The detective attempted a wet gurgle, dropped to his knees, right shoulder hitting the floor with a hard thud. Then came the shudder and the spasms, hands clutching both sides of his neck as a dark pool collected beneath him. Slick and shiny, black as tar.

The man was slipping away. He would never see the cottonwoods in the Bosque again, or the copper skies of New Mexico in the summertime. He would never know what was in that black gym bag.

"There," Gabriel murmured, wiping the blood from his

mouth with the back of his hand. "Are you pleased now?"

There was no reply. No round of applause. Gabriel expected Demon to crow his knowledge of life and death, regale him with stories of how he fell to earth in a blaze of lightning, wings scorched even before he touched the ground.

"Did I fail?" Gabriel hated to ask, but imagined the killing to be a death worthy of Demon's expectations, a mark he had earlier fallen short of.

The silence was unnerving.

Gabriel studied the corpse, squinted at it for a second or two. He re-sheathed the knife and slipped it in his pocket, didn't want to ask any more questions, wanted to save himself the indignity of another lecture.

The eyes were bulbous and there was no life in them. It suddenly struck him as odd that there had been a living, moving body less than a few minutes ago and now it was a limp mass on his kitchen floor. Something in Gabriel's dreams resonated with this scene, not so much the death itself, but the helplessness of the intruder. Where Gabriel had extraordinary discernment, the type that Demon called near-divine, this man had not been able to sense anything at all. Certainly not death at the end of another passing day.

A tear collected in the corner of Gabriel's eye and he was aware he had not been this emotional for years. He studied the man's face, the curve of the body, the wavy hair, and through a haze of tears he could see the man was morphing into someone else.

"You knew!" he cried, hearing the deafening pulse in his ears. "Why didn't you tell me!"

Demon was up there in that suffocating silence, spiraling higher and higher in the endless void of space. A flying gargoyle banking first to the left and then to the right, picking up speed and shrieking in an ear-piercing crescendo.

Gabriel pressed two hands against his ears, rocking back and forth at a heralding din of trumpets that seemed to phrase an impending finale. A sudden burst of light and the pain in his skull ebbed like the surge of an ocean upon a rocky shore.

"Wake up," he said, stabbing dead flesh with a knuckle. He lifted himself off the bloody floor and staggered about in a viscous pool.

"Don't torture yourself," Demon whispered, voice drifting in and out. "Death... life, none of it matters."

But it did matter. Like it mattered the first time Gabriel stepped on a sleepy butterfly on the lawn. He had been six then.

"Everything has to die," Demon whispered on a downward spiral, coming to land on the kitchen counter as if he had burst through a roof that wasn't there. "You just gave it a leg up."

Gabriel closed his eyes and when he opened them again the man looked like he was homeless or a drunk looking for money to feed his craving. But the thoughts were empty this time as if Gabriel was trying to confirm something he knew to be false. Had no right.

"Of course you have rights," Demon muttered. "All people have rights. You are the king of your own castle, the lord of all you survey. Isn't that right, Gabriel? Isn't that the truth?"

Gabriel shook his head and backed away from the scene as if it had taken on a filthy stench. "Get me out of these clothes," he whimpered, scratching at his chest, his arms, his legs. "Get me out of here."

"Just as I thought," Demon said. "Feeble. Like all manflesh. You're no better than the dirt you came from."

TWENTY-EIGHT

The Emergency Response Teams pulled out of San Rafael Avenue just after midnight, ambulance shrieking down University Boulevard toward Lomas. The scene was owned by the police now, front yard barred by a yellow ribbon of tape, warning: CRIME SCENE–DO NOT CROSS.

Two officers flanked the front door eyeing the curious public and the responding officer was jotting down a few statements and making a witness list. An Asian woman was barely able to choke out a statement, said Zarah had not been seen for two days and the dog was a mess. No food, no water. Could have been three days for all she knew.

Malin stood on the curb hugging a notepad, eyes drawn to a sprinkle of rain in the beam of a street lamp. She turned her mind to the victim, Zarah Thai, a young woman who lived alone with her dog, ordered a pizza like she did every Friday night. She was found tied to a chair and gagged and had somehow managed to chew through the brown packing tape in her mouth. She had been vomiting on and off for twenty-four hours. This wasn't the work of a street thug, a gang, or a sophisticated assassin. It was too personal for that.

Malin's mind returned to Paddy Brody because to her he was showing all the classic signs of restlessness. She had likely shaken him up a little, made him nervous, made him look in his rearview mirror a little more often than he used to. Tried calling him a few times, but he never answered, and the word *transparent* kept buzzing around in her head.

A cackling laugh brought Malin's mind back to the present, Unit Commander Roach was sharing a joke with an agent. It wasn't until Roach raised his voice to officer Maynard, who was hunched over the roof of his unit and shaking his head vigorously, that she realized what had happened. Surveillance had failed. Her belly was already smoldering with hot needles of dread.

She took a gulp of fresh air and then another. Every crime scene stayed in her head, blinking in and out until the next one came along. In this case, there were ribbons of twisted cord hanging from the back of a chair and a puckered area rug spattered with dried blood and vomit. Tiny heels had hammered and hammered on that hardwood floor in the vain hope someone would hear her.

All the other rooms appeared undisturbed, no sign of a struggle, and one window had been smashed by the responding officer. Most of the other windows wouldn't budge, wood frames warped from the recent rains or painted shut some years before.

Make-up was scattered about on the dressing table and there was an open pot of moisturizer with a deep indentation in the cream. All bagged and taken, including a fluorescent green tennis racket Malin had found behind the bedroom door. Then there had been the inevitable disagreement between the police officers and detectives as to how the perp got in and subtle whispers about Maynard.

Malin watched the Field Investigators and a group of Crime Scene Specialists as they emptied trash cans and nodded to each other in a silent language only they knew. Matt Black brought out a pizza box sealed in a plastic bag and swinging from two fingers. Dark hair in a schoolboy cut and a cheeky grin, he stood beside her silently for a few moments, lips forming words around a stutter. He clearly read the wretchedness on her face and went off on one of his little-known-facts rampage.

"Lucky she wasn't gagged with duct tape," he said. "Wouldn't have stood a chance."

Malin thought about that for a moment. It meant the crime hadn't been well thought through. Meant the killer was getting sloppy.

"Sugar cane, almonds, wheat... they all contain a little cyanide," he said. "Green potatoes contain glycol alkaloid. Too much of that and you'd be in a polished mahogany casket with a cream interior."

"And how does that have anything to do with a pizza?" Malin asked.

"I've seen pizza sprinkled with Romano and Parmesan. But I can't say I've ever seen one powdered with Rodenticide. Nor have I ever heard of anyone eating such a high dose."

"She must have been hungry."

"I think what you meant to say was, why didn't she notice anything odd about the taste before she polished off three quarters of it? Thing is, they usually come in pellets, only this was ground down and mixed with extra mature cheddar. Of course we'll run tests, but that's my gut feeling."

Malin felt her stomach contract. Matt would have stuck a nose and a finger in it if he had to.

"We had rats in the stables when I was a kid," he said with a sad smile this time. "No amount of sign language could have coaxed my mom's deaf pug out of those feed bins. Ate over three pounds of it right there in front of her. Took a few teaspoons of hydrogen peroxide before he threw up. Then came the activated charcoal, the plasma transfusion and treatments of vitamin K. But he survived."

Malin loved dogs, couldn't abide the thought of one

dying from rat poison. "I hope Zarah will be OK."

Matt gave a brief nod and then walked toward the criminalistics motor home. He paused in the middle of the street in front of Commander Roach, then turned and stared at her with a lopsided grin. "Want to go out for lunch sometime?"

"I don't think I could eat anything after seeing that."

Matt gave her a curt nod. "Temeke's in the living room measuring the distance from the wall to the doggie door. He'll be out soon."

Malin blew out a large cloud of breath and thanked him. Never thought Matt liked her. Not like that.

She glanced through the front door, saw the back of Temeke's head peering over the inner tape at the core of the crime scene. Black as midnight and damn fine. A man who read forensics textbooks every night, majored in psychology and criminal justice and had a brain like a sponge when it came to character patterns. She felt a rollercoaster of adrenalin, couldn't stop stealing looks at him.

He was a bugger too. At least, that's how the British described each other, and he was uncompromising and tenacious to a fault. In short, he stood out from his peers because of his background; behavioral science training wasn't for everyone. That's why Hackett kept him, even at the risk of losing a certain rapport he had gained with District Attorney Theodore L. Meyer.

She glanced down at the notepad in her hand, the diagram of the sitting room and the victim's chair. Two words she always wrote in the margin. This time; *anger, separation.* She was never sure where these words came from, a primal sense, a whisper that seemed to wedge them there.

She stayed by the front door and smiled at the young Asian woman who was trying to dab her nose with a handkerchief. The man beside her gripped the collar of an energetic Dalmatian whose lips were wrapped around a butcher's bone.

Malin wondered if Zarah Thai had been a specific target, vulnerable as she was. The pizza box came from a recognized chain of restaurants and for one naïve moment Malin wondered if it had been an accident. But no ground up rat poison mixed with cheddar cheese was an accident. It was more likely a spiteful afterthought.

A jealous boyfriend? It certainly wasn't spontaneous, rather orchestrated by someone who knew Zarah liked pizza, or knew she regularly ordered one on a particular night.

Malin considered a man with a key to the house, but that didn't wash, not with the threat of a police unit outside. She thought of someone in a neighboring house who had access to the back yard, or someone who had been inside the house all the time. Poison was too subtle for a man and she jumped to the natural conclusion that it had to be a woman.

She also jumped at the loud sigh behind her. Temeke was on the doorstep, slipping off a pair of shoe covers and gloves and slapping them on the lid of a nearby trash can. He walked further out into the street, lit a cigarette and then turned around to face her.

"Notice the word on the kitchen doorframe?"

She hadn't but she nodded all the same.

"E-S-T-H-E-R-I." He paused for a second to take a drag. "What else did you find out about Paddy Brody?"

"Glad you got my messages, sir." He gave her a look as if to say *yeah so you followed Paddy and Adel to a gloomy wood, who gives a crap,* and flapped a hand to invite her to continue.

"I tried to call him. No answer," she said. "So I called his roommate. He said Paddy has counseling with Pastor Razz at Clemency Baptist Church on Thursday afternoons and classes at Gibson on Monday and Wednesday. Said

Paddy could get weird sometimes. Started talking in his sleep about Lily Delgado. Thought you might be interested."

"Time to bring Mr. Brody in."

Malin could see a ripple of excitement on his face before he became distracted by the open door.

"They're still bloody measuring and drawing sketches, Marl. Poor girl must have been in agony, stomach stripped down to the quick. Damn lucky she was found by a nosy neighbor."

He jutted his chin at the man and the Dalmatian, and then came up close enough that she could feel his breath on her cheek. "Found the dog outside the front door, whining and scratching at the paint. Neighbor rapped on the window of the cop car, roused young officer Maynard over there from his forty winks and told him to get his ass into gear. Since there was no answer when he rang the bell, Maynard muscled his way through the garden gate and broke a window. And there was poor Zarah Thai tied up and unconscious. Of course, he never saw anyone go in. Or out, for that matter."

"Why are we always hurting for witnesses?" It was Malin's turn to sigh.

"I bet that's every copper's cry." He flicked a hand at the responding officer and asked to look at his notepad. "Anyone I need to talk to?"

Officer Maynard shook his head. "All I saw was a pizza van. Guy rang the bell and left the box on the doorstep."

"Did you get the license plate? Nah, I didn't think you did. Color."

"Gray."

Temeke's head snapped up. "What did he look like—"

"Black woolen hat, dark hair down to his collar. Five seven, a hundred and twenty-five pounds, or thereabouts. It happened so fast. The van was rattling down the street before I had time to think about it. None of the neighbor's saw him."

"Bloody typical, isn't it. All glued to the TV, blinds drawn, no one doing neighborhood watch. It's a pity because we are entitled to know the methods maniacs use to destroy lives." Temeke gave a tight grin and eyed the Unit Commander on the other side of the street. He gave Maynard a dismissive nod and turned back to Malin.

"Look on the bright side, love. At least you don't have to deal with that skinny old git over there fog-horning into his hanky. We're lucky to have Hackett. If he had half the brains of Roach we'd have been given our marching orders by now."

A fleeting glance told Malin the balding Commander standing in front of the motor home was no pushover. Roach had a somber face, steel gray hair and what Temeke frequently described as a poncey scent. He hated smoking and if he found so much as a whiff on his patch, the offender was sent packing for violating the crime scene.

"Aren't you going back inside?" Roach shouted, finger pointed at Temeke.

"I've already been, sir," Temeke replied, clearly sounding puzzled at such an obvious question.

"What's that smell?"

"Smell, sir?" Temeke threw the cigarette behind him, gave it a cursory glance and ground it under his heel.

"Should have gotten here sooner. You'd have caught him in the act." Roach straightened up, walked on over and stood right in front of Malin. He listened intently as Temeke introduced her.

"I'm glad you're here to look after Temeke."

"Look after him, sir? I wasn't aware he needed looking after."

"You'd be surprised what he'll get up to unsupervised." Roach looked at her and did not add that he expected her to agree with him. But it was implied in a quirky smile. "I heard you got a little bonus."

"A bonus, sir?"

"Hackett only rewards the best," he said, tapping his nose.

Malin stood still, breath suspended, wondering what type of gratuity he was referring to and how little it really was. She felt her spirits rise. About time those ridiculous hours she'd been pulling were noticed for once, especially the entire reorganization of the cold case files which were a shambles before she was hired. And here was Temeke scuffing moodily at the remains of his cigarette on the pavement because no one had said anything to him. She wanted to laugh.

"Awful, what happened." Roach narrowed his eyes and looked past them at the house. "Things are getting worse out here, drugs, gangs, murder... and we've not even made a dent in it. I was only going over the figures with my sergeant this morning. Criminal mischief, dead bodies, behavioral problems, DUI, and that's only if you don't factor in traffic stops—"

"It's not gangs," Malin spoke up. She sensed Temeke's head snap around, sensed his scrutiny.

"You don't think so?" Roach said. "'Cause it's important to me what you think. That's why I asked you both here."

"I think it's a lone assassin, sir. Someone with a personal grudge. A revenge thing... you know."

"Can't say I do."

"Including Alice Delgado, we've got three murders and one attempted murder. I say *including Alice Delgado* because all the victims went to Los Poblanos Academy. At the same time."

"Alice Delgado was a suicide."

"What if it wasn't? What if it was somehow staged... made to look like a suicide? These aren't a bunch of thugs executing girls with a bullet through the head. It's too exotic for that. Feels personal, don't you think?"

"If indeed they are linked."

"What if they all played tennis at Tanoan Country Club? What if they all had the same sexual partner?"

"It would be unusual to have the same sexual partner, my dear. We don't have harems in New Mexico. Don't have the stomach for it. Or the culture."

"No, of course not, sir."

Roach's eyes moved past hers to the front door of the house and he nodded to someone inside. "If you'll excuse me," he said, eyes forward as he brushed past her.

Malin walked back to the car with Temeke in silence, turned on the ignition and headlights, and then rubbed her hands against the air vents. "He jumped at the sexual partner comment. Wasn't interested in tennis."

"Some people prefer sex to tennis. And a small portion of tennis could be termed as erotica. Seen how short those skirts are?" Temeke lit up another cigarette and switched his attention to officer Maynard, whose car pulled out of the road first. "Poor old bugger. Can't see him making sergeant any time soon."

"More victims... how does it look if we can't protect them?"

"Thinking about Adel Martinez?"

"I'm thinking about better surveillance."

"Volunteering?"

"Commander Roach has assigned two officers day and night. But Adel's getting past them. And since suspects are still pretty thin on the ground, someone needs to stay in the house."

"Not our area, Marl. But I'll put in a good word at Southeast Area Command. And no, I won't mention you followed Mr. Brody to a restaurant the other night and that Ms. Martinez was packing illegal goodies down that tight little blouse of hers. Or that you didn't bring her home when you had the chance. Don't want to ruin that nice bonus now, do we?"

Malin merely snorted. Temeke offering her services to Detective Suzi Cornwell was the last thing she needed, but she knew the case, knew the witness. It was likely Suzi would agree.

Temeke looked unnerved, like he knew there was something strange out there. "Did you notice the Dalmatian? Sodding big dog. Sodding big lamb shank and all." He whistled softly to show he was impressed, raised his butt off the seat a little to retrieve a ringing phone.

"Yeah," she murmured, and then it hit her. The doggie door wasn't big enough for a full grown man, but it would certainly accommodate a boy.

Temeke turned slowly to face her, phone pressed against his ear.

"Go ahead, Luis… She's what? You've got to be bloody kidding."

TWENTY-NINE

Temeke glanced at the gray skinned girl and picked up the letter.

I look around the house and I see her picture. I call her name and when she doesn't answer it feels like a punch in the chest. I see the garage where my dad used to work, all his tools laid out as if he would come back any second and just pick them up again.

It scares me and it haunts me.

Then I go into my sister's room, smell her clothes, sit on her bed and wait a while. I listen to the silence and to the wind outside and then I cry when I lie on her bed. I remember the last thing we did together, how the sun slanted across the room as we laughed, I remember exactly where she stood and how. What she wore. Her hair, the color of it and how long it was.

I pray I won't wake up because of the pain. It hurts so much. My heart shudders a little. It's breaking. Maybe enough to kill me. It's the cloudy days that make it worse and the rain when it comes. So many tears. And when the sun comes out I feel a little better.

But she was happy. That's the only thing that keeps the lump from my throat growing bigger and bigger. Both of us... were happy.

He didn't know how to explain it, except to say that Lily had been kidnapped, kept in a basement, fed nothing more than left-overs through a grate in the door. Said she heard a solid beat that escalated now and again, a motor of some kind.

There were squeals of delight when Valerie saw her that Tuesday morning, hands brushing her cheeks, arms and whatever else she could feel. Parents always wanted to touch and smell, and they had questions... so many questions.

Lily lay in a hospital bed with an officer on duty outside. She was muttering about the color of days, some gray, some white, some red. Temeke didn't know what she meant, couldn't imagine the pain, didn't want to fill her in with what had happened to Zarah Thai either. Her upper lip had been split open and her eye socket was a rare shade of blue.

"I can see a white metal bed and a window. I like the view," she said.

"What can you see?" he asked, leaning in a little and smelling the scent of her.

"A lawn, the Pepper Pot, Alice..." She smiled and then frowned. "But it's all a dream, isn't it?"

Temeke knew she was remembering Los Poblanos, high stone walls, stone benches and secret paths in the Lion's Mouth. She had been happy when Alice was there.

"Yes, it's all a dream."

She said she couldn't remember how it happened, who had left her on the hard shoulder of Alameda bridge in the dark. But someone found her, one arm dangling over the parapet, fingers twitching from the cold. No shoes, no socks, no coat.

Lily said she saw the winding river and heard the rumble of a car. Said she ached all over, felt the pain in her chest, couldn't breathe, couldn't blink and her eyelids were swollen. One kind soul had stopped, parked a few feet from where she fell. She remembered because she was able to lift her head, saw him through strands of wet hair that clung to her cheeks. He kept asking for her name, gave her a coat and stayed with her until the ambulance came.

Temeke sat for a brief moment in silence, while Valerie Delgado fumbled with her purse, muttered something about how much better it would be if Temeke and Lily were alone. She walked out of the room, face lowered as if she was somehow ashamed.

She shouldn't have been, thought Temeke. None of it was her fault.

"Mom outside?" Lily murmured.

"Yes," he said. "Want me to fetch her?"

"In a little while."

Lily shivered, asked for a cup of tea and turned her head toward the window at a light patter of rain against the glass. Said she didn't dare fall asleep. She'd only dream if she did.

"You're a little banged up, that's all," he said, walking toward the window and pulling the blinds down half way. "We'll find the man who did this. You'll see."

Sad they couldn't find the man who waited with Lily until the ambulance came. Temeke wondered if she was seeing things through the lens of terror and the slit of a black eye.

He studied her long and hard before he spoke, noticed the set of her mouth was sad. She had a certain presence he couldn't define.

"Name's Detective Temeke. I just want to ask a few questions if that's OK?"

"The same guy who caught that Norwegian killer before Christmas?" She seemed to wait for him to nod. "It was all over the news. So you're the big crime fighter they're always talking about."

"Who's talking?"

"Everyone. All the school kids know you. All the boys want to be like you."

For all his faults, Temeke had no idea he had a

following. He often gave talks at schools, did roadshows at the mall with the K-9 unit and he was usually chased out without a smile.

"How are you feeling?" he said.

"Tired."

He sat down again, elbows on his thighs as he leaned forward a little. "I'm glad you're home. I'm glad you're OK."

A nurse brought in a cup of tea and Lily seemed to take a cautious sip. Again there was silence, curiously pleasant this time and he was in no hurry to break it.

"You look different from the TV," she said, and he caught her glancing at his right hand. There was no sign of a ring, or any visible indentation on the fourth finger. It was long gone now.

He turned on the micro-recorder he kept in his pocket and placed it on the overbed table. "Witness interview with Lily Delgado, Rust Hospital. Conversation begins..." he checked his watch, "at ten fifteen a.m. From the beginning, Lily, tell me what happened?"

She took another sip of hot tea, a steady blush creeping across her face as if she was suddenly self-conscious. "It was Friday afternoon when I went to get the mail. He drove up to the curb, asked me if I wanted to go for a walk."

"Who asked you?"

"Paddy... Paddy Brody."

"Where you expecting him?"

"No."

"When was the last time you saw him?"

Lily squinted at a ray of sun that slipped under the blinds. "About two weeks ago."

"Where did you go?"

"To the woods. We had a few smokes, talked. He asked if he could kiss me. I said no."

"Why did you say no?"

"He's dating someone, a friend from school."

"Did he try to kiss you?"

"No, sir. Paddy wouldn't do that."

"He must like you a lot."

"He always says so."

Temeke saw the flicker of a smile at the corners of her mouth, the heavy lidded stare. He reminded himself he was a professional, a man hunter, always looking for a challenge. And here he was locked into two hazel eyes and he felt the irresistible need to pretend it wasn't happening.

"Were you drinking?" he asked. It would be no use lying about a few drinks. She couldn't deceive him for a minute.

"Wine. I... I blacked out."

"Fainted? Knocked out... what?"

Her eyes seemed to take in every detail, seemed to glide over his denim shirt, collar open to the second button and cuffs turned up beyond the wrist. Everything in the room went very quiet, the scent of fresh soap was very noticeable.

"Lily... Did you faint? Or were you knocked out?"

Lily blinked back the tears, as if she felt the shudder before the memory came. "I think it was the wine. There was something in the wine."

"Take your time."

"H-He was shouting at me."

"Paddy?"

"No, someone else."

"Can you describe him?"

"Dark. Everything went blurry, the kind of blurry when you know you're in danger. I tried to calm him down, but he hit me. Then I knew it was real. I pleaded with him, but he was cussing, telling me to shut up. I don't know what I must have said to make him so angry. I-I kept thinking, I don't know where I am. I need help. The more

I pleaded, the angrier he got. And then he dragged one finger across his throat, said he was going to kill me."

Temeke felt like he was standing at the end of a very long tunnel which seemed to ease in and out with each breath. "You could see this in the dark."

"Yes, the moon was light enough. I could taste blood. I thought my right eye was shattered."

"When they brought you in, your eyes were a little swollen, and your hair was matted with leaves. But there wasn't much blood. Just a few bruises and scrapes."

"I went numb. I didn't know what to do. Then he hit me again, wouldn't stop. I told myself to let go, to just roll with it. So I played dead."

"For how long? How long were you on the ground?"

She went quiet then, eyes appearing to trail the underside of his left arm. She was lost in a detached haze.

"Lily," he said, a little firmer this time. "How long were you on the ground?"

Her eyes snapped back to his face and she gripped that plastic tea cup and gave it another chance. "When I woke up," she said, trying to swallow, trying perhaps to get a grip on what it was she actually saw. "I could see stars, the moon. I thought I was lying in a grave. Buried alive."

"You wouldn't have been buried if you could see stars."

It would have been darker than hell itself if she'd been covered in soil and there would be no room to move. He noticed something flicker across her face and he struggled with a wrenching feeling of uncertainty. "And then what happened?"

"I was blindfolded, taken along a track. Something stung my arm. I heard the sliding door of a van, woke up in the dark... a basement. It was really cold."

"Do you have any enemies, an ex-boyfriend, someone who might want to harm you?"

"No."

"Can you describe the basement?"

She said she couldn't really, it was too dark to see anything except stone walls and candles.

"Was there anyone else with you?"

"No. I was alone."

"Why would someone want to kidnap you, Lily?"

"Because of the curses."

"What curses?"

She took a deep breath, brow furrowing as she began to explain it. "Alice found them in a book."

"An Esoterica," he said, growing increasingly more tired of the book.

"Yes... but we thought it was all a game, just make-believe."

"Until Alice died." He leaned back in his chair, found his eyes sliding down to her lips, but only for a second. "You've read it, haven't you, Lily? A sisterhood of six."

He summoned up the page from memory and the paragraph he knew by heart. *"For it is said, the first woman to disobey shall be buried alive, the second shall have her limbs severed, the third shall be cast into a fire, the fourth shall be drowned, the fifth shall be poisoned and the sixth shall be starved of air.* Do you remember how Alice died?"

Lily turned her head to the window again, mind drifting to somewhere he couldn't go. And then they widened as she turned to look at him, the type of look a person gave when they were suddenly surer than they had ever been about anything.

"She cut herself."

THIRTY

Temeke sat at his desk at five o'clock in the afternoon, sipping a cup of stewed coffee and wondering where all the sunlight had gone. A white cloud rolled in from the northwest scored with wavy indentations like ripples on an ocean bed, and he began to superimpose each crime scene in his head, sensing something more.

He called Officer Watts, asked her to drive out and take a look at the scene where Lily last saw Paddy, to determine boundaries and to stay under that tree until the Field Examiners arrived.

He couldn't get the voices in the cornfield out of his head, uncertain whether they had anything to do with the latest rash of crimes. Since the killings had escalated to fever pitch, he couldn't delay the composite sketches any longer.

Malin was on the phone, leaving another message for Paddy Brody. Here was a case that started out as one missing female and had escalated into a full-scale murder investigation. There was something in the ICRIIS entries that bothered him, something he didn't see coming, a sliver of detail that had eluded him when he'd received those thick binders.

From the photographs of Alice Delgado, it was clear the water in the tub was streaked with blood, that a young, healthy woman had slashed herself with a knife. But what the report failed to mention was a tiny slit in the bottom of that double hung window where he could vaguely make out a stand of cottonwoods and a gray wintry sky. The report mentioned that the reporting officer had had to turn the light on when he entered the bathroom because Alice had been bathing in the dark. Around nine o'clock at night, it said.

The temperatures had been in the low thirties then, a little on the cold side to leave a window open and there was a light sprinkling of snow on the trees. Temeke knew he wouldn't have seen the parapet, the sloping roof and the fire escape from inside the bathroom, but he had seen it from the parking lot.

Fingerprints? Plenty. All female. All accounted for. But could someone have been with Alice when she died? Someone who could have used that open window as a means of escape?

Not if the window was broken as Miss Baca had mentioned. *The window used to stick a little. It's secure now.*

He felt a surge of exhilaration as he studied those files, venturing into an undiscovered place, to track, to snare, to find the truth. But in all his time at the Behavioral Institute, nothing had prepared him for a trip down loony street.

"When's Paddy Brody coming in?" he asked Malin as she put the phone down.

"In one hour. Sarge left a message after lunch to remind him."

"When you followed him on Saturday night, was he calm? Worked up?"

Malin seemed to study his face for a few seconds before responding. "Calm. Adel was worked up."

"Bad withdrawals?"

"Something like that. Los Poblanos is a competitive environment, sir, and the teenagers are all from high income families. Plenty of money to buy Adderall."

"Only none of these girls have ADHD."

"It only takes one person to convince a doctor," she said in a tone which could have been mistaken for impatience. "I called Dr. Vasillion. He said Alice's pathology report mentioned she wasn't taking any regular medication at the time, but it showed traces of methylphenidate and an enlarged heart. He said alcohol can cause methylphenidate to be released into the bloodstream too fast. It can also cause seizures, psychosis and hallucinations. We'll need a blood sample from Paddy Brody."

"Any news on Zarah Thai?"

"She's stable today. They're still not letting anyone see her."

Temeke's mind began to fire in all directions, to Lily, to Zarah and sliding back to Paddy Brody. If anyone convinced a doctor they had ADHD, got a prescription for simulates and then handed them around a college campus, jail time was a severe consequence. If they were addicted and couldn't get a prescription refill, suicide was a close second.

"Valerie Delgado said Alice had no suicidal symptoms," he said, "no boyfriend problems, no medical issues. If Alice was dabbling in study drugs, she was getting them from someone else."

"Paddy Brody had a contact on the south side of town. Said he owed someone money. Dealers don't like being ripped." Malin went quiet all of a sudden as if she was counting down the seconds. "He also told Adel he was going to find Lily. And now she's been found."

Temeke's mind turned over the angles, wondered if they were being played in a way he would never understand. He started to see a pattern, and a single thought kept eating at him. That an arcane book had been guiding the actions of this serial killer.

"How's Lily doing?" Malin asked.

"Bloody scared. Who wouldn't be after being drugged, taken on a joy ride to who-knows-where and then dumped in the street two weeks later? Couldn't remember anything in between. Forensics combed the parapets and the roadway on Alameda Bridge. Found nothing. Not even a piece of wool from her bloody sweater."

"I'll listen to the tape" she said, chin cupped in both hands, eyes searching the screen.

That was the thing about Malin. In the five brief months she'd been at Northwest Area Command, he had seen a mettle in that tender spirit and an unhurried method he rather craved. The freckles along the bridge of her nose stood out when she was angry, only today they were soft, almost undistinguishable against that buttery skin.

"I'll be seeing her again," Temeke said, suppressing a sigh. "She was staring me up and down like I was a six hundred pounder with quadruple chins and a massive gut."

Malin gave him a look somewhere between curiosity and regret, he couldn't work out which. His impression was that she was desperately trying to look cheerful and failing.

"So, you'll tell Mr. Brody about the blood sample?" she asked.

"No. You will. And get those bloody sketches out to the public. Oh, and did you get that search warrant?"

He saw her nod and took the envelope she handed him. Took a small screwdriver from his desk drawer and slipped it in his jacket pocket. "I'd like to see exactly what Mr. Brody does for a living."

"He's a student. You can't possibly imagine the state of his house."

Temeke could. It was probably creepy and a darn site colder than his. "It's a bizarre trail, Marl. And it's getting more bizarre by the minute. Paddy Brody can make every bloody excuse he wants about the dictates of a demonic book. He was willing to be part of it."

"You know the stats, sir. All drug users have psych issues. Paddy's no different, no matter how he holds himself. He was in an art gallery when Kenzie Voorhees was killed and he was in class when Asha Samadi disappeared. Both these locations are only three miles away from where the victims lived."

"Are you questioning the witnesses statements?"

"I agree it's a stretch," she said, eyes following a dust mote hanging in a thin shaft of light. "But what if he took a break and no one saw him leave?"

THIRTY-ONE

Paddy was a no show and that made Temeke nervous. He snapped the file shut and herded Malin outside to the parking lot. It was seven o'clock in the evening and if it wasn't for the traffic, they would have got to Paddy's house faster.

"Matt called," she said at last. "It was rat poison. There were traces of it in Zarah's vomit."

"I expect you're going to tell me there wasn't a bleeding stitch of whoever did this. Not even a toenail clipping."

Malin shook her head and blew out a loud sigh. "Nope."

Temeke looked at his wrist watch and pointed at the curb. "Pull up here. By the lamppost."

"By the way, sir, before you nip around the back with that screwdriver, I won't mention you broke into Mr. Brody's house or that you didn't wait to use the search warrant. Don't want to ruin your good name now, do we?"

Temeke gave her the benefit of a wide grin. "All it takes is a bit of nerve in khaki, Marl. But I appreciate your kind consideration."

He left her shivering inside his drafty jeep, told her to keep a lookout. Hammered away at the front door, listened to the wind in the trees and waited for a moment. No shuffling footsteps from within, no harsh voice demanding who he was. Temeke was confident he could eliminate any possibility that Paddy might still be in the house.

Low in a black sky, a full moon bathed the street in an eerie gray and he stood silently for a moment, analyzing the shadows and sounds. Pulling on a pair of latex gloves and tucking a flashlight under one arm, he sprinted around the back to a small yard dotted with waist-high weeds. The back door was furnished with a spring bolt, would have been nice and easy with a shopper's card, only it was locked.

There were three windows at the back of the house, all slide-up sashes. He shone the flashlight at three latch locks and found one unfastened. No need to prize the window up with a screwdriver and jimmy it around.

The house he entered was barely furnished. A couch, a coffee table and two bar stools pushed under the lip of a small kitchen counter. There was the distinct aroma of clean linen, an air freshener scent he recognized from the car wash.

A black binder lay on the couch, labeled *AFAM 190b African American Art from 1941 - present*. Alongside it was a pad of Post-it notes, but nowhere could Temeke see a notepad or any writing materials. Not that he was going to leave young Paddy a note, college lined pads were a staple he remembered from his own school days.

No cars in the garage, bare shelves except for two suitcases and three spare tires leaning against the wall. The laundry room, which connected the garage to the kitchen, was neat and tidy and as he walked back into the living room, he sensed the oppressive silence always present in an empty house.

In the kitchen there were two items in the sink, a white coffee mug with a slogan marked in a tightly kerned thriller font. *We've all got pieces of crazy in us. Some larger pieces than others.* And a cast iron bowl featuring a five-toed dragon, an imperial Chinese design. In the cupboard nearest the sink were two cans of Pyin Green Tea and Kyaukme Black Tea, a selection of noodles and a slab of dark chocolate. The fridge was well stocked and fresh by the smell of it.

Temeke assumed the bedrooms were beyond the living room and walked toward a closed door, hand hovering over his weapon as he pushed down on the handle. The bed was made, top sheet turned down over a blanket and a tee shirt folded neatly on the pillow. Fresh air wafted in from a small crack in the bathroom window, fresh as baby breath. It seemed the very picture of a Myanmar serviceman.

The map over the bed was of Burma's longest river, the Irrawaddy, and to the east, the shorter Salween river emptying into the Gulf of Martaban between the ancient cities of Pegu and Thaton.

A small niche in the wall housed a meditating Buddha made of cast iron and surrounded by flowers and incense. Temeke felt like he'd stumbled across a reserved and hallowed place and should have taken his shoes off at the door.

The second bedroom was in stark contrast to the first, stale and dark. Temeke tilted his head and scanned the floor under the mattress, took a good look at the space between that and the frame. A gray plaid comforter had been pulled up over the pillow, a half-ass effort, he thought, of making the bed. There were no pictures, no personal items to speak of, except a can of shaving cream and a packet of disposable razors in the bathroom cabinet.

In the closet, clothes hung from wire coat hangers and there were two pairs of shoes on the floor, size ten, scuffed and well worn. In the chest of drawers he found underwear, tee shirts and belts and there was a pile of wrinkled clothes in the corner by the door as if Paddy had been too lazy to hang them up. Temeke had no idea what he was looking for.

The more he thought about Alice Delgado's death, the more it presented a problem. What if Paddy was a middle level drug dealer as Malin claimed? What if he sold Smarts to Alice, who in turn sold them to someone else? Once Alice received the money she would then have to pay it back to Paddy. But what if that *someone else* didn't give Alice her money? Coupled with the fifteen hundred Paddy was owed might explain why Alice wound up dead. This type of drug dealing hierarchy would have worked for Temeke if it wasn't for the fact that the students were filthy rich.

He let his eyes graze over the place, no landline, no telephone jack in any room, but by the front door on a small hall table was a notepad. He reached for it just as the cell phone vibrated in his pocket.

"Roommate's just pulled up," Malin said. "You'd better get out of there."

Temeke stood still, held his breath for a moment and listened to the traffic outside. He scuttled to a front window and peered out into the street. There was a man in the driver's seat of a car holding a phone to his ear. He was clearly in no hurry, but if Temeke wasn't quick enough the daft old sod would find him behind a curtain and wonder how he'd got in.

The rumble of the garage door, the squeal of brakes, the deep throated growl of an engine, then silence. The sound signaled that Temeke's allotted time had run out.

The first thing he noticed was the address scribbled on the top sheet of the notepad. 9718 Guadalupe Trail. The second was that the address was two houses down from his and on the other side of the street. The old ruin.

The third was his heart rate. No longer a gentle patter but a hectic drumming as if something was about to burst out of his chest.

The fourth was a buzzing in his ears as his body propelled itself forward, floorboards creaking underfoot.

All he could hear was the rasp of his breathing as he opened the front door, saw clouds pressing against the rooftops like a crowd of lead-gray faces.

He braced himself against a cold draft, shot out into the street just as Maun Tung sauntered into the living room.

THIRTY-TWO

Malin and Temeke pulled into Guadalupe Trail at nine thirty at night and parked behind a chain of units, light bars glowing. Malin spotted the white Honda Accord abandoned on a narrow track between a tall hedge and the west side of a derelict house. A driver would have been hard pushed to have seen it from the road.

"It's his car," she said, eyes snapping further up the road to Temeke's house.

Reporters stood behind yellow tape, speaking into microphones and waiting impatiently for the moment when a body was brought out. One female dressed in a Hermes scarf and a green swing coat caught her eye. Jennifer Danes was standing close to a camera crew who were recording the incident on the Friday evening news.

Temeke said little as they walked toward the house, black eyes flicking back and forth as if he was looking for something. Traces, she thought, tracks, irrefutable evidence that he could somehow see in the dark, something he could clutch onto because right now there was nothing else.

She examined the license plate on the Honda, noting the absence of tags, and peered down into the passenger seat where a sheet of paper caught her eye. Handwritten directions to the house and a dollar number – one hundred and fifty. Temeke matched the writing to the note left in the house. It was Paddy's all right.

The south wall was pockmarked as if it had been rammed with a wrecking ball and yellow tape ran all the way to the back yard, a mere huddle of weeds that led to a cornfield. Peeling stucco flashed in fierce blues and reds and Malin eased her way between two units and an ambulance, nodded at an officer with an attendance log who checked his watch and summoned her in.

Officer Manning was in the cornfield shouting to his K-9. Malin could see the remote control flashing on Brock's collar as he appeared to be herding a flock of quail toward the house.

She stood two feet from the back door, watching a Field Investigator dressed in protective clothing who was marking a bloody footprint on the threshold. It was pointing toward the back yard, where only the faint indentation of a second print suggested the perpetrator might have been in a hurry.

Malin held her breath from the familiar metallic stench and one of the worst bloodbaths she had ever seen. The doctor was talking to Temeke, saying how the thin trickle of blood from the victim's neck once started out as a pumping geyser and now coated nearly three walls. There was blunt force trauma to the back of his head, victim was in full rigor. Said his name was Paddy Brody.

It was worse when you knew them, once suspected them and then found out they weren't the sick perpetrators of the crime you were trying to investigate. Shame and sadness came in one quick surge and she forced herself to take a breath, tried to calm her racing pulse.

Temeke was leaning against the outside wall near a crate of evidence bags, mouth opening and closing like a fish. "Not bloody fast enough, was I?"

"You called them as soon as you could," she reminded, shivering a little under her coat.

He seemed to flinch involuntarily as if he was about to lose the one last thread of evidence he had to solve the case. "You can never underestimate the meanderings of an art student, especially one with the morals of a tom cat. It's a bleeding crack house. Has been for years. Who the hell was he meeting?"

Malin peered back into the kitchen which was already taped off, crime scene specialists mapping and marking and recording descriptions of the scene. A young man meticulously cleared Coke cans and fast food wrappers into evidence bags, and the doctor collected samples with forceps and placed them in metal evidence buttons. Malin wasn't allowed any further.

Temeke pushed himself away from the wall when Matt Black hovered at the doorway in a white bunny suit. He was holding up a cell phone bagged in clear plastic and what appeared to be an old metal iron. "We think he was struck from behind with this. Looks like he had a text two days ago. Someone called *D* asking him to come over to grandma's for a ride."

Malin knew the word *grandma's* was slang for a meeting place and as for *ride* it could have referred to sexual favors.

"Looks like he was collecting money."

Temeke responded to Matt with the customary ribaldry and Malin sniffed back a bite of anger. The knot in her stomach wouldn't go away, nor would the feeling that she was peering through the glass of a fisheye lens and everything she saw was curved and distorted.

"There's a handprint on the inside door frame," Matt said, leaning back a little and studying it for a moment. "Thumb's facing forward. Killer probably tried to steady himself on the way out. Floor's slippery. Pauline's checking the blood arcs. But she thinks the killer came at him from behind the door. He was already here."

"Prints?" Temeke asked.

"He must have worn gloves."

"How tall was the deceased?"

"Seventy-two inches. About six feet. There's some cash in a coffee can," Matt whispered, "a grand at a peek."

"Under all the coffee grinds or in full view?"

Matt gave a small smile. "He could have brought it with him. Maybe it was already there. Hookers... drug dealers, they all take cash."

"Do you think this is the primary crime scene?"

"The doc said it was."

Malin watched three heads bobbing back and forth behind the kitchen window, saw Pauline Bailey, the blood spatter analyst, and gave her a quick wave.

"Mr. Brody hadn't been here before," Malin said, hands pressed inside her pockets. She tried to form words through the constriction in her throat, and coughed a few times. "The address was in the car on the passenger seat. And there was a dollar amount. Probably cash he was owed."

Matt nodded and gave her a small smile before ambling toward a Field Examiner who was squatting about ten feet away from the house in the back yard. He seemed to be leaning over a muddy path that led to the cornfield and shouting something about a set of footprints. Size nine, Vibram sole, same as a duty boot.

"Get those in plaster," Matt shouted back.

"I hope they're not yours," Malin murmured, staring at Temeke's yawning mouth. It was a common man's boot and size.

More flashlights, more shouts from a patrol officer trying to deter Captain Fowler from lifting the tape to let Hackett past. Hackett stood there with a cashmere coat draped over his shoulders, chin lowered and peering over his glasses.

"Temeke!" he shouted. "What have we got?"

"Got, sir?" A spent match dropped into the dirt. Temeke lit a cigarette. "Terrible business. I wouldn't go in there if I were you, not after that nice dinner you've just had."

"Who is it?"

"Well, it's not a bunch of old biddies playing poker, that's for sure."

"Get out of my way!"

"Before you go, sir, Detective Santiago and Lieutenant Alvarez were supposed to meet the victim at two o'clock this afternoon," Temeke continued, pointing with his cigarette. "This explains why the poor old sod didn't show up. Must have got the surprise of his life. I thought it was a nasty case of hara-kiri when they found him. It was his throat, sir. Sliced from here to here and the kitchen's a nasty mess. I didn't touch anything, I promise."

Hackett gave a tolerant smile. "Doctor Vasillion or Doctor Henderson?"

"Dr. V. He's bringing the deceased out now, sir. Twenty-two-year-old male. Patrick Brody, art student at Gibson."

It was the black body bag carried by two examiners that claimed Hackett's interest and quickly wiped the smile from his face. Dr. Vasillion followed behind, jutted a chin greeting to Hackett.

"Homicide," the doctor confirmed, staring down at the body. He peeled off his gloves in two quick snaps and stuffed them in the top of his bag. "We'll know more after the exam. Given the temperature, I'd put time of death at around twenty-two to twenty-four hours. Two slices to the carotid and jugular here and here." He lifted his head and motioned to the left and right.

Malin was hardly able to pay attention to the steady stream of chatter, thoughts jumbled and where no scenario, no matter how intricate, seemed to fit into place. She recognized the tension under her hair, the sour surge in her gut, and stumbled a few feet from the house to inhale a gust of wind. Judging by the cuts, the killer hadn't hesitated for a second.

"Makes you want to down a large whisky, doesn't it?" Temeke said over her right shoulder.

"I don't drink," she reminded him, watching the blistering end of a lighted cigarette.

"Pauline's a bloody trooper. Imagine what it must be like having to analyze every tiny speck of blood, every smear, and wonder how it all happened. Said our unspecified subject would have been covered in blood 'cause there was plenty of it on the grass and leaves outside. Got a male intern with her this time. Smells like he threw up over here."

Malin rolled her eyes and walked ten feet to her right. Couldn't get the brutal visual out of her head, thick hair coated in blood and the staring eyes that had once been so blue. He wasn't a bad kid, a little confused that's all. But lying there on that hard wood floor eliminated the only suspect they had.

Temeke was right there beside her, puffing out smoke at her elbow. He raised his eyes to the sky as he had done five minutes earlier, and five minutes before that. "A guy like that doesn't need to visit a hooker."

Malin counted off a few more possibilities of her own. "A friend of a friend, a drug deal gone wrong—"

"Besides the girls, did Paddy mention any names when you saw him?"

"Demon. I don't know if it's a code name for a drug, or the person Paddy came to meet."

"Why here?"

All Malin could think of was a rundown old house in close proximity to Temeke's. She winced and turned her back on it all, walked toward the car with a determined stride. She could feel the warmth of Temeke's breath against her cheek, and tensed when she heard the tone of his voice.

"Someone was watching me the other night," he said, confirming her worst fears. "Young man, late teens, early twenties, between one twenty-five, one thirty. I followed him all the way through that cornfield. He was talking to a female."

Lean at one hundred and twenty-five pounds, Malin thought. "What did the female look like?"

"I didn't see her." Temeke took a deep drag and then crushed the cigarette under his foot. "But I'd recognize the man if I saw him again."

THIRTY-THREE

Gabriel opened his eyes and thought he was in The Lion's Mouth. There was a peace about the place, rows of tall, weathered trunks and a muddy path pitted by human feet. Fir trees made a hollow, resonant whisper and sunlight streamed in between the branches.

He wanted to be back in the light where the spirits of family run free. He wanted to be one of them, away from this infernal darkness.

He rested now, warm and tired, heard a familiar roar in the distance. The Outlaw Biker Club met along the main drag into Corrales, road names emblazoned on their jackets and lounging with attitude on their tricked out motorcycles. In a strange way he envied them, the freedom and the thrill of all those 'twisties' on the hairpin turns. And he missed the homemade meals in the Fat Mule and the compassion of an aging waitress.

It was dark, but then he didn't expect it to be anything different at that time of night. He knew Demon was there with him, a shape huddled against the wall and oddly translucent in the moonlight, oddly quiet.

His lips were moving, emitting no sound. But there was a mocking tinge to it and if Gabriel really listened, he could hear the soft strains of a song he once knew. Something about a garden, breath and dirt.

Gabriel never understood the words until now. Dirt was man, a filthy creature who was given authority over the animals and the earth. And when Dirt needed a mate he was given one from his own rib because Master loved Dirt more than Demon.

"Such an extravagant gesture. Such favoritism," Demon muttered.

Gabriel had always felt sorry for Demon and he almost did now. But there was one thing that scared him and that was Demon's power. His never-ending energy, the incredible fight that was still left in him, the passion to destroy a race that had taken away the Master's favor.

"You must understand," Demon said, "you are made in Master's image. You are perfect."

Gabriel liked the sound of that. *Perfect.* It had a nice ring to it and he almost thought he was.

"But you are also imperfect. Oh, yes, it was all Master's plan. The original pair, lying down together and making more of their hideous race. A royal priesthood. You are testament to that, a museum piece that my kind study through a thin veil we can no longer walk through."

"What do you mean?"

"Regret... is what I mean. There are moments when I grieve, moments when I remember the first sunset, the first moonset. And then I wonder what it must be like to live. I expect this is all ancient history to you."

It was all a myth to Gabriel. Old-fashioned language that had no place in a modern world. A load of crock.

He stared at the shadow against the wall, wondered what the draw had been, what made him gravitate toward such a terrible choice. From an innocent man to a murderer, all in the span of two years. And then a thought struck him.

"If I am royal... then what are you?"

"Ah, now there's a story." Demon dropped his voice to a conspiratorial whisper and smiled.

Gabriel didn't like that smile.

"I am one of many. A legion of prowlers tasked with

turning the priesthood away from fellowship with Master. It seemed like a good idea at the time, stalking the herd, herding the stalked. So vulnerable, so frail... out there in the wild. Trouble is, it's a gigantic waste of time and I'm getting rather tired of it. You would if you knew how it all ends. Oh, I forget, you already do."

"I don't know anything."

"No, but you will. You'll remember the stuff they taught you at school, all those righteous little stories. They have a funny way of creeping back into the mind when you least expect it. You won't get lost then, will you?"

Gabriel was lost. Horribly so. All he wanted to do was get revenge, slash their tires, key their cars, crush their everything. Sometimes he was overcome with a rage so thick he'd fall into the deep black, legs kicking, arms flailing, not knowing what had put him there. Those *righteous little stories* were as calming as an antique clock, pendulum and cogs ticking their way through time. Soft and rhythmic. It put him to sleep.

"You told me those stories were make-believe," Gabriel said. "Especially the one about the man who had a vision—"

"John."

"...on that island. You said he was hallucinating from sunstroke."

"The island was a little scant of trees."

Gabriel hardly remembered those classes at school, but what he did remember were the pictures of Patmos, a desolate island in the Aegean Sea. Caves, rocky bays and not a hint of shade in sight. He began to wonder if Demon had been there, whether he was as ancient as he said he was.

"I'm old and tired," Demon said over Gabriel's thoughts. "Probably time we said goodbye. After all, an unwilling host is hardly worth dining with. Look at you. You don't fool me. And you won't fool them."

"They don't know me."

"I know you. Remember how we met? You were quite different then. You believed me."

Gabriel wanted to expel every nuance of that memory and dash the deep whispers from his mind. He replayed the scene in that quaint little wood in front of the school, recalled how Demon's voice had called out to him, risen above the rest. How he preyed upon Gabriel in waking and dreaming moments.

It was no use. There was no quick escape this time. That voice was outfitted with every witty comeback, and slick remark, wooing Gabriel until he was his. "You said it was all a hoax."

"A very elaborate one," Demon murmured. "But there are stories, and there are stories. Around-the-campfire-stories, midnight-night-feast-stories, horror stories, love stories. You have to admit, my stories were the best."

The smile Gabriel hated was back again, and the laugh when it came terrified him.

"And they were the best, my friend," Demon whispered, "because they were all lies."

THIRTY-FOUR

Malin watched a cylinder of ash drop from Temeke's cigarette before he took a drag, smoke exiting through his nose. The office was slowly fogging up to the density of a low hanging rain cloud and it was pointless hanging *no smoking* signs on the wall. He ignored every one of them.

There were two more in the boardroom, each torn down with an angry snarl. This wasn't the seventies where crystal ash trays sat on every desk and a decorative pedestal outside the elevator. He'd flipped, that's all. Willing the axe to drop on his career because he was no longer part of an elite team.

Temeke dropped the cigarette in his coffee cup, gave a disdainful sniff and walked beside her down the corridor with a file under one arm.

"Blimey, this is going to be a downer," he said. "Why can't we just send her a letter with the bad news? Duke City Police logo on the letterhead. You could frame something like that."

"How would you feel? You can be such a jerk sometimes."

"Of course, I'm sorry for her, Marl. I'm sorry for him too. How he died. She's going to be in shock for a day or two."

Malin always preferred the personal touch. You could tell a bunch by a person's reaction, the way they look up or down, the shock, the tears. And sometimes there weren't any tears. Like today.

"He can't be..." Adel looked from Malin to Temeke, shook her head a few times. "He can't be."

"It was a terrible thing finding him there. Of course it was quick. That type of thing usually is." Temeke tapped the file against the edge of the desk a few times before setting it on the surface. "When did you last see Paddy?"

"Last Saturday night."

"Did he come to your house?" Temeke leaned forward and frowned a little. "Because the surveillance officer never recorded it."

Malin knew he was trying to listen to the speech inflection, trying to match it to the female voice he'd heard in the cornfield. Bottom line, Paddy's description did not match the man Temeke had seen that night.

"No. I met him somewhere."

"Corrales Café wasn't it?"

"How did—"

"It's law enforcement, love. Got eyes everywhere. Should have told that nice surveillance officer you were going for a drive. He was worried sick. Incidentally, how did you get out without being seen?"

"Over the back wall," she said, picking at her fingernails. "Albuquerque Yellow Cab met me up the street. You can check."

"Oh, I intend to. But just to make you feel comfortable, Detective Santiago here will be staying with you from now on. Don't want any pizza vans turning up at your door. Awful what happened to Zarah Thai. You were saying?"

Adel gave him a frown and lowered her eyes. "I needed a few Smarts. He gave me all he had."

"Did you give him any money?"

"No, sir."

Malin pitched in. "You know it's illegal to give prescription drugs to other people?"

Adel was really crying now. Mumbling something about wishing Paddy hadn't taken so many because he would still be alive. "He's addicted... can't last a day without them."

"He gave them to all of you, didn't he?" Malin said, remembering Paddy's crushed in head and the bag of Smarts they found in his pocket. "Made a killing on the side."

It was a shot in the dark, nothing to say it was Paddy's fault the girls all wound up dead, but when the nod came it gave a Malin jolt.

"Paddy never loved me. Not the way I thought he did."

"*Womanizer's* the word that springs to mind," Malin said. "I wouldn't blame you if you wanted to get even, give him a taste of his own medicine."

"I hated it... but I couldn't stop it."

Temeke was clearly holding out on the details, the real reason Paddy had died. Malin had seen him do it a hundred times, especially with the drug dealers they picked up on the street, the ones who had no idea how the crack got down the pockets of their pants because they claimed the pants weren't theirs. He would likely hit Adel with that gruesome bit of news. The bit where Paddy hadn't died from an overdose, rather he had been slit from ear to ear and left in a puddle of blood. It was all in the file.

Temeke did it with every suspect. And Adel was a suspect because out of four dead and two in hospital she was the only one left kicking.

"Got ADHD?" Temeke cocked his head sideways and almost winked.

"No, sir. We just use it to study."

"Whose prescription?"

Adel shook her head, shrugged and wiped an eye. She wasn't talking.

Temeke gave Adel a box of tissues. "Miss Baca an old

dragon?"

"It's a school for gifted students, what do you think? My dad said if I didn't get good grades he'd take away my car."

"I doubt getting good grades is hard for a gifted student."

Adel's eyes narrowed. "Do you even know what the pressure's like?"

"Seems like your day was one round of pleasure judging by the amount of spare time you had. Let's face it, it takes an hour here and there to have a séance, thirty minutes to enforce the power of levitation, at least ten minutes for a smoke down the nature trail and one for a bit of casual sex. Mustn't forget the hours you all spent reading that book, mixing herbs and pulling feathers off a sodding roadrunner in the potting shed. When did you have time to study?"

"It was just kid's stuff."

"You do realize roadrunners are a protected species? State bird and all that. There'll be a fine."

"I don't know about any birds."

Malin wriggled in her chair, would have appreciated details on the roadrunner an hour ago. Animal cruelty was a fourth degree felony.

"I thought there was someone following us that night," Adel said.

"Care to describe that person?"

"Medium height, black coat, dark jeans."

A black coat? Malin thought. She was wearing a black coat.

"It was the beanie he was wearing that made me wonder... Homeless, all spaced out like he was on something. I couldn't think where I'd seen him before, but there was someone just like him on campus a few weeks ago, digging around in the trash."

The question on Malin's mind came bouncing back

hard. What man? And had he seen her? She hadn't been aware of another soul in the woods that night. Thought she'd been thorough.

Temeke sniffed. "Can't be homeless if he was digging around in the trash on campus one minute and outside Corrales Café the next. A good few miles between Gibson and the West side. Must have wheels."

"I never saw another car in the parking lot. Do you think someone's stalking me?"

Adel's eyes seem to bore into Temeke's and never once did they roam over Malin. At a guess, Malin knew Adel hadn't seen her that night. She would have recognized her if she had.

"I specialize in stalkers, love." Temeke seemed to be digging a hole in his cheek with a finger. Something was bothering him. "So, Paddy was going to find Lily?"

Malin stifled a chuckle. Adel had not communicated that piece of information and judging by a wrinkled brow, she must have been wondering how he could have known. Temeke was pushing her into a corner and he was taking pleasure in watching her squirm.

"He told me he knew where she was."

Well, not exactly, thought Malin. It wasn't quite how she remembered it. Paddy had said, *I think I know where she is.*

Temeke ran a finger over a pack of cigarettes on the table, probably craving a smoke now the questions were getting close to the mark. "Paddy gave you an overnight bag. Care to tell us what was in it?"

Adel looked down at the table, eyes running over each score and nick as if she was trying to make a shape out of them. "Just clothes."

"Why would he bring you clothes?"

"I left them when I stayed the night."

Malin wondered who Adel was covering for, who she was afraid of.

"So you knew he was sleeping with other women?" Temeke said, offering her a cigarette.

Adel shook her head and blinked at him through the lenses of her glasses. "The signs were all there. I just didn't want to believe it."

"You see I'm trying to understand why an intelligent male would see the sense in all of this. Unless he was hurting for his next fix."

Temeke slipped the photograph of Paddy Brody's blood-spattered remains from the file and laid it face up on the table.

"And why a perfectly intelligent male would go to a crack house on a whim. Because he died, you see. Got hacked to pieces. You wouldn't know anyone who would do such a thing?"

THIRTY-FIVE

I saw you set the candle in water, watched it burn until it went out. Were you thinking of me?

Gabriel saw the eyes he longed for, bursts of memory seen through a gauzy curtain where gray silhouettes moved at random and the room was alive with whispers.

Sometimes he heard the sounds of crying, sometimes screams. Then silence as the night began to talk to him, all within a tangle of nightmares. He remembered the friends who shared this hell, friends marked with the same broken presence he knew so well. Friends who had passed on and left him abandoned and alone. Why did they have to do that?

He saw it in detail now, the chairs, the tables, the hierarchy of the place. Her hierarchy. He didn't belong, she'd made that clear enough.

He couldn't decide what was worse. Girls being teased and humiliated in the locker rooms with cruel words that made no sense, or boys doing the macho thing, trying to get noticed, trying to keep their egos intact. Boys who hid behind a blank, indifferent mask, saying few words but just enough to get them by. And they say a man is only as good as his word.

He wondered how he could do better, make better, see better. It wasn't like he didn't know. There were classmates, teachers, friends who could attest to a strong religious stance at school. Not like he hadn't heard it all before and wondered.

He just didn't want it rammed down his throat, that was all.

There was a pastor on 19th Street who came to the school to counsel and read scripture. What was his name? A man you warmed to because he had a sense of understanding hopelessness. He'd told Gabriel once that if a man claims to be in the light and hates someone, he is still in the dark.

The dark was a cold, lonely place where people go to die. Trouble was, Gabriel was very much alive and it all seemed wrong somehow. He was done kidding himself. Whenever he heard the distant sound of an airplane in the sky he thought of home. Bright sunny days as a child with a swollen diaper between his knees, looking up into the clouds to see where that sound was coming from.

His gut turned with the thought and his nostrils filled with the smells of childhood. Freshly mown grass, a girl's laughter, his mother's voice. What had gone wrong?

Then a new thought. If he turned himself in to the police, the screeching, the needling and the pain would stop. The shakes would stop. The vomiting, the sweats... Anything was better than this.

There was another way, and that was take his own life. The longer he waited, the more he wondered.

Demon never once portrayed himself as anything other than powerful and killing Paddy Brody had been a Herculean job. It didn't seem possible for one man. Quick as a flash Gabriel's whole world went muddy, with slashes of red and gray, and the scent of rust. The hatred seemed to accelerate one minute and dissipate the next, and he was never sure how to draw back the curtain to let in the light. He'd tried often enough and kept seeing things, orange eyes and dark shapes. It was starting to get to him.

Only a man knows how another man feels, the despair,

the degradation, the panic. And the punch, when it came, hurt Gabriel right down to his secret place.

Change is good, so they say.

Shards of memories meant only one thing. His past was broken, swept up and thrown away. Today was new. It felt different, as if something vital was missing, and it wasn't until he talked himself into drawing back the curtains of the room, squinting through a shaft of sunlight that he realized what it was.

He wasn't sad any more.

THIRTY-SIX

Malin rolled her shoulders and stared out of the window of the house on Columbia Drive. How Temeke had managed to pull this off she would never know. But that winning British tongue had a way with words and Detective Suzi Cornwell couldn't resist him.

The road was frosted in the moonlight and she tried to shake off the feeling of sadness and duty. A day of checking the university campus for witnesses of the homeless man Adel had described turned up no leads. No one seemed to remember much about him because no one ever looks the homeless in the eye.

Paddy Brody's house had been cleared of all his personal effects and his roommate was a nervous wreck. She'd tried to calm the poor man down, tried to make him understand it was unlikely he was on the killer's hit list. But what right had she to say that?

A kettle rumbled in the kitchen, made her tense sitting there with a small overnight bag listening to the infernal clink of cups and saucers.

"Here," Adel said, placing two mugs of tea on the coffee table next to a cell phone.

A small crop top revealed the glimmer of a belly piercing, thighs sticklike and encased in a pair of yoga pants. She sat on the couch, pale eyes jittering behind stylish glasses. Exhaustion or a nervous tic? Malin couldn't decide which.

"Sugar?"

Malin shook her head and took the tea black. She sat on a chair decorated with hunchback flute players so typical of the southwest. It was a darn sight more comfortable than perching on bar stools in front of the kitchen counter with your back to the action.

"You took my iPad," Adel said. "I only use it to study."

"If you've deleted anything, we'll find it," Malin said. "Not worth the trouble really."

"Only pictures of Paddy and me." Adel ran a finger under one eye, caught a tear before it slipped away.

Malin half expected her to launch into how she met this cool-ass guy she was crying over now, how he was the year's best catch. And how the heck did he die in that rat infested ruin?

Get a grip, Malin told herself, feeling the sweat break out between her shoulders. Adel wouldn't ask how Paddy died because she hadn't asked how Zarah Thai was either.

"I want to know why he was there," Adel said. "I want to understand."

Malin studied the bleak gaze, the half open mouth and tried to place the accent she was hearing. Wondered if she could mimic it if she had to. "We think he took a phone call from someone. A drug dealer, perhaps. Did he ever snort or inject anything other than amphetamines?"

"No."

"Ever complain of stomach cramps? Get aggressive?"

"I don't think so."

Malin tried to imagine the flotsam of users who came and went from the crack house on Guadalupe Trail, twitching and staggering with their dark rimmed eyes. "There's a range of symptoms. You'd recognize them if you saw them. Fever, nausea, hallucinations–"

"Alice had hallucinations." Adel stared at the window, glasses reflecting the setting sun, a spotlight in a dark sky.

Little by little, she was remembering.

"What's the thing you most remember about Alice?" Malin asked.

"Always laughing and cracking jokes." Adel blew into her mug and placed it back on the coffee table. "Every embarrassment became a funny story at dinnertime and with her, it didn't matter if you failed a test or your grades plummeted. She said everything would turn out fine. You felt happy when you were with her, like you could forget everything bad that had happened. After class, we'd go upstairs and sit on Asha's Persian rug and drink wine, tell stories… act them out sometimes. You know what I liked best about her? She wasn't beautiful in the obvious sense. It kind of crept up on you. None of it went to her head."

Malin remembered the picture. Long hair with traces of red… "Perfect, then."

"All the guys thought so."

"How tall?" Malin knew, she just wondered if Adel knew.

"Five foot five, six, maybe."

"Fat? Thin?"

"Stocky. She worked out a lot. Liked to keep in shape."

"Did she play sports?"

"Tennis mostly."

"What about you?"

"Modeling, swimming. I wasn't good at tennis."

"But Alice was."

Adel nodded and wiped her hands on her thighs. "She was always beating Zarah."

"Something to be proud of. Did you like Zarah?"

"I liked everyone. But I liked Alice best. Thought she was brave. She never cried after her dad died."

"Holding it in isn't good."

"She did it for us."

Malin felt a familiar stirring in her gut, giddy, as in

stepping off a carousel that had spun too fast. Her mother's voice seemed to creep into the back of her mind. *The oldest child is always the most sensitive. They're the protectors.*

"She found this book," Adel murmured. "It was full of symbolism and rituals. And demons. It changed us. There was no way to undo it."

"Why?"

"Because someone took the book."

"Who?"

"Baca. She took everything. Nosing around in our private things."

"She was protecting you." Malin took a sip of tea. "Remember what Alice did? She spread ashes around her bed so she could find footprints in the morning. She found some, didn't she?"

Adel shrugged. "Alice said if you believed, things happened. Good things. Like getting A's and the boy you liked. Of course, everyone liked Paddy. Flirted with him whenever they could."

"Did you start dating Paddy after Alice died?"

"Yes.

Malin suspected it was *before*, but she wasn't going to push it.

"Do you believe your actions can be controlled by supernatural forces?" Adel clasped her hands together and pushed them down between her knees. "That they can be influenced mysteriously?"

"By magic, you mean?"

"Yes."

"No."

"Well, they can. I'm not talking about a magician who carries a crystal ball for scrying. I'm talking about a questing demon who carries everything he needs in here." Adel tapped the side of her head. "The type that moves from place to place, occupies the space between mortals and angels. Something that can change a man from the inside out."

Malin tried to stop the frown and the upturned mouth, but Adel had already sensed it.

"I know you don't believe me," Adel said. "But it's true. He lives in the desert, in ruins, in outhouses, and on roofs. Alice once said he takes up three quarters of the human mind. Did you know the angel of death keeps his tools in a synagogue?"

"No... I didn't."

"He can't procreate. He has to use the semen of Adam to make his own kind and then he uses a woman to birth it. Makes you think, doesn't it?"

Malin was thinking. The front door was only a few feet away and the thought of staying the night with a quirky girl and a bad spirit seemed like a bad idea.

Adel turned her head slightly, eyes following a faint shadow of light that arced around the room. The headlights of a passing car. "He's frightening to look at during the day. But at night he looks like a man."

A man? The cogs in Malin's mind began to turn. "Then Alice should have found human feet around her bed that night. Not bird's feet. Someone was having her on."

Adel leaned forward a little. Her hands were now tucked under her thighs and Malin was sure she saw her shiver.

"Awful what happened to Zarah," Malin said, trying to keep her mind on the matter. Trying to understand why Adel hadn't mentioned it. "Awful to think she could have died."

Adel nodded, gazed out of the window toward the road and the police unit that had pulled out to make way for another on the next shift. "Do you know what drives a demon away? Spitting... bribery... the bells on a priest's skirt—"

"Psalms," Malin blurted out over the rim of her teacup. "As do quite a number of verses in scripture."

"Scripture?" Adel uttered as if she found the concept alien. "That is – if I'm honest – a bit old fashioned. You need to understand, this demon is very much part of this world. He might go away for a time but he always comes back. I could say... he's right behind you. But you'd take a peek, see nothing and then expect me to say *monkeys always look*. But he's everywhere."

The *Esoterica* made reference to a demon who had no face, who caused illness and death, and whose powers were fiercest during a waning moon. A demon who worked in concert with man because he could do nothing on his own. A demon who was invisible, except at night. A *familiar*.

Malin decided to get things straight, to evaluate the case correctly in order to keep the profile realistic. Demons weren't tangible. But a cold-blooded killer was. A man who hunted his victims and killed them in their own homes. A stalker... a predator, a revenge killer. Someone known to the victims, close to them, dependent on them. A killer who remained under police radar, not because he was fashioned from smoke and vapor, but because he was always moving. Always changing.

The cell phone clattered along the surface of the table and Adel lunged for it.

"This is Adel," she said, body twisting around to an end table and reaching for a notepad. "Who? No, I don't have it. Is this... The Spring Fair... OK. I'll try."

Maybe because Adel was staring at the phone as if it had burned her ear, maybe because the caller had hung up without saying goodbye, but there was something odd about that call. Malin had overheard a male voice pressing Adel to find the book and bring it to the Fair.

"Is everything OK?"

Adel's lips were parted and there was a faraway stare

in her eyes that gave Malin the impression the caller was someone she hadn't spoken to in a while.

"Are you using, Adel?"

"Why do you say that?"

"You look nervous."

Malin felt like she was stumbling around in a mine shaft with a broken flashlight. Why didn't the killer fit a profit killer or a team killer? He had no sexual motif. The crimes were sudden, brutal and quick and had garnered no witnesses. Except for Zarah Thai whose rambling speech and hallucinations had kept law enforcement away, although she repeatedly inquired about her dog.

Not one person had come forward with any information, which roused the possibility that the killer was a person who looked, acted and sounded normal. A next-door neighbor. A workmate.

"This demon..." Malin asked, studying the cell phone on the table. "What's his name?"

"We just call him Demon. That's all I know."

"But what does he look like?"

Adel's eyes scuttling up and down the walls while running a finger along her lower lip. "Sometimes kind, sometimes mean. He's so random. You never know which side you'll get."

"Moody, volatile? I need words. I need to gauge the mood, to see a face."

Adel drew her arms around her waist and shuddered. "Two faces. One looks into the future. And one into the past."

Malin felt a sudden rush of heat followed by a stirring chill. She knew she was onto something, kept seeing a figure that seemed vaguely familiar, but she was too far away to see the face.

"Can you see him now?"

Adel squinted and stiffened. "All the time."

THIRTY-SEVEN

Wrought-iron gates crept open and a guard waved Temeke through to Los Poblanos Academy. The driveway was crammed with black Suburbans and a limousine that took up the equivalent of three parking spaces. It was six o'clock in the evening, bloody March already and a dinner party he hadn't expected.

"Hello, sir. Greetings, greetings." A man rushed forward and bowed, starched white kurta buttoned to his throat. "Come, come. Yes, sir."

Temeke smiled, appreciating the warmth of a Pakistani gentleman, at least he assumed he was Pakistani. He introduced himself as *Ravi* and rattled on about cricket.

"I pray to God England always win," Ravi said. "Andrew Strauss, marvelous batter. Do you remember Bangladesh at Birmingham? Most glorious—"

They cut through a courtyard to avoid the guests, through sweeping archways to a large kitchen. But in all the spaciousness, Temeke noted how Spartan it was.

"Chef Moose," Ravi whispered, jutting his chin at a young man who was giving Puccini's *Nessun Dorma* a surprisingly good shot.

Moose was a striking young man with keen eyes and a starched chef coat that hung from a slender frame. Temeke couldn't think for the life of him where he'd seen him before. In his line of business it was usually a six pack, a trawl of police lineups all gift-wrapped in a three ring binder. Better still, wrestled to the ground in a jangle of cuffs behind the old Bernalillo Courthouse.

"Pastor Razz. Very good man." Ravi nodded at a portly African American who was peering under pot lids and pitching a fit at the lobsters in the sink. Temeke had met him before.

Moose stopped mid-key when he saw them in the doorway and Pastor Razz gave a wide smile. Temeke assumed it was the black polo shirt and khaki pants, and a Glock in his belt. He must have had the words *Duke City Police* written all over him.

"Good to see you," Pastor Razz grabbed Temeke's hand and gave it a sturdy shake.

He pointed to a door opposite the kitchen and led Temeke into a small office with a mission style bench and a polished mahogany desk. Behind it was a black and white photograph of Georgia O'Keeffe with a faraway smile and hands splayed over one exposed breast. There was a second photograph of an old man smoking a pipe in one of the downtown Albuquerque alleyways. It reminded him of a drug deal some years back.

"It's been almost six months," Razz said. "The Eriksen case?"

Temeke rubbed a hand over his bald head. "I'm wondering if this one's tougher."

"I counseled Lily Delgado, if it helps. Although—"

"Confidentiality. Yeah, I know."

Pastor Razz lowered his head and placed his hands flat on the desk. "There is an enemy we cannot see. It doesn't mean he isn't real. If it takes tempting you in secret… slander, stealing, sex, drugs, he'll go there. Whatever it takes to crush you. Have you ever killed anyone?"

The question took Temeke by surprise, but he got a kick out of Razz's sharp-eyed nature.

"A few years ago," Temeke said, "there was a rising

tide of drug traffickers DCPD had no chance of controlling. I was downtown when it happened. Followed my Glock toward a locked dumpster, sensing something up ahead."

Temeke could still feel his heart booming in his chest, muscles knotted with adrenalin.

"I stopped when I saw the muzzle of an AR-15. I told him to drop his weapon. But he didn't hear. Didn't want to hear. So I aimed, shot twice, watched the body jerk and heard the clatter of that brute of a rifle. I turned him over and cuffed him even though he was dead. We always follow procedure."

"Then you understand how to defend yourself. How to rid yourself of the threat. But what if you had no gun? No training. What then?"

Clacking heels in the corridor wiped the smile from Razz's face and brought both men to their feet.

"Ah, there you are, detective," Miss Baca said, shaking his hand and showing Razz the door with a snap of her fingers. Her perfume seemed to provoke an allergic reaction and Temeke began to sneeze.

"It's the juniper," she said, wrestling with a tissue from a box on the desk and handing it to him. "I was glad to hear you'd found Lily Delgado. As much as I hate it, I think we need the National Guard to surround the school until this terrible person is caught."

Temeke sneezed loudly and covered both nostrils with the tiny tissue. He sat down again.

"This monster makes people disappear, burst into flames and then delivers poisonous pizza. I bet he's from New York and speaks Italian," she said, nodding and pointing a finger. "And he intends to do the same to the rest of us."

"There's no need to assume he's a terrorist, ma'am, or that he's from New York."

"All the pizzerias across the nation could be at risk.

And we've got two dead girls already."

"I have a few questions about Adel Martinez, ma'am. There's something I'd like you to see. Were you aware she had ADHD?"

"I'm perfectly sure that she didn't."

"Seen these?"

Temeke took a small evidence bag from his jacket pocket and placed it on the desk between them. He noted the downward slant of her eyes and the slightly parted lips. She leaned in toward the evidence bag, mouth moving, but he heard no words. *Go on, tell her it's Adderall. She looks like she could use a bloody good laugh.*

"Omeprazole," she whispered, sounding out the name. "Never heard of it."

He felt an uneasy twinge. She had either seen the medication or she hadn't. And if she hadn't, he could have read her all wrong and he didn't like that feeling at all.

"Take a closer look," he said, pushing the bag toward her.

"You people should be checking cars for New York plates instead of asking innocent citizens to look at pills."

"Ma'am?" Temeke heard his voice rising by a major third. "The name on the bottle is Adel Martinez, one of your former students. As you can see, she was taking Omeprazole for an ulcer. Only, these aren't Omeprazole. They're Amphetamines."

Miss Baca only managed to whimper the first syllable and then, "No one here takes amphetamines. It's in the contract both parents and students are required to sign."

"You insist on the highest grades, ma'am. The school board insists on it. The last time we met you said there was simply no wiggle room. Students are given one chance to raise their grades to an A. Anything less requires disciplinary action. What type of disciplinary action?"

"Detention, garden duties." She hitched her shoulder a little, not a shrug, more like an unconscious attempt to readjust her posture. "Cleaning windows, that kind of thing."

Cleaning windows... Temeke thought about the fire escape and the bathroom window, the same window Alice may have looked out of during her final hours. He just wasn't sure how it tied into the investigation, but something in that tight little list of duties made his stomach curl. "You said the window was broken, used to stick a little."

"Yes," she lowered her head, even colored a little as if it was something she had overlooked.

"The book... why didn't you give it to the police sooner?"

"I didn't think it was important."

"A missing girl and a couple of murders are important. Someone was running a lucrative business handing out drugs to students who were struggling to get straight A's. You wouldn't know who that *someone* was, would you?"

Temeke knew his deliberate allusion to some of Miss Baca's students would be lost on her if she knew nothing about it. He wasn't sure yet if she was shooting straight and that made him jumpy.

"This is ridiculous," she said. "Why would anyone do that?"

"When did you raise the fees?"

"Three years ago."

"Ten thousand a semester is quite a jump from when Alice Delgado started. I understand they were seven thousand then."

"The upkeep of this school has taken its toll. And as you know there was a fire ten years ago."

Upkeep or no upkeep, Temeke thought, the school had had far more than just a lick of bloody paint. It was palatial, and serving lobster on the school's anniversary was a luxury reserved only for the rich.

"I understand the building, contents and store are insured against theft, fire, explosion and stampeding animals for the sum of three million."

Her eyes widened. "I can't believe it."

"Neither could I." Temeke gave her the benefit of his blackest stare. "I doubt there's more than ten grand of stock in the place now and I'd be surprised if that was paid for. Tell me about Chef Moose?"

"He worked at the Frontier on Central before he came here," she said, handing back the evidence bag. "He was a little banged up, shall we say."

"Not sure the kitchen's the right place for an ex-con. He may not have told you his real name."

"His name's Moose Ham. It's on his driver's license. You can check if you like." A barely perceptible pause before her face tightened and her eyes blazed. "Are you insinuating I employ illegal immigrants?"

"They get about."

"Not here they don't. All my employees go through a thorough screening."

Temeke realized he was losing it and one more snide comment would give Hackett the legitimate excuse he needed to bounce him. All he seemed to do these days was stagger from one disaster to the next.

"Moose is a fine chef. It's time someone gave him a chance."

Temeke gave her a sideways smile and heaved himself from the chair. "First impressions are always big in law enforcement. So, I'll be keeping an open mind. Any chance I could talk to him?"

THIRTY-EIGHT

Clouds moved fast toward the iced sliver of a moon and Malin thought she saw a blur of movement in the front yard of Columbia Drive. It was only the shadows cast by the clouds and a scuttle of leaves across the pavement.

Sitting on the couch and staring through a window smeared with a year's worth of dust gave her time to think, time to watch a beam of light as it spilled through the trees, a strobe from the neighbor's garage. A coyote perhaps? Something was slinking along the wall out there, black as midnight, unless she was seeing things.

Demon. The name made her flesh ripple. Whatever it was, whoever it was, even if she had to venture into the dirty alleys and shady denizens of the Albuquerque drug world, she would find him. The murders had all the features of a serial, and lab tests had been rushed to the top of the autopsy line. She wanted to file away all the mug shots in the database, wanted time to wander around the house while Adel and her roommate slept.

The clock on the mantel reminded her it was midnight and her mind drifted back a few hours, rewinding Adel's words, trying to understand how she fitted in to all this. Malin knew she was getting ahead of herself, imagining a young woman burning with hatred and fingers curled around the handle of a knife.

As far as Alice's autopsy report claimed, Alice was five feet five inches, stocky, firm, and by no means overweight. By contrast, Adel was lean, had upper arms you could snap and a mind that quite frankly wasn't sharp enough to mastermind a poisoning or a gas explosion. She also wasn't the type to fire off a few rounds and deck a crowd either. But she could have slit a wrist if she was under the influence.

Malin instinctively turned her head and gazed into Adel's bedroom. It was about ten feet from where she sat, door half open and only the right side of the bed was visible. One hand lay on the edge of the mattress, fingers twitching as if caught in a nightmare. For one brief second, Malin wondered if there had ever been any trace evidence under those painted nails.

So what did Alice say that made you kill her? What did she do? Did you have the knife in your pocket all the time? What were you looking for?

Malin pulled her mind away from the scene and walked toward Sarah Hughes' bedroom first. Window barred and locked, no access from the outside with a cruiser parked along the curb. Moonlight shone through the open blinds and onto a dark-skinned girl, rounded limbs with the plumpness of baby fat.

Adel's bedroom was next door; a rocker, a small white dresser about six feet from the bed and a cell phone charged and ready to use. A nightlight cast a scroll pattern on the ceiling and a dream catcher hung from a curtain rod. No sign of that overnight bag. Malin had looked hard enough.

Adel lay on her back, hair thrown over the pillow, sheet turned down to her hips. Malin could just make out the faintest pulse on a bare stomach and the quiver of a belly ring. The more she watched Adel, the more troubled she felt.

Paddy had pissed off a lot of girls, leading them on, casting them off. A guy like that was bound to come to a sticky end one way or another. But did Adel's jealousy merit killing all those women? Judging by the vacillating moods, the idea wasn't exactly off the charts. Malin could file the theory as possible, not probable, but the question kept hovering in the back of her mind.

There was only one thing for it. Tilting her head back in that ringing silence, she crept further into the bedroom and reached for Adel's cell phone. Scrolling through two calls from someone called Tammy in Admissions, she found a local one without a name. It was a number worth memorizing.

She pressed the phone against her ear, heard four rings before it went through to voicemail.

Hi, you know who this is. If you don't leave your name and number, I will find you.

Nailed it. The hesitation in the male voice was a dead giveaway, identical to the one Adel was meeting at The Spring Fair.

Malin caught a flicker of movement from the bed, pressed END and replaced the phone on the dresser where she found it. Adel was restless, one knee lifted as if she was about to turn over and a deep moan slipped through open lips.

Malin tensed, felt a prickle of adrenalin as it powered through her body and she mumbled rapidly to herself. One slip, one tiny mistake, and Adel would wake up. Malin lurched for the door, had to keep moving, had to keep alert, had to write that number down before she forgot it.

The pad was there by the couch and the pen seemed to tremble in her hand before she could get a grip. She tore off a sheet, stuffed it in her pocket, and swallowed hard before the hunger pain hit.

Couldn't stop thinking about the only witness they had left. It wasn't by some confluence of fate that Zarah Thai had become a victim. She was part of a group, a sick and twisted sisterhood that may have created a monster in all that alchemy and magic. She was a material witness, the last person to have seen the killer. But the entire case couldn't rest on the word of a tortured young woman and it was doubtful she would be available for interview until the end of the week.

Malin checked the kitchen drawers for handwritten notes, phone numbers, anything that might pin Adel to the same pizza delivery company that Zarah used. Nothing.

She resisted the urge to go outside, to breathe in a lungful of fresh air. The patio doors would only make a noise and wake up the one person she didn't want to meet in a dark corridor.

Returning to the living room, she crouched in front of a bookshelf, dragged a finger across the spines of fifteen cookery books, two vampire novels, a *Webster's Collegiate Dictionary* and a book on the *Cumbres & Toltec Scenic Railroad*.

She sat down on the couch and checked her phone. Wingman was sending a message.

Wingman: I'm back, my dear. Want to talk?

Malin felt relieved, as if she had finally found her rhythm. I'm babysitting. Trying to keep a clear mind.

Wingman: On the Delgado case? I saw it on the news. Terrible business. Remember the Rocky and Bullwinkle show? Might be before your time. It was a radio program with pictures. Thought I'd watch it. Have a good laugh.

It was no good assuming Wingman was just making small talk. None of his words were wasted and most were code for something to do with the case, which, of course, he would have fully acquainted himself with. She quickly googled the show, trying to keep the grin from her face.

Malin: You mean that flying squirrel?

Wingman: Now that was cheating, Malin. You just googled it.

She actually trembled for a few moments, until she realized he wasn't watching her from some satellite in outer space. Nor was he in the cruiser outside the house laughing his head off.

Three little dots. He was typing again.

Wingman: First, I want you to imagine you're at the crime scene. We won't say the gas explosion because you weren't among the first responders, neither were you invited because no one saw a connection. Let's pick this week's front page news. Mr. Brody. The techs, the blood spatter analyst and the videographer are looking at evidence inside that small room. They look up, see you and move back so you can approach. What's the first thing you see? A crowd of white coveralls? Or a body?

Malin: I wasn't allowed in. But I saw enough from the door. Young man, early twenties, fully clothed, lying on his stomach, neck slashed, one hand grasping the wound. There was blood spatter on three walls and a gloved handprint on the door frame.

Wingman: On the face of it, yes. But what does that tell you?

Malin took the obvious shot. Head and hands intact. The killer didn't care to hide the victim's identity. He slipped in the blood on the way out, tried to steady himself against the doorframe. I'd like to hear your opinion.

Wingman: I'd like to hear yours.

Malin knew he was waiting, knew he was making her work for this one. Someone he knew. Someone who surprised him. One disappearance, two deaths, one which appeared like an accident, the other like a suicide. Both within a few weeks of one another and within an eight mile radius. It looks like the killer has no intention of cooling off. Connection, Los Poblanos Academy. Certainly not random.

Wingman: Good. Now you're thinking like a profiler. Just one last thing before I let you go. I think you know who did it. You just don't know how.

A slew of useless tips turned up nothing and Malin was stumped. No sooner did she think she was on the right track than her mind became muddied by a killer who continued to creep under the radar. The first words that popped into her head were *member of staff*, but it didn't seem right somehow.

She flicked a quick look toward Adel's bedroom and watched a shadow on the wall. Her mind replayed the items in that room; the dream catcher twitching slightly in a draft of air. There were no open windows, just the soughing of the air vents above the door.

"Adel?" Malin called out, leaning forward slightly so she could see the bed. "Are you awake?"

Silence. Adel wasn't awake. She was out cold.

Malin looked down at her phone and saw Wingman had signed off. Probably wanted her to dwell on what he'd just said, wanted her to decipher the code. She was beginning to see a pattern in these virtual appointments. He'd disappear for a time, a week maybe, a month, and then he'd be back again when she least expected it.

Rocky and Bullwinkle, a squirrel and a stupid moose. A partnership. She felt strange, but *strange* didn't equal what she theorized in those short few minutes.

The techs, the blood spatter analyst and the videographer were bagging evidence inside that small room.

There were only a few people allowed on the scene that night. She dialed Temeke's number. "Where are you right now?"

"Out and about."

She felt a heightened stillness in the air, brain ticking and churning. Was that a dog barking on the phone and in unison to the one outside? Temeke didn't have a dog. "You here?"

"Couldn't sleep, love. Keep wondering how Adel Martinez managed to elude surveillance the other night. Everything all right with you?"

"Yeah. Everything's good here." Malin stood and crossed the room to the window. She couldn't see him outside. Must have been mistaken. "I've got a number I need traced."

"Consider it done."

She took the slip of paper out of her pocket, relayed the number and then asked for the names of the technicians at the Brody scene.

"Matt Black, Carol Turner, Neil Sanchez, Pauline Bailey... I forgot the name of her intern," he said. "The usual crew. Why?"

Matt Black. Malin tried on the name for size, even whispered it a few times. Matt may have liked her enough to ask her out. But he didn't hate Temeke enough to denigrate him or have the power to get him removed. The only other person was Hackett and quite frankly he was a tired old man with respect for Temeke because his solve stats were higher than any of the other detectives in homicide. "I think someone's stalking me on the internet."

There, she'd finally spat it out. He'd be mad, of course. Especially if she told him Wingman had an interest in the case and madder still if she admitted how long she'd known him.

"As long as he doesn't have a deadly weapon," Temeke said, "because that's when people start talking. Who do you know with a deadly weapon? Oh, yeah, half of bloody law enforcement."

"Don't be cute." Malin huffed out a large breath.

"I hope you're not busy tomorrow night because we're meeting with the chef of Los Poblanos," he said. "Good food always loosens up the tongue. He had a thing with Adel. Said Alice was a knockout and all. The type a man can only dream about."

THIRTY-NINE

"So what have we got?" Luis asked, staring from one to the other, obviously waiting for the best punchline the Duke City Police Department had to offer.

"Adel Martinez took a call, sir," Malin said. "I could hear a man's voice asking if she had the book and to bring it to the Corrales Spring Fair. I checked her cell phone while she was sleeping, asked Temeke to trace a number. It was registered to a Gabriel Mann, false ID, old address."

"This book." Temeke set the leather bound book on the top of Luis' desk and scooted it over. "Seems it's hot property. Demonology. Your favorite genre."

Luis gave Temeke a narrow-eyed look. "You'll be seeing Ms. Martinez again?"

"As soon as yawner here gets some kip."

"There is something else." Malin attempted a smile, but the edges of her mouth barely forced a crease. Her head kept bobbing on that lean stalk of a neck and her eyes had begun to water. "I left a message for Mr. Mann pretending I was Adel Martinez. Told him I had found the book and confirmed my meeting with him at the Fair this weekend."

"There's no proof, Luis, not until we catch him in the act," Temeke said.

Luis lost his smile, seemed to be honing in on that last comment. "Seems like you were caught in the act. Hackett received another complaint about you sitting astride a wall in Ms. Hughes' back yard last night. Officer Jarvis gave a positive ID."

Temeke could feel Malin's intense focus. "Ms. Martinez mentioned climbing over the wall a few times. I was checking to see how easy it was."

"Damn it, bro Don't you have anything else?"

Temeke knew there was no way out and neither one of them had any substantial evidence. With Malin looking ominously on the verge of collapse, a theory was the best he could offer.

"So far the killings are all in Albuquerque, Luis. Geographical radius about eight miles. Victims are adult white females between the ages of nineteen and twenty-three, different ethnic groups, same socioeconomic status, and they all knew each other. Two vics dead, one missing and one in hospital under twenty-four hour surveillance. All within a month."

"I agree, a compressed timeframe. What's the connection?"

"All these victims went to Los Poblanos Academy," Malin chimed in.

"According to the principal," Temeke said, "they made up a tight-knit group. Six girls including Adel Martinez."

Luis nodded slightly. "So, you're working on the proposition that all three victims, plus two potential victims, were perpetrated by the same person?"

"It's possible. And it looks personal," Temeke said. "We'll be meeting with Mr. Moose Ham, chef at Los Poblanos Academy. Small time drug dealer, been in and out a few times. Good looking guy."

"I'm not following?"

"In the industry, Luis, looks and background are considered a clue."

"Based on statistics and probable behavior would you

say Mr. Ham fits the profile?"

"No, sir. He's a witness."

"Then what type of person do you see?"

Temeke had a light bulb moment in the nick of time. "I'm seeing a man who might have been sexually abused, terrorized, or even bullied. Went on a bender, probably killed the Samadi girl before trying to make the Voorhees incident look like an accident. Shame about the Belmonte drowning, but we were bloody lucky to get to Zarah Thai before it was too late."

"You know what I see? I see a high profile case that isn't any further along that it was a month ago and I see homicide scrutinizing the lead detective because they don't think he's up for it. They say your last name spells *trouble, dead loss, embarrassment to the police department.* I'd like to see things change."

"Maybe this will add a little inspiration." Temeke pointed at the book. "You might want to read it because whoever killed these women had a vested interest in the occult."

Luis raised the edge of his upper lip and gave an eye roll. "Any staging of the bodies? Religious symbols?"

"None. All murders took place inside their homes, except for Rosa Belmonte. I doubt she was lured. Had singing practice every Friday night at the Waterfalls Studios on 528. Parked by the river to eat waffle fries and honey mustard sauce from the Burger Giant. We know because she paid with a debit card. So someone was watching her."

Luis opened the book and flipped through a few pages. "Amphetamines heighten the libido."

"Also known to cause hallucinations, insomnia and headache," Malin said.

Temeke couldn't speculate as to how many students were taking them and he felt himself roiling with unwanted pity for the ones who had become addicted.

"I've questioned how they had managed to call in a repeat prescription, sir, because according to Miss Baca, no one had ADHD."

"So these students must have been getting them from a pill mill?" Luis said, rattling of a few rogue pharmacies in the valley.

"There's something ancient and disturbing about that book," Temeke said, eyeing it from behind a smile. "It's not like – other books."

"It's just a book," Luis said, then conceded, "Pretty weird book. Martinez into all of this?"

"She was conversant with it," Malin said. "Gave me the chills."

A stir of ideas seemed to break apart in Temeke's mind like a flurry of moths and he kept wondering why he couldn't match Adel's voice to the woman he'd heard in the field.

"Charlie Miller at Minerd's," Malin said. "The scrap place… he mentioned a man with dark hair. Someone Zarah Thai could positively identify."

Luis looked maddeningly uninspired. "Who's on surveillance at the Martinez place this week?"

"Officers Jarvis, Hinkley and Toledo. I'm on tonight," Malin begrudgingly volunteered.

Luis' face dipped closer to the page he was reading, lines etched deep into the skin at his forehead. "Do you really think Martinez lured Paddy Brody into that crack house and slit him up like a pig?"

Temeke sniffed and sat up straight. "No, sir. I don't."

FORTY

It was nestled in the north valley. The restaurant with bright bundles of red chile hanging from the porch and large French doors, once a private home in the midst of a clutch of cottonwoods.

Malin hadn't set foot in it since her mother died. She briefly glanced up between the leaves at clouds presently drifting in a clear blue sky, sun streaming down onto one of the restaurant's five garden patios. She would have enjoyed having dinner with Temeke if it hadn't been for Moose Ham, a man whose hands you wanted to sweep for gunshot residue.

"You might not think I like to read," Moose said, "but I do. I go to that library on 2nd Street, sit by the window."

"What are you reading?"

"A book on holocaust survivors. Left a bookmark in it last Wednesday."

"Didn't feel like checking it out?

"Library card's out of date." Moose sneezed and focused intently at a nearby pot of gamma grass. "It was last Saturday around two o'clock in the afternoon. I saw this girl walking between the shelves and there was a cop behind her. She was looking for something in the science fiction section. I knew her from the school. Used to meet me outside the kitchens while I was having a smoke. We'd drink a glass of wine... stuff, you know."

"Get drunk?"

"Sometimes?"

"Intimate?"

"Always."

"What was her name?" Temeke asked.

"Adel Martinez I had two salted caramel cake pops in my pocket. Thought she'd like one. Then I got this strange feeling." Moose patted his belly and gave an apologetic smile. "She was with that big ass cop because of the murders, right?"

Temeke said nothing, but when he did speak his voice was calm, belying the pressures he faced every day. "Have you heard from her since she left?"

"Nah, she had the hots for someone else." Moose sucked down the last of his iced tea and nodded at the waiter for a refill. "So, I was disappointed, but you can't blame her. Thought I was some meth fairy."

This got a raised eyebrow from Temeke. It was Malin's cue to take over the rest of the interview.

"Who was the other guy?" she asked.

"Paddy Brody. I'm sorry he's gone. One of the few who came into the kitchen at the end of the day and thanked me for my service. Made me feel special."

"How did you feel when you heard he'd been murdered?"

"Gutted. But something didn't sit right. Adel started hanging out with him after Alice died. Paddy told me it was like being a bull in a cowshed. Course, I said something stupid like 'must be nice' but he didn't seem to think so. All he cared about was Alice's little sister 'cause she didn't take it too well."

"Lily?" Malin looked at Moose head-on, saw him nod slightly.

"Alice was wild... fun, you know. Left a big hole. I think Paddy got closer to Lily after that. A protection thing, not a physical thing. I never saw them touch. You see stuff when you're working in the kitchens. The back door looks onto the parking lot and that's where they all hung out. But Adel was jealous."

Malin gave Temeke a brief glance before looking across at Moose. "Ever give Adel cigarettes?"

Moose gave a tight nod. "Weed. I gave her a few tokes now and then."

"Do amphetamines, that kind of thing?"

"No way, dude. Cleaner than I've ever been."

Which would be true, Malin thought, since he had a full-time job with regular drug screening. As for the weed... nobody seemed to count that these days. "Did Adel have a temper? Get violent?"

"Pastor Razz and I used to walk in the grounds when it got dark. We'd sit on a bench in the Lion's Mouth. He'd pray, I'd listen. Anyway, I heard voices in the parking lot one evening, shouting and carrying on. Adel and Kenzie. Something about how their stash had gone missing. How it was time someone had a real taste of hell."

"Who was the *someone*?"

"I didn't get a name." Moose leaned in a little and wrapped both hands around his iced tea. He copped a brief glance at Temeke and took a sip. "Those insane-ass witches were in the attic with a few bottles of hooch. Paddy was scared. Told me Adel suspected he was sleeping around, threatened to raise a demon. It all went south after that. If you ask me, that's motive enough?"

Temeke shrugged. "Not necessarily."

"C'mon, man, surely you don't think the killings in the news are random?"

"You think they were specifically targeted?"

Moose nodded, wiped one moist eye with the heel of his hand. "I found a book on Baca's desk. There was a piece of paper in the back, so I took it."

Moose placed the torn out page on the table. Likely an epilogue of sorts with a six pointed star in the header and the letters A-M-K-G-E-R at each corner.

During a waxing moon, he must then take six women to wife, six firstborn girls of wealth and position. Each will be called after the six corners of the sacred place, north, south, east, west, and all that is in its roof and floor – symbols by which they may be summoned.

Arezo – longed for, Mahtab – light of the moon, Kohinoor – mountain of light, Gulshan – garden of roses, Estheri – like a star and Roshan – the bright one.

For he, himself, is the Sun.

FORTY-ONE

The house was exactly as Gabriel envisioned. A beautiful slice of wonderland at the end of a long drive, wraparound cottonwoods covered in snow and a dark green lawn that looked out of place against the wintry grays of the neighboring yards.

He understood there was something calming in those ancient trees, an earlier memory in a sudden gust. Of sunshine and early blooms and the distinct fragrance of honeysuckle. Another child and a woman between them. Linked like family.

Gabriel couldn't see their faces anymore but he could feel her fingers, hear the shrill sound of a child's giggle. The woman stooped and hooked one arm around his waist, settling him against her hip.

"Look," she said, pointing upward. "Can you see it?"

Gabriel could if he thought hard enough. A humming bird hovering for a moment and then darting back and forth between the leaves. He kept staring at patches of blue between the branches just in case it came back to occupy the same space it once had.

"Why did it go, mommy?" he asked, no longer seeing the blur of tiny wings.

"A voice in the wind. Or maybe the change in the temperature, the season. But somehow they know."

"Will it speak to us?"

"Yes, if you listen." The woman turned her face

upward again, sunlight bronzing her cheeks. "There... did you hear that?"

Gabriel did. A soft susurration in the gamma grass and a float of tumbleweed across the drive. A small voice that said something so quickly he couldn't make out the exact words. But the wind was talking. Just like she said it would.

"Snow!" he shouted, pointing with a gloved finger.

Tiny flakes filtered down and then a cascade of snow that slipped through the air with a soft hiss. It was the occasional branch letting go of its load.

"What does the voice look like?" he asked.

"You know," the girl said. "You've seen him."

There was a sense the girl meant something else and Gabriel nodded. He didn't really understand. He hadn't really seen. "Is he big?"

"Naww," she said, giggling in that infectious way she did. "He's bigger than big."

"Big as a tree?"

"Yes, silly!" she shouted.

The sound released a flurry of humming birds, hundreds and thousands of tiny brown creatures and the whispery pulse of wings. Gabriel breathed in as the flock enveloped them and the woman smiled at the girl, cooing only at her.

There was something brittle about the girl – not on the outside, but on the inside – something that spiked now and then, something only Gabriel could sense.

It scared him when they shared the same room. She was restless with daring, telling him there were ghosts in the closet and how the stuffed bear on the toy box came alive at night. Gabriel watched those beady eyes for hours and if he was careful he would catch them winking. Mostly, he kept his head under the covers so he couldn't see them at all.

"You can play Prince Charming," she would whisper.

"And you can kiss me if you like."

He liked kissing her soft cheeks and braiding her hair. She was always the princess.

A blustery wind ruffled through the trees above them, stirring a lanyard on a nearby flagpole. The girl was silent, threads of hair fluttering against her back as she navigated a channel of brown water in a pair of boots. Her jeans were wet to the ankles and she didn't seem to care.

"C'mon, you slowpokes," she urged, eyes and skin ablaze in a shaft of sunlight. "Last person to the front door is a jackass!"

And then she was off, streaking through the trees until she dissolved into the bark of a sycamore. The sudden separation hit Gabriel in the chest and his heart was a tight spikey thing that stung and hurt inside. He knew he would gag if he didn't snap out of it.

The drive opened to a wide loop and he almost sobbed as he approached the house. Why did people have to die?

Sometimes he dreamed of a blackened body seen through a kitchen window, mouth wide open, teeth visible behind strands of darkened and twisted lips. Sometimes he saw the white nubs of broken fingers on a Persian carpet, a girl in a black dress, head thrown sideways and hair glistening with what had come out of the crack in her skull.

Neither had faces or voices.

The detective was bound to remember. It would all come flooding back. When he was shaving perhaps or cleaning his teeth, or vacuuming. Do detectives vacuum?

They were already bound with blood, because it was blood that first brought them together. Yes, the detective would remember.

Gabriel was immortal, but even as the sun rose earlier in the mornings chasing the last sprinkling of snow between the roots of trees and thawing icicles from gutters, something in his subconscious told him his luck was running out.

There was a face on the news, a face that had gone viral, a face he hardly recognized. Looked like any crackhead lowlife and it made him smile.

The picture dwindled into the crunch of gravel under his feet and the chatter of birds. There were three things he had to do today. Break into the house. Find the book. And destroy it.

Then Demon, the deceiver, would be gone.

FORTY-TWO

Temeke had fifteen minutes until he met with Adel Martinez and he wasn't looking forward to listening to her account of slashed throats and unusual accidents with gas.

Suspect? Unlikely. Working with an accomplice... possibly. If he deprived her of sleep or bathroom facilities, he might get a name for *composite-man*. Besides, there was nothing like returning home with the pride of capture on his face.

A buzzing down his trouser leg. He wriggled the phone out of his pocket and swiveled in his chair. "Yes, love?"

"I'm at the hospital," Malin said in a voice charged with significance. "Zarah Thai's nurse said she'll be available this afternoon at two. Want to meet me here?"

"Sounds like a date."

"And Lily Delgado was discharged this morning. So you're on tonight. Might want to take her for a walk out back. In the trees."

"It's bloody freezing out back, Marl."

"Sometimes taking a victim back to where it all happened might help her remember."

Temeke could tell by the tremor in her voice and the eerie silences she used after each sentence she was trying to tell him to be careful. "A jug of whisky would be quicker. Might loosen her tongue a little."

"Oh, and Hackett wants to call a press conference to take the heat off the situation. About two o'clock."

Temeke couldn't resist a smile. Malin was getting too sharp-witted for her own good and talking to a key witness was the best *out* they could possibly have for not attending another press dominated fiasco.

"I was following the penalty trail in that creepy book," she said, reciting a few lines from memory. *The first woman to disobey shall be buried alive, the second shall have her limbs severed, the third shall be cast into a fire, the fourth shall be drowned, the fifth shall be poisoned and the sixth shall be suffocated.* We know Alice was the first in that group to die, even though hers was an apparent suicide. But what if her Lilin name was *Arezo*, meaning *longed for*. Then there's a long gap between her death and Asha's disappearance, but it doesn't necessarily separate the two incidents. This would make Asha the second in these recent spree killings."

Temeke felt a flush of hot and cold tingling behind his ears and something shuddered deep inside. It was too critical a link to ignore.

"If she is the second then the name carved on the door frame confirms it. *M-A-H-T-A-B*." Malin reworked the spelling out loud. "Light of the moon. Since there was nothing left of the Voorhees house, we can assume *Kohinoor* was scratched on a doorframe somewhere. Mountain of light?"

"Yeah, a big-ass mountain of light," Temeke agreed. He wasn't sure how he felt about it, but there was a sense of urgency that raced through his veins.

"*Gulshan* was written on the flood gauge, sir. Garden of Roses. Rosa? As for the last two, we can ask Adel Martinez and Zarah Thai what their Lilin names were. It's clear the meanings defined each woman while they lived. What if the killer's trying to connect those names to their deaths?"

Temeke couldn't see the connection of *light* or *moon* to Asha Samadi, but it was the notion she fell into the category of being buried alive that made him itch under the skin. Wherever she was, they had to find her soon. "Or he's trying to mislead us with amateurish post-mortem scribblings to disguise what a raving bloody nutcase he is."

He ended the call, rushed down the stairs to Sandra's office and hammered a fist on the closed door. Creaking and pattering came from within and the door was opened a chink. Two angry eyes surveyed him and a claw pulled the door open further.

"Come on in," Fowler said as he walked over to Sandra's desk and pressed his big fat ass on the corner.

There was a half-eaten box of chocolate cream puffs beside the monitor and judging by the trajectory of crumbs, Fowler had wolfed down most of them.

"Could I have a word, Sandra?" Temeke saw the exchange of looks. "In private."

"By the way," Fowler said, giving in to an eye-roll on the way out. "Hackett wants to see you. He was in earlier, screaming blue murder because someone left a cigarette butt in the elevator."

Temeke had to raise his voice over a slamming door and the loud hammering of keys. "One cream puff and you've bought my soul. Do me a favor, love. Call all the mortuaries in Albuquerque and ask them for a list of burials from say February 3rd to the 8th."

"Righto. There's well over twenty mortuaries in Albuquerque and, while I'm at it, at least fourteen cemeteries. It might take a while, sir. Which victim?"

"Asha Samadi," he said between chews and keeping his tone as drab as he was feeling.

"She could have been buried in the woods."

Temeke didn't want to consider that option, but Sandra was right. There were other places besides cemeteries to bury the dead. Walls, dumpsters, barrels...

"What exactly am I looking for, sir?" she asked.

"I'm hoping for a name that might point to where Asha is. I'm sick of speculating, sick of not having any facts to report and sick of making a complete balls-up of everything I do."

The phone on Sandra's desk gave a long drawn-out wail and she pressed the intercom. "Go ahead, Sarge."

"Can you tell Temeke his nooner's just cancelled."

FORTY-THREE

Temeke forced himself to stop pacing and to sit down in Hackett's office. It never felt good to be summoned for an audience and to cap it all, the bastard was always late. Made his victims wait forty minutes at a trot and stare out of that big rectangular window.

At night it was like a motherboard of sparkling circuitry, something Hackett thought was pleasing and reminded him of his responsibility to the city of Albuquerque. He was proud of his substation, proud of his officers. When thirteen of his best were out paddling in the Rio Grande searching for guns tossed out of a car after a crime had been committed, he stood on the Alameda bridge and cheered them on. Became the Commander the police department deemed their best role model.

Temeke had spent his afternoon searching public records nationwide for current and past addresses for Adel Martinez, including any bankruptcy listings and liens. He was surprised to find she had been pulled over in the University campus a month ago for DUI.

Dozy cow.

Hackett's assistant, Cat Spears brought in a large tray of coffee and biscottis and set them down on the desk. Before she could offer Temeke a cup Hackett breezed in, sweeping the coat from his shoulders like Zorro.

"I've put officer Watts in charge of the Delgado house tonight."

"Why's that, sir?"

"Because I need you to look into something. I got your report," he said, collapsing in his chair and pulling off his glasses. "Names on door posts... the killer's possible MO. But the trouble is, we still haven't found Asha Samadi. Time's running out."

Good job Hackett didn't need reminding most cases take years to solve, Temeke thought. He would have yelled his bloody lungs off then. "I'm afraid so, sir."

"Have you seen the headlines?" There was a threatening note in his voice.

"I haven't had that privilege, sir."

"It says, *All The Officers And All Hackett's Men, Couldn't Put Samadi Together Again*. Who's leaking all this classified and humiliating information to the Press!"

Temeke tensed at the sound of a fist on the desk and a filing tray jumped in response. "Jennifer Danes. It's about time someone filed an injunction."

"Listen," Hackett said, blowing his nose loudly and dabbing the corners of his eyes with the same handkerchief. "Asha Samadi's father wants her found before he returns to Riyadh –" the lip quivered, "– or he'll sue."

"Bit unrealistic, isn't it? We've got no idea where she is!"

"I know that. But he's sick of all the *I'll keep you updated* nonsense."

"I'm being as creative as I can, sir."

"The only thing creative about you is your version of the truth. If I wasn't so busy with my health and other important matters, I'd go out and look for her myself."

"Relax, sir. Have a cookie."

Cat poured two steaming cups of coffee and balanced a caramel drizzled biscotti on each saucer before busying herself with the filing cabinet.

"All this stress," Hackett said. "Julie says I'm

twitching in my sleep."

"Quite normal, sir. All dogs do that."

"I want the girl found, do you hear?" Hackett's finger sawed away at an itch under his nose. "Every bit of her."

"I hope she hasn't been packed into three difference suitcases and tossed into the river, sir. You know how strong those currents are. Part of her could be in Mexico by Christmas."

Hackett looked shaken rigid and had to grip onto the edge of the desk. "It must be awful to be a father. Of course, you wouldn't know a thing about that. You… with your sick jokes and disgusting sense of humor."

"Just trying to take the edge off, sir."

"My blood pressure's up in the two hundreds, Temeke. Can't have Julie knowing. She can be very protective."

"Wouldn't tell a soul."

"I hope it's not cancer."

"You don't have cancer, not with all that great food you keep eating. Where was it last week? The Rancher's Club?"

Hackett's eye's flicked up. "You watching me?"

"Listen. Officer Dempsey – you must remember her – got a pair like two Christmas puddings."

The culinary allusion gave Hackett the necessary mental picture and he appeared to brightened up.

"Well, she was told she had breast cancer three years ago, sir. Refused chemo, wasn't going to pump more poison into her bloodstream. Decided to drink vegetables instead. Not a trace of cancer left in that tight little body. All went down the toilet."

Hackett seemed to nod in appreciation. He was the type of man who cost a fortune, running up restaurant bills and cholesterol levels and trawling The Mayo Clinic for a particularly elusive type of disease he thought he had. Retirement wasn't far in the future, but Temeke knew if Hackett could swing it earlier and at full pay he'd be a very happy man.

"Sandra asked me to give this to you." Hackett fished two pieces of paper from a landfill on his desk. "Recent burials. And what's all this witchcraft stuff Alvarez keeps alluding to? Says he's been studying it in a book."

"I heard he was a bit eccentric, sir, but I didn't know in which direction."

"I used to make fun of all that spiritual stuff in the old days, but now…"

"It's quite the thing these days. And now we have information that implies Asha might have been buried in a cemetery. Yeah, go on, sir, have a good laugh."

"It's not a laughing matter, Temeke. And what makes you think she's buried in a cemetery?"

"Because no one would think of looking there." Temeke hoped his theory wasn't about to be booted up the ass. "A name on a headstone, an object… anything might be significant in locating her. Just a feeling."

"Been smoking in the elevator?"

Temeke raised his rear off the seat and shook his head. "I wouldn't dream of it."

He slipped out into the corridor, smelling fresh air for the first time in twenty minutes. His office was more sanitary than walking through a wall of sneeze and he settled in his chair.

The pages he had been given showed a list of names, church affiliation and places of burial, all in date order. On the fourth page there were two names that intrigued him and the burial dates were within three days of each other.

Roger Lightfoot and Marie-Claire Santos, both recent burials at Calvary Cemetery on Southern.

Apart from the reference to *light* in the first name, the second was a closer bet. The eighteenth century French folk song, Au Clair de la Lune was translated as 'By the Light of the Moon'. The name itself meant *clear* or *bright* and Temeke wondered if it was close enough.

There was a third option listed at Vista Bella Memory Gardens on Sara Road. Poonam Kapoor. Burial date, February 12.

Hunching forward he tapped the keys, clicking through several links that gave the same mind-numbing meaning.

Poonam, a Hindu/Sanskrit name meaning, *full moon*.

FORTY-FOUR

Every bloody graveyard was like a junkyard, Temeke thought, discarded scrap spreading out toward the boundaries as if it would soon take over the city. He stared out of the mortuary window at a row of granite tiles sparkling under a harsh sun.

"Peaceful, isn't it?" said a voice.

Temeke turned to see a pasty-faced funeral assistant dressed in a black jacket and a bow tie. He extended his hand and his badge, knowing the elusive peace the assistant hoped for was short-lived.

"I'm looking for Poonam Kapoor," Temeke said. "Recently deceased?"

The assistant held up a finger and bounced into an office behind the reception desk. He pulled open the drawer of a filing cabinet, finger tapping row after row of plastic labels until he found the one he wanted.

"The deceased's full name is Poonam Eva Kapoor. Burial February 12th. Row five at the west end of the plot."

"So, she wasn't cremated?" Temeke felt his spirits lift.

"Oddly enough, no. Her mother wasn't Hindu."

Temeke walked alone to the site, counting seven people gathered by the columbarium niches in the center of the gardens and a lone man praying over a stone cross in the far northwest corner. The city seemed to stretch languidly around the cemetery, houses a pale gold in the distance and further out there was downtown Albuquerque tingling with life.

Poonam Kapoor's headstone stood in a secluded place beneath a large cottonwood tree where the wind keened softly through the upper branches, scattering the last of the winter leaves on the ground. He gazed at a patch of raw dirt about six feet long where a lizard scurried between the rocks.

"It may be nothing," Temeke muttered, standing about five feet from the grave, "but it's all we've got."

He lowered himself to a crouch, not knowing what to expect. Twelve roses slouched in a green memorial vase, petals scattered over the base of the headstone.

He looked up between the branches of the tree at a clear blue sky. Could Poonam hear the rustling leaves? Could she even see the sky? If Malin had been there she would have said no. The dead are dead. They can neither see nor hear.

It was a bit terminal in his opinion, a bit harsh. *How come our forefathers said they'd watch over us from the sky if it was a load of cobblers?*

Temeke had an uncomfortable relationship with religion, having been raised by a mother who was confirmed Church of England, a woman who spent her last days wittering on about Revelation and the beast, and how important it was to know where you were going after death. And then there was his dad who never gave a toss about where he was headed after death. As long as it wasn't Key West. Too bloody hot.

Temeke looked out at a row of headstones that ran toward the southern boundaries to gauge the shadows until a cloud blocked out the sun for a moment. He looked up again, unaware of any clouds in the sky on his last examination. There was always one that snuck up behind you and it took a few seconds to work out where it had come from.

He began a soft-footed prowl of the periphery, winding his way cautiously inward, sometimes crouching with his head to one side. From certain angles, you could discern things by a freshly mown lawn, especially one where each blade of grass held a single droplet of water. It was strangely hypnotic. He could see no recent footprints, just the wide cutting path left by a four-wheeled mower.

The other two deceased names were listed at Calvary Cemetery on Southern. It was about a fifteen minute drive and Temeke knew he had barely enough time to make it before his meeting with Malin.

He felt vulnerable standing there on his own, as if someone was sighting him from forty yards. He could almost feel the heat of a bead on the back of his neck and turned a half circle, giving the parking lot a cursory glance. His eyes then swung to his right where a row of gravestones gave off short shadows at that time of day.

He didn't like the silence, wondering if there was something he had overlooked and he didn't want his titanic reputation as a badass detective thrown to the wind. The whole unit would be in a turmoil, especially if he couldn't close this case.

Voices were muffled near the columbarium niches, branches groaned, things scuttled. Temeke looked around, visualizing the place at night... seeing a young woman struggling at the edge of the gravesite until she hung motionless in the arms of her attacker.

Long, dark hair and brown pleading eyes. Temeke couldn't get past the violence, the cruelty, the terrible thing he knew he would find. So much talent wasted in a single, vicious moment.

He felt a dry wind against his scalp, heard the gentle pulse of crickets and closed his eyes. Held his breath.

Oh, God, Asha... I hope you were already dead.

Sealed in the earth unable to move, unable to breathe,

unable to shout for help. Seeing only black and asking yourself… is this a dream I'll wake from in a few seconds?

Temeke opened his eyes. His head was already invaded by dark images, leafy shadows and silence, and yet here was a neat landscape with spurting sprinklers that threatened to give him an enema if he didn't get moving.

Get a grip. Forget the emotion. There's no time for it.

His eyes took in two burgeoning roots at the base of the tree and between them a flake of bark and a pile of wood shavings. A chipmunk or a squirrel perhaps. His eyes raced up the trunk to where a name had been scored in the smooth undercoat. His pulse spiked.

Mahtab.

Slipping the phone out of his pocket he got Luis on the first ring, told him what he'd found, careful not to betray the excitement in his voice.

"She's here, Luis. I can feel it."

He was lightheaded, felt a prickling in the back of his neck, wanted to kneel down and scoop all the topsoil off the grave right down to the casket itself. He didn't care how dark that place was or what he might see. He just wanted Asha.

Luis didn't comment for a long time and then he finally spoke. "We'll need a court order, Temeke. It won't be today."

FORTY-FIVE

Malin glanced over the pristine waiting room, feeling the sense of a presence. Any watcher would be obvious among gray walls and black upholstery, and everyone in the hospital seemed to be reading. Her eyes took in four men slouched on the tandem seating against the wall, one gave her an approving once-over and then lowered his eyes. It wasn't him.

She focused down the hallway to a large potted parlor palm where a flash of black moved behind the wall. A triage nurse perhaps? Some wore black scrubs and gray lanyards and those who worked with the surgeons wore disposable pony caps in sky blue.

Temeke sat beside her on a chair that was two sizes too small, fingers drumming against his thighs like an expectant father. "How's Adel?" he said.

"She's a good cook. Pasta and veal tonight."

"Take a sandwich, will you, love? Save us both a sleepless night." He rubbed a hand over his head where beads of sweat sparkled under recessed lighting. "What's taking so long? You'll say a prayer to hurry things up?"

Malin could always read the humor past those faint laugh lines. She knew he believed in the power of prayer just as long as he didn't have to say one himself.

He popped a knuckle and gazed down at the parking lot through a floor-to-ceiling window and muttered something about where could he find some handy earth digging equipment to open that grave.

"Stop whining," Malin said.

"I hate hospitals." His eyes raced over the contents of the room and paused at Once-Over. "What's he bloody staring at?"

Malin shifted slightly as a willowy figure in blue scrubs walked down the hall toward them and gave a tentative smile.

"Detective Santiago?"

Malin showed her badge and introduced Temeke, hoping the interview had not been cancelled.

"You can go ahead and see Zarah now. But I do advise short visits to start with. About ten minutes?"

They both nodded and followed her down the hall to where an officer sat outside a large room with an ensuite bathroom. It reminded Malin of an earlier visit she and Temeke had made over a month ago. The Mayor of Albuquerque had suffered from a gunshot wound during a home invasion.

Zarah was in bed, propped up against a stack of pillows, slender arms resting on the sheet. She was alone, but the sight of two empty chairs on the other side of the bed indicated to Malin that her parents had tactfully left.

Malin took the chair nearest to the bed, reached into her jacket pocket and pulled out a micro-recorder. Her questions had to count given the unrealistic timeframe they'd been given. She gave names, time and date.

"We'd like to talk to you about what happened that night, what you saw. Is that OK, Zarah?"

"You want to talk about the man," Zarah said, small eyes following Temeke as he sat on the couch under the window.

"If you like."

Zarah's mouth was a thin line that turned down a little at the corners, as if the fine layer of skin that stretched over her square cheekbones prevented a full smile.

"Tell us what happened."

"I don't know how he got in. But he was right there," Zarah murmured. "I-I saw him. It was horrible."

Malin realized it must have been and said how sorry she was. She needed a face, a positive ID. "What did he look like?"

"Dark. And his skin was... s-so white. That's how I knew it was him."

"Who?"

Zarah sobbed for a while and then said something so quietly Malin almost missed it. "Demon."

Malin tried to imagine what a demon looked like, but it was like trying to summon a hideous version of Mr. Tumnus. She pulled out the composite sketch and got a resounding yes, from Zarah.

"How did he get in?" Malin asked.

"Like the trail of sand through a keyhole. A draft under the door. You can't stop him."

Malin pondered this without reacting, waited a moment for the twitch in Zarah's mouth to formulate the next words.

"I wanted to run but my stomach hurt so bad. I couldn't move my arms."

"Did he say anything?"

Zarah's sobs turned into a moue of unease. "He said Asha was dead and buried, that s-she didn't suffer."

"Did he say where she was?"

"No. But he knew I kissed Paddy in the parking lot at school. We'd been so careful." Zarah wiped her eyes with a wrist and stared at the bowl of soup. "He said there was poison in my pizza. He told me I was going to die."

"Why... why would he do that to you?"

"He accused me of saying he was evil. But I never said that."

"Were you scared?"

"Yes, I was scared. What do you think I was feeling?

You don't understand. He'll never stop. Not until he's killed all of us... all the sisterhood."

"Tell me about the sisterhood. Tell me how it all started."

"Nobility. The chosen ones. That's how it started."

"Who chose them?"

"Alice."

"Alice wasn't born into the aristocracy. She was a racing driver's daughter."

"Her name means *Nobility*."

"Can you explain how Alice became the leader of this group? Majority vote?"

Zarah frowned then and began picking at the blanket, fingers toying with a tail of wool. She was gaunt, thinner than Malin expected and the lavender blanket almost matched the shadows under her eyes. Despite Zarah's faded appearance, Malin had a hard time rousing any compassion for her.

"Alice was a Lilin. She read the book, knew how it all worked."

It struck Malin as comical in a frenzied, high-pitched giggling kind of way. She could imagine six girls spending entire nights cavorting naked with demons. But a suspicion soon drowned out the humor. It was the sense that all six girls believed Alice had the necessary powers to summon this Demon and the necessary powers to dismiss him. Weren't even Lilin subject to an unholy background check?

"What made you want to be a Lilin?" Malin asked.

"Alice said if I joined I could have anything I wanted."

"And you believed her?"

"Sometimes we played out our fantasies on each other. Sometimes we played them out on someone else."

Malin felt her stomach tighten, saw Temeke's motionless face and realized he had sensed it too. "But something happened, didn't it?"

"We thought it would make everything better… but it doesn't. Makes you empty inside. Even Alice questioned what Demon meant when he said she was marked for greater things. They were vile things. When she refused to be part of his… collection, he threw it back in her face. Told her she was damned."

The nurse came in and took a seat at the computer beside the bed. Malin realized they were running out of time.

"That's when she stopped believing him." Zarah lowered her eyes and began to inspect the thread of wool wrapped around her finger. "And so did we."

FORTY-SIX

They drove through winding backstreets toward the junction of 19th and Pat D'Arco Highway. Temeke felt a twitch of impatience as Luis turned north, doing fifty-eight in that nice black charger to cut through the Friday night traffic.

If it wasn't the smoke stack from the semiconductor factory or the stench from a nearby sewage plant, it was the chimney of the bloody crematorium. Lucky for the pine tree air freshener hanging from the rearview mirror, Temeke only caught a whiff now and then.

"Would have been five days prior to exhumation according to the Environmental Health Office," Luis said as he made a sharp right on Sarah Road. "Someone's at the site now checking the nameplate on the casket corresponds to the one on the license. I hope we're right about this one. Miss Kapoor's parents are understandably upset. Gave us permission to exhume their daughter on the condition we don't tamper with her casket."

"Can't the DA override that?"

"If we need to take a look inside, then, yes."

It was that once yawning pit that bothered Temeke, the notion that Malin's nightmares had been fueled by a girl running blindly in the night. It was where she was running to that interested him. "The Kapoors... what type of people are they?"

"Father was a landowner and a trader. Married an

American Caucasian in 1972 which threw any kids outside the Indian caste system. He was a Viasya, third tier if that's what you call it. They won't be present."

It explained why the girl was buried in a conventional plot. A single thought gnawed away at Temeke. *What if Asha Samadi's remains weren't there?*

"You and I haven't talked in a while," Luis said, seeming to hesitate for a moment. "About personal stuff. Is there anything you need?"

Temeke wanted to talk about Serena but he knew it was off limits. *Do you miss me?* he asked her in his head. And then he thought, to hell with it. "I'd like my wife back."

Luis brushed one hand over the dash at a pile of dust only he could see. Tidy squirrel.

"Last time I saw her was Thursday," he said. "I remember it was Thursday because there was a two dollops for the price of one at Cold Stone Creamery. So I got in line. She was a few cars ahead shaking a fist at the talking menu board. I love my sister, bro, but I'm not sure you want her back. She's put on at least fifty pounds and the back tires of that little Scion are flatter than a gunny sack."

Temeke felt the tremor in his gut, rubbed his mouth to hide a smile. He gazed at Luis without blinking and before he could explore that disturbing thought he realized the big guy was serious. "I like big girls, Luis. Always have."

"Give it time."

They pulled in past two flag poles on an emerald hill, turning right at the split in the road where four parking spaces had been allotted to invalid drivers. The main parking lot was devoid of visitors, taken over now by the criminalistics motorhome, an environmental health minivan, a fleet of law enforcement and Dr. Vasillion's team.

Temeke felt a rush of hope as he got out of the car,

glancing up the hill at a forensics tent. The sun streamed red and gold through a billow of massing clouds on the horizon and the sound of screeching pulleys from the crane-lift announced the start of the exhumation. He switched off his phone.

Making his way up the hill, he wondered how Malin was doing at Adel Martinez's house, whether she was watching her back. While here he was staring at silent mounds of earth, headstones connected by green paths; an idyllic setting. He noticed a dust devil spiraling between two stone angels in the rising wind and a soft keening as if he could almost hear the trumpets they were playing.

He suited up in coveralls while listening to an eerie silence as the rig shut down. Temeke tensed as he walked into the tent, saw the casket and clods of dirt spilling from the lid. The glimmer of a brass nameplate coupled with a bilious stench almost made him gag.

"Nothing in the topsoil," cried a voice from behind a hazmat mask. "Checking underneath."

Temeke stepped forward a few paces, suddenly floodlit by inspection lamps and feeling as if he was standing on a dangerous precipice. An overpowering burn-your-hair-off odor wafted up from the pit and he slapped a hand over his mouth.

The photographer began shooting overviews and close-ups, and two field examiners descended in protective suits to begin their careful examination. It was ten agonizing minutes before the sight of blue vinyl burst through the earth in the shape of a seventy-two inch shower curtain.

They laid it on a stretcher and Dr. Vasillion unwrapped the gruesome package, verbalizing each tiny observation for his assistant to record. Temeke felt the whump of blood from his head as he staggered against Luis.

"It's her," Temeke said, voicing her full name, date of birth and last known address.

What he saw was a young woman in a black sheath dress, head turned sideways from the weight of the casket. Her neck was draped with pearls and there was a smear of dried blood at her throat. White nubs of cartilage peeked out from the right third and fourth finger. Made Temeke tremble, made him nauseous. Her hair had been tied in a chignon and the wind tugged at a lock above her forehead, giving the impression of life for one false second.

She didn't deserve to be dumped.

"Was she already...?" Temeke's mind hesitated at finishing the sentence. He recalled the amount of blood at the primary scene on Cornell Drive, but he had to know for sure.

"I'll send the report over tomorrow," Dr. Vasillion said.

The first woman to disobey shall be buried alive... The sight of her lying there called to mind the recital at Popejoy Hall, ten fingers flitting gracefully over the piano keys where now there were eight.

The question was, did she fight back?

Temeke peeled off his coveralls, leaving the technicians to process the scene. Silent thoughts echoed in his head as he staggered back to the car, until his attention snapped back to Luis' voice.

"You OK?"

Temeke wasn't sure he was, but he was darn sure about one thing. "This wasn't a chance encounter or a one-night-stand gone wrong. It wasn't a symbolic sacrifice either. It was a druggy, burnt-out psycho on a revenge kick and with any luck the perp might have left traces of himself all over her. Unless he was suited up."

"Chemical tape and goggles..." Luis jutted his chin at the crime scene techs and nodded as if he noted the ingenuity of it. "'Course, you'd need to work in a place like that. Storm's coming."

Luis looked up at the clouds, hair flattened by a sudden

gust of wind.

Temeke wasn't worried about the storm. It was a face that suddenly came to mind. A face in a white suit, a face he recalled on his last case. Pauline Bailey's former intern.

The car radio burst through his thoughts, a plaintive voice trying to raise them. He slowly lit a cigarette before announcing his whereabouts into the microphone.

"I've been trying to call you for ages," It was Malin. "Adel Martinez... she's missing."

FORTY-SEVEN

Temeke arrived at Columbia Drive and adrenalin hit his nerves like a double shot of espresso. There was a light burning over the porch and the huddled figure of Detective Suzi Cornwell, punching a text into her cell phone with one finger.

Temeke stiffened at the sight of a cordoned off front yard and two Crown Vics parked against the curb, light bars flashing at full tilt. An elderly man in a housecoat had wandered out onto a neighboring yard, eyes screwed up against the rain. Officers must have been searching his house.

At this stage of the case, the victims were all apparent drug users – a problem in Temeke's mind because it widened his field of suspects. According to Hackett the public was concerned over these deaths, echoing one nagging question: Who's taking our girls? Local news stations were asking if these women had any enemies in the drug world.

Suzi was pressed against the front door trying to keep the rain off her hair. "What have we got?" he asked.

"What was I thinking?" She blew hot air into her hands. "I told Roach it was a bad idea to let your lot in. Well, she's gone. And you know the strangest thing? Adel Martinez doesn't strike me as the type of girl who could find her way out of a paper bag."

"Did you know she was a Lilin?" Temeke said,

knowing Suzi was hinting at Malin's incompetence.

"Off the record," Suzi said, moving a little closer, "if Martinez is one of these made-up Lilins—"

"Which she is."

"She's probably taken off on her broomstick." Suzi brushed a blonde curl off her forehead and looked up at him with clear blue eyes. "Might explain why no one saw her."

"You're not taking this seriously, are you?"

"Is there any reason why I should?"

"Since this is not my scene, as you correctly point out, I'll leave you with the broomstick issue. No doubt you'll have to extend the area of your search and a few more men. She could be in outer space."

Bright red lips widened to a smile and she was giggling now. She was also standing too close within the limits of his personal space and he was aware of a thick flowery scent following her like an echo.

"Tell me," she said, blinking away a drop of rain. "Are the rumors true?"

"What rumors?"

"That you're a single man?"

His fingertips began to tingle in his jacket pocket as if they had touched a clump of ice and were warming up again. "Separated," he corrected.

"We should have lunch."

"Not many great restaurants in your neck of the woods."

"Who said anything about my neck of the woods."

Temeke's mind went back to the conversation Captain Fowler had had with Hackett in the board room, the one about Suzi Cornwell becoming a third spoke in their cozy world.

"My treat," she said, sensing his hesitation.

"Good. Let's talk soon then." He heard a dog barking and glanced up the street at a Belgian Malinois and a dog handler. "I see you put officer Manning's K-9 to work. Looks like he's parked his ass in front of the neighbor's house. Bang goes your broomstick theory."

"What do you know about dogs?"

"I know Brock's canine teeth are made of titanium and I know he's telling us this is where he needs to be. Adel must have jumped over the wall between her house and theirs, walked straight through the front yard and hitched a ride out of the Dodge. A four-year-old could work that one out, love."

Temeke muscled his way past her and squeezed in through a half open door. Cold air seeped in behind him and he closed it with a bang.

"What the bloody hell happened?" He followed Malin into the bathroom, wind whipping the shower curtain through the open window. He could hear a woman crying down the hall. "Did Adel slither out of there all naked and wet? Bet that gave the neighbors something to gawp at."

"She took her phone, purse... probably jeans and a black sweater." Malin was rubbing the back of her neck with one hand and pointing at the window with the other. "The window's three feet by two. I just measured it. I should have followed *her* that night, not Paddy."

Malin led him to the living room, dimly lit and thickly carpeted. "Now you're here you might as well take off that wet coat."

Temeke shrugged off his leather jacket and hooked it over a chair. "Who's relieving you tonight?"

"Officer Jarvis. Midnight."

"Where's Sarah Hughes?"

Malin sat on the couch, head to one side, watching him. "She's in her room, crying her eyes out. Maggie's with her. I'll freaking kill Adel!"

"Now remember, Marl, forgiveness is the vernacular of Christianity."

"Where could she possibly have gone?"

"I doubt the dozy cow's sipping Chardonnay and dipping her feet in a Jacuzzi. Let's think about this for a minute. Was she happy, angry, upset?"

"Upset. Said she felt boxed in, smothered. Can't blame her with all the police attention she's been getting. She also said, and I quote, 'I'm glad Paddy's dead because now no one else can have him'. Maggie found a note Adel must have written. Found it on the kitchen counter."

"What's it say?"

"First off, you're the one who doesn't like coincidence and it's a coincidence Zarah Thai's alert and talking. Let's just say Adel had a plan when she told me she was going to take a shower."

"Shall we toss for it, Marl? Cause the way I see it Adel doesn't have the balls to kill anyone. Hasn't exactly been lifting weights on the sly, has she? And her voice is nothing like the one I heard in the cornfield. If you're worried about Zarah, don't be. She's got more security than Governor Bendish."

"The killer... there's been no cooling-off period, sir."

Temeke knew this was the most dangerous time, when the killer began to lose his grip on reality, no organization, no planning, just an orgy of bloodbaths. As in the case of Ted Bundy, his mind had become so chaotic leading to decompensation, recklessness and mistakes, it was surprising he could function at all. Temeke refrained from digging into that deteriorated and rotting psyche because Bundy had worked alone.

He was also conscious of a wave of wretchedness as he relived an interview with an earlier serial killer whose stories were a rats' nest of hallucinations, lies and fantasy. A getting-off on the torment he forced his victims to endure, reliving it, taking pleasure in it – so much so – Temeke no longer wanted to encounter that kind of evil.

This killer was another he would have to confront, to study the coldness of those eyes, the nothingness, until he was drained and incapacitated. Until he eventually lost his mind.

Malin took the note and handed it to him. "Read this."

He allowed his eyes to skim over the words in the note, knowing they were significant.

Sarah, everything's OK. I just went out to get something. I'll be back before you know it.

He felt the tension in his spine at the first crack of thunder outside and the wind whistling against the side of the house. Judging by Brock's announcement Adel had been picked up outside the neighbor's house. And possibly by someone she knew.

It was Malin's voice that made him realize he had been staring at a slick wall of rain against the window for too long. He forced down the vile images, forced himself back into driving mode.

"Adel mentioned something about a questing demon, the type that moves around a lot, lives rough, homeless. Like the intersections before the freeway, or general dosser territory on 2nd and 3rd Street. It's a weak thread, sir, but I can't help thinking he's the answer."

"I'm counting on him sticking out, Marl. A man called Demon… a man with a demon tattoo dressed in Goth clothing. Sounds like a few familiar faces in the International District. Someone might have noticed him."

The dense area around Central was a possibility, once called the warzone due to low income and crime. Temeke felt a spike of hope. The chances of picking up his trail were strong.

"I knew this would happen. Haven't slept a wink for the past two nights." she said, patting her chest. "I could feel it in here every time I prayed."

It was during times like these that Temeke wished he had an *in* with God, and he began to wonder what specialized coms Malin used to raise him. "Listen, I know how you're feeling, love. But you can't be in every room."

Temeke felt his phone shudder, saw a message from Dr. Vasillion's office and pressed the speaker button. The words came out in a fluent stream like an eager sprinter who had bolted before the starting pistol.

"The blood on the doorframe belonged to Paddy Brody, but not the handprint. Blunt force trauma caused by the antique iron. Heavy... it would have taken some strength, but it would have brought him down. Easier to get a quick slice to the throat then."

"And Ms. Samadi?"

"Asha Samadi was killed in the house and latterly moved to the cemetery. A blow to the right of the cranium and above the ear was made by an object with a sharp edge. Consistent with the metal poker your boys sent over. Contusions to the forehead suggest her head was thrown forward onto the stretcher bar below the music rack. She was playing the piano when she died."

"Would that explain the blood spurts?"

"Not the first blow. There would have been bleeding into the cranial cavity at this site. But the second and subsequent strikes would have caused spattering, rather than a strong stream. Depends how close the assailant was to the victim."

"Of course, the crime scene was compromised, doc. The roommate was there for a few days trampling in all the good stuff."

Temeke tapped the phone off, dragging a wrist over his forehead. Blood typing was fast. DNA not so fast.

"Listen, love. I need to wash all this stink off before going to Valerie Delgado's." Temeke studied a brave smile. "You should go home. Cornwell's requesting it."

He felt a draft of warm air on the back of his neck, gooseflesh raising on his arms. He didn't want to leave Malin when she was chugging along on the last gallon of energy, battling whatever dark forces were at work in her mind.

"One more thing." He could see she was examining him, wondering what he was going to say next. "Remember Pauline Bailey's intern on the Oliver case? Find out what her name was, will you?"

FORTY-EIGHT

Temeke relit an old cigarette butt he had found in his top pocket and dribbled the smoke from his nose. Two more drags and the rest of it was posted through a gap in the car window.

He was proud of Malin and the way she handled the interviews, and he was proud of her profiling skills. She could match the best of them and in keeping with being a truthful lawman, he would state it to her personally.

He also had a bad feeling in the pit of his stomach and tried to fight the impulse to pull over and throw up. His stomach was rebelling against the absence of food and a sudden hike of adrenalin that threatened to put his mind on overload.

Something was wrong the minute he turned into his driveway. The rain was coming down harder now against his windshield and in the moonlight he could see an ornamental tree stooping in the wind. There were tracks across his lawn, a kidney-shaped piece of artificial grass which the New Mexico water service wholeheartedly supported. He was too lazy to walk around it to get to his mailbox and his feet had worn a path down the middle.

It struck him that the screen over Serena's old quilting room window was lying against the exterior wall. Either the hardware had rusted and caused it to pop out, or someone had removed it. And if someone had removed it, they might still be in the house.

Turning off the ignition, he reached inside his jacket and drew his weapon. Over the patter of rain he could hear the sound of breathing as if he was sharing the same space with someone else. Not someone, something. He wasn't imagining it.

He turned and scanned the driveway, cloudy from jeep exhaust. It was full of shadows. Nothing between the trees, no movement, no signs of life.

It could have been Fats Riley's dog chuffing in the long grass. But that was unlikely since the old wooden kennel was saturated with rainwater and there would have been a few loud barks as Temeke drove in.

He frowned, eyes weaving in and out of the stand of cottonwoods. Back and forth, back and forth, and returning to the tree closest to the gate. There was something about it and he looked toward the ground first and then up into the branches. Still nothing.

He tried to take in what might be lurking behind the undulating stems of buffalo grass and a slouching desert willow. Then his heart did a wheelie because something had moved from behind the tree and without making a sound. And that something had been real close.

His senses told him it was gone even though his instincts screamed at him to go after it. Too fast for a human, more intuitive like a scavenging coyote.

Wind gusted across a sea of green, swirling leaves and tumbleweeds not yet flattened by the rain. Steadying the weapon in front of him, he eased his way through the front door where two wings of the house fanned out from a large hallway and the kitchen beyond. He checked the patio door, windows, kitchen, closets and living room. All in order, just as he had left them.

He checked the quilting room, heard his own breath, harsh and dry in his throat, and a stillness in the air he was used to. The flip lock on the vertical window was broken, possibly someone using a flat tip screwdriver and a few hard taps with a mallet. Possibly years of opening and closing until the hardware gave out. What would anyone want in Sparta? The name he fondly called his house now most of the furniture and valuables were gone.

The screen had been removed. Fact. The intruder was on foot. Fact. Ergo there would be some muddy footprints around here, on the tile, the carpet...

Nada. Yet he couldn't help feeling the essence of a second person who puffed out a breath of air every time he did. He looked over his shoulder before leaping up the stairs two steps at a time and was met with an angry meow on the landing. It gave him a start.

Dodger. The next time he caught the bugger crapping in the laundry basket the gun in his hand might accidentally go off.

He checked all the places an intruder would hide, stood for a while listening to the soughing of the heater and the scratch of a tree branch against the bathroom window. All familiar sounds.

The vague footprint when he found it was a boot sole, half on the carpet and half on the tile floor of the bathroom. Serena never wore boots. But he did.

He called himself a few choice names, re-holstered his gun and sat down on the end of his bed. The stink that came off his body was more important than chasing ghosts, or even food right now. If there had been anyone in the house they were long gone.

Laying out a fresh set of clothes, he peeled off his harness and hooked it behind the bathroom door. He liked to watch that gun from the shower, inseparable as if it was part of his skin. And he liked the door half open so he could see the bedroom and the hall beyond.

Hot water stabbed at his back and legs and he allowed his mind to swim with images of an open grave, a pale skinned girl, the brutality of it all. This case wasn't a family massacre but it sure felt like one. Temeke had been exposed to sexual homicide many times and although there was no evidence of sexual assault, the use of a knife could be construed as a substitute for penetration. Worst of all, he sensed the perp reveled in the excitement of the killing and there was no doubt in Temeke's mind the man was still executing his mission.

There were signs he was unraveling and didn't seem to care about the chaos of each violent attack. Signs he wanted to escape the terror of his existence, signs he might have wanted to give himself up. Yet, after the field investigators had sifted through every inch of the crime scene it had been curiously clean of trace evidence.

A continual hum followed by a clacking sound pulled him back to the present. His phone was buzzing on the countertop, dangerously close to the sink. He could tell by the tone in Luis' voice there had been a development of some kind.

"Bad news. Cornwell's team still haven't found Adel Martinez and someone leaked her picture to the press. Good news. Manager called in an abandoned van outside the Dollar store on Southern an hour ago. Gay. 1972 Chevy. Back tire was flat and there was oil all over the road. Looks like someone's been living in it for a while. Security footage picked up a man last night, sometime around nine o'clock. He was wearing a black beanie, dark hair. Got out of the truck and walked into the store. And then ten minutes later he was walking with a bag toward Unser. The manager's off this week, but she said she'd come in if you could make it in half an hour. I'll tell Mrs. Delgado you'll be late."

Temeke dressed hurriedly, shrugged on his harness and coat and made for the refrigerator. The soup would have to wait, but there was a half-eaten bean burrito and a can of Coke he could wolf down on the way.

Pushing his foot down on the gas, he shot past the Delgado turnoff and roared up the hill on 528 to Southern.

He chugged down the Coke and took a few bites of the burrito, made a face. It was older than he thought.

He couldn't reach the store fast enough. A positive ID was gold dust and someone living in a van had to yield all kinds of DNA.

"Your manager," Temeke said, showing his badge to the store clerk.

He didn't have to wait. A thin woman with blonde hair and dark roots wobbled toward him on four inch heels. Didn't look like an old slapper. Didn't look a bullshitter either.

"Graciella Fish," she said, escorting him to the greeting card aisle. She lowered her voice to a whisper. "Staff get antsy when they see guns."

Temeke cleared his throat. "Tell me about the man you saw."

"Looked real pale and sickly. Up from the grave he rose, know what I mean? You look like you ain't feeling too good either," she said, getting a little closer to make sure he wasn't some crazy person. "What'chu detectives eat these days?"

"Tall? Short?" Temeke asked, not in the slightest bit interested in food and wondering why the bloody hell she had to remind him he hadn't eaten a decent meal in six hours.

"Eyes like this, know what I'm' saying?" She stretched her index and third finger out wide in front of her face. "Thought he'd had a few but his voice weren't slurred."

"Accent?"

"Talked normal. You get all sorts in here. But this one I'd remember. About my height, five ten," she grinned.

Realistically more like five six, he thought, peering at a pair of metallic leather platform pumps.

"Thin-ish, white skin, black hair. Didn't look like he were staying at the Holiday Inn. Looked more like he were sleeping rough."

"You've him before?"

"Nuh-uh. But he did remind me of a picture I once saw in a spirit store."

"How did he pay? Debit, credit?"

"Cash."

Temeke's mind was racing. What did white-skin-black-hair buy? What did he touch? There would be prints around here somewhere. And prints didn't take long to run. "What food did he get?"

Graciella was sharper than he gave her credit for. "Bought some popcorn and a few Cokes. Wore black leather gloves, hon. Packing light I should say. But if he bought popcorn, he had to have a microwave to pop it in."

"See which way he went?"

"Went that way," she said, pointing in a vaguely northerly direction.

White-skin-black-hair was a canny drunk if he hiked out on Unser toward Northern. There was nothing much out there except sand and tumbleweeds, and row upon row of new houses, empty now after the 2008 downturn.

And model homes equipped with electricity. The thought gave him a shiver of anticipation. Anyone could break in and make themselves comfortable for a night or two.

He thanked her quickly, gave her his card and asked if she wouldn't mind working with the composite sketch artist.

"A guy like that… slinging dope," she said, giving him the down-turned mouth and the sorry eyes. "Might already be dead. Might have been taken up in the sky."

Temeke made for the door, knew instinctively what was coming next. But she was right behind him in two teetering strides.

"Got Jesus?" she whispered. "He's coming soon, and you don't want to be giving someone a ticket and finding there's no one in the driver's seat 'cause they've been Raptured. No one knows when it'll happen. Two men working in a field, and then one of them disappears. Two women in the hairdressers, and one of them is gone. You better hope you ain't still pulling people over and arresting them, 'cause if you are, that means you've been left behind."

Temeke made a dive for the front seat of his car, couldn't shake her off fast enough. He was conscious of a brisk wind through the open window as he clocked fifty down 528 toward Bazan Loop.

FORTY-NINE

Temeke studied the arch of her throat, red hair cut to her jaw. Not Alice, but closer to her than he had ever been. He sat there for a long time watching Lily cry, watching those gold, glossy eyes in the candlelight.

"I'm sorry you had to hear it from me," he said, knowing the wound had been reopened, making it all fresh again.

Temeke hadn't thought how Paddy must have felt in those last moments. Whether he panicked as he lay there bleeding out, whether he tried to cry out. There was nothing he could say to make those tears go away and the red eyes she kept rubbing.

There was always a steady patter of questions in his head and the more he thought about the killer, the more he wanted to hunt him down, push him up against a wall, make him talk. He wondered where all this pent up hatred was coming from.

"You heard Zarah Thai pulled through?" he said, wondering why they had to sit in the dining room with a five-tapered candelabra on the table for light.

"Mom told me."

"And Adel Martinez?" He studied her face, reading the eagerness to see what he would say next. "She's home now."

It was a lie. Crack-head Adel was out there in the boonies sharpening her next knife or whatever it was she had up her sleeve. He had no wish to frighten Lily.

"Ever done drugs?" He asked, writing the words, *blood test* in his notebook.

"No, sir."

He believed her. Cheeks and hands had a rosy tinge, fingernails white and neatly filed. The bruising on her eye was concealed with make-up and her lip was no longer an angry red. She was easy to read, eyes grazing over him and calculating how strong he was, how single. All women did it, no matter their age.

"We've met before, haven't we?" he asked, wanting her to remember another time, another case.

She shook her head. "I don't think so."

But she should have remembered a large living room, impressive now he thought of it. There was blood on the carpet, a line of spatters that had arced from the couch where the victim had been shot at close range. When Temeke arrived on the scene he saw Pauline Bailey and a female intern. Lily was her name.

He grunted and opened the manila folder he'd brought. Took out a photograph of a man with a phone pressed to his ear outside Clemency Baptist Church, a photo Malin had taken with her cell phone. "Is this Paddy Brody?"

"That's him."

"Where did he park his car that day?"

Her eyes slipped past him to the window and the driveway beyond. "Down the road so mom wouldn't see it."

"She wouldn't approve?"

Lily nodded.

"Not very gentlemanly to take a lady into the woods and then leave her there," Temeke said. Not a question.

He saw the confusion in her eyes, the shrug, the glint of a white tooth behind an attempted smile. He knew the woods Lily described were less than thirty feet from the house, but he wanted to see where Paddy had taken her, wanted to see that secret place for himself.

"Let's go back to our last conversation, shall we? The one where you described the incident before the kidnap. You said you and Paddy were together under the trees, drinking and talking. What was the last thing you remember?"

"The sound of the zipper on his bag. The smell of wine. How he told me not to feel lonely because he promised he'd always be there. I put my head on his shoulder and when I woke up he was gone."

"How did you feel?"

"Sore, especially here," Lily said, tapping the top of her arm.

An interesting comment, he thought, going for the physical rather than the emotional. Most would have described the feeling as *abandoned* or *afraid*. Better still, she might have been angry after he had promised never to leave her.

Temeke could see the faint outline of a puncture wound, a neat little red dot. He hoped the bastard hadn't stuck her while she was asleep.

"I didn't wake up under the trees. It was a basement," she said.

"Can you explain how you got there?"

She traced the outline of a drip of wax with one finger, watching it turn a cloudy white. "No."

"How big was the basement?"

"Long... narrow. Wine racks and stone walls."

"You said it was dark," he reminded, feeling the knot of a scowl between his eyes.

"There was a candle at the far end. It flickered sometimes, so there must have been air coming from a vent. I couldn't see the door."

The room was likely L-shaped, door concealed around the corner at the short end, or the wine racks covered the only exit there was. Temeke stared down at the photo on the table, pulse a little faster now. "Were you attracted to Paddy?"

"No, we're just friends."

He noted the use of the present tense. "Ever seen him use a syringe? Diabetic, that kind of thing?"

"No, sir, never."

Her response only added another gallon of creepy to a case Temeke couldn't get to grips with. Although, contrary to Hackett's whining about finding Asha Samadi, he didn't think he'd done too badly. "Like to show me where you last saw Paddy?"

Lily pulled a coat from a hanger in the hall closet, brown sheepskin with wide lapels. She was slender, jeans hugging her hips and thighs and a concave belly tucked neatly behind a brown leather belt. When she bent over to do up a shoelace, it was the small rectangle of flesh peeking out between her jeans and her shirt that bothered him. Irregular strips like fleshy Braille and timeworn welts that could only have been done by a birch.

Temeke wondered if she knew how hard he studied her, whether she even sensed what he was looking for.

"It's cold outside," Valerie said, padding to the front door in a pair of slippers.

"I'll look after her." He pulled on his coat and checking the pocket for his flashlight. "Won't be long, love. About ten... fifteen minutes?"

They followed the lane to where it curved around the loop, cutting west between the trees to a small bridge. There was a light patter of rain against the leaves, not enough to force them back around again. Temeke was conscious of the creeping sense of a presence, an animal perhaps? He'd seen a coyote once, drinking at the water's edge and nosing for eggs in the reeds.

A bitter odor of wet detritus stung his nostrils as they neared the bridge, horse droppings visible in the beam of a street lamp and silence jarred by the shriek of an owl.

Lily's arms were buried in the pockets of her jacket, shoulders slightly hunched. She was nervous alright, kept looking over her shoulder to check Temeke was still there.

But Temeke didn't catch up, felt like he was wading through mud, listening to the silence of the cold and the wind tearing through long-needled pines. He wanted to watch from a distance, examine what Lily would do when she saw the place, gauge the level of torment. Because there would be torment after a nightmare like that.

Lily jerked her chin to where the brown limbs of a cottonwood stretched to the sky and beneath it a huddle of young coyote willow.

"There," she said, sleeves pulled down to her fingertips and pointing. "That's the secret place."

Temeke swept the flashlight beam across the grass. Yellow tape drooped between three trees, a large boundary preserved by Officer Watts for processing. It had yielded a rotten mattress, the frame of a child's stroller caught in the lower branch of a tree, a plastic doll and a pair of size eight tennis shoes wrapped around an overhead powerline. No dried blood or other fluids that might explain the cuts and bruises to Lily's face.

The grass was flat where two people might have lounged in the shadows and a rough tree trunk to lean against. Moonlight filtered between the branches, reminding Temeke the street lamps were the only light they had. He scanned the ground, looking for depressions, unusual clearings where dirt had been scratched away and where a surrounding tree trunk might offer up a single word scratched in the bark. But it was too dark to see.

"Did you meet here all the time?"

"We used to meet after school. Talked about Alice. How it used to be."

"The past has a way of catching up with us, doesn't it?"

Lily must have noticed the subtle change in Temeke's

voice, took two steps toward him, blinking in the sharp strobe lighting from the restaurant. It fell on the pale angles of her face and he could see her eyes now, as clearly as if they were engraved on every tree.

So beautiful, he thought. Someone should paint her. But there was something she wasn't saying and Temeke searched feverishly for a loose thread, anything to force her to unravel.

"Did Paddy look out for you?" he asked, keeping it personal.

"Oh, yes," she said, eyes skimming over the grass toward the river. "He was afraid of what Adel might do."

FIFTY

Temeke had no idea why the words stayed with him, why all of his training begged at him to dig deeper. He slipped the flashlight into his coat pocket, stuffed his hands in there too. It wasn't cold, more of a chill that came and went with every gust. He rolled his shoulders and asked Lily if she was cold. Whether she wanted to go home.

"I'm OK," she said.

A drop of rain smacked against his head, then another and another. He offered her a smoke and struck a match on a nearby tree, cupping his hands around the flame. He caught a sweet fragrance as she leaned toward him, oranges, he thought, but he couldn't be sure.

"I try to imagine what Alice would look like now," Lily said, hair beaded with rain. "Whether she would have been married to Paddy or someone else."

Temeke's mind had been tracking on the kidnap rather than Alice, and the comment came as a surprise.

"Tell me about her," he said, estimating when they would get back to the house and how many hours of sleep he might get. The unexpected topic of conversation had snapped his focus back to the routine necessities of life, no matter how empty his was.

"She was the most exciting person I have ever known. As much as people resented her, they were drawn to her. Sure, the craziness was entertaining, none of us ever got tired of it. Alice was beautiful. She was brilliant, something you desperately wanted to be. I remember the first time Paddy ever saw her. It was like his eyes were opened. He was so sure of himself, talking about literature, art, spirituality. I was the only one who could see how alike they were. But Adel was like a spider on the edge of a web, watching until the time was right. I saw that too."

"Did you like Adel?"

"I did at first. Then I saw why she wanted to be friends with me. A sprat to catch a mackerel, isn't that what they call it? The others were just as bad. Flirting and carrying on. Adel tried to take Paddy away from us. But we were family. She shouldn't have interfered."

"Us?"

Lily hooked an arm through his, took a few steps north along the path. It was an oddly familiar gesture, possessive even. "Alice was more than a sister. She was my best friend. We shared everything."

Temeke felt his brows arch and he turned his head sideways to study her. From the psychological reports he had read, both girls had been raised in a calm, stress-free environment. Alice was articulate, considered advanced for her age, and at the age of six her IQ was somewhere in the 140s. Her school grades were exceptional until her father died, then her whole world became a dark world of antidepressants, weight gain and detentions.

"Want to know a secret?" Lily said.

Temeke did.

"Paddy asked me out first. But I was scared. Never had a boyfriend before." She made a face and then braved a smiled. "But I think he liked that."

"The fact that you weren't interested?"

"The fact that I was a virgin."

Was, he thought. And was she still? Or had she been lured into Paddy's web like all the others? Then there was the breath of an answer, so soft he could have dreamed it.

"No, Paddy never touched me," she said, turning to face him. "I wouldn't let him. Is that so bad?"

"No. It's admirable."

"I hated what he did. All those lies. I didn't think he was like that."

"Some people change."

He noticed how cool her voice had become, how intense her gaze. She was so like her sister he had to look away.

"He betrayed Alice, going off like that," she said. "And it wasn't just Adel."

"Nobody's perfect."

"But she was. Alice made me feel safe. And sometimes it wasn't safe."

"At school?" He had often wondered about the discipline.

"Dad was raised Pentecostal. When he was a kid they weren't allowed to dance or sing in the house. It was forbidden. That's why mom sent us to boarding school. It was better that way."

"Were you happy there?"

"Yes."

"And that's where you met Paddy," said Temeke. *Paddy the player. High-on-drugs Paddy.*

Something flickered behind those eyes. She nodded slightly, not speaking. The cigarette slipped out of her fingers, sparks flying in the undergrowth and then a hiss as it sputtered against the wet grass.

"I knew Adel had the hots for him. Eyes following him everywhere and then she'd pretend not to look. I told Alice. Told her not to trust her." Placing a hand against her chest, she took a deep breath and straightened. "We had tea in the Pepper Pot one afternoon. Fall I think it was. I remember Alice saying, 'when all the excitement of the chase dies away, there's only regret and the overpowering sensation of loss.' She was crying when she said it. I think that's what started all the rituals."

"So she could prolong the fantasy?"

"So she could control it."

Lily continued to walk a ways and then stopped in front of him, face tilted upward to catch the rain. The wind cut through the trees, rattling the leaves and sending ripples across the water. She stood there for a while, face quite still and childlike, and a little afraid.

"Paddy was like dad. Had a twinkle in his eye. Liked the excitement of it all, had to be challenged. You can't blame Alice for loving him. But then..."

"But then she didn't," Temeke said, finishing the sentence for her.

"Then she cursed them... Adel, Zarah, Asha, Kenzie. And Paddy. Began cutting herself after that."

"I don't remember the report saying she had other cuts?"

"No, there weren't any. She'd let the cuts heal over time and then on that last day, she asked me to get a fillet knife from the kitchens, one with a narrow blade so she could bleed the demons out. And she reopened those wounds... in exactly the same place."

"You saw her do it?"

Lily gasped for breath. She was really crying now. "The bathroom door was locked. I shouted and shouted but she wouldn't let me in. I ran downstairs, outside... to the fire escape, but the French doors were locked and the window... it wouldn't budge. I pushed and pushed..."

It was all plain as day as if Temeke could see it in real time. He took a few steps forward, but her hands flew up to ward him off.

"I called her name, tried to stop it. But she couldn't hear me."

"You can't blame yourself," he said, It was a bloody lame thing to say in light of her suffering, but he couldn't think of anything else.

"It was Demon."

"There's no such thing, love," he said, feeling his mind shudder with denial.

"He killed her."

Temeke was aware his breathing was deep and labored and he was hit with a sense of déjà vu. A girl standing a few feet away, hair clinging in wet threads, inaccessible like a masterpiece you couldn't touch.

Then she tilted her head toward him. Something was bothering her. "Can't you feel it? He's here. Hunting."

Dropping his cigarette in a puddle, Temeke watched it fizzle and die. When he looked up again she seemed to have moved closer as if she had floated toward him in those brief seconds. Her hands dropped and the coat opened a little and he could see the line of her shirt, the top of her jeans and the L-shaped buckle. He could smell faint traces of orange blossom and patchouli now.

She seemed to recognize his attention for what it was, one she might have experienced before and hated. Taking a step backwards, she wrapped the coat around her and shivered.

He sensed the formality between them, watched her eyes chase something in the darkness. The isolated sound of a car rushing by and the groan of an overhead branch. The sense they were being watched, a spider-sense so strong that he beckoned Lily behind him, reached into his jacket and drew his weapon.

His skin began to crawl with a crippling terror, eyes sweeping the shadows an inch at a time, trying to take in what he couldn't see. No movement, no sounds, other than the steady patter of rain.

A weight seemed to push down on his head, an ancient presence that goaded his subconscious and grinned at him from a dark corner. The thing was rooted to the scene and hanging in the air like a bad smell. He had no idea what was giving him this flight-or-fight sensation. He gazed over the rim of the horizon working his way in until he was sure there was no one there.

The warmth of Lily's cheek pressed against his back distracted him and he turned to face her. She rubbed her forearm as if to smooth away any goosebumps and her eyes seemed to look through him.

"You felt that, didn't you?"

He felt her if that's what she meant. She reminded him of a wild animal, ears back and hackles raised and he followed her line of vision trying to see what had caught her attention, trying to understand what had made her posture stiffen.

"A hateful, ugly thing," she said, pointing a finger towards an insubstantial shape behind a cluster of cattails.

Now there was a description that was going to fester, Temeke thought, taking a few seconds to realize how close he came to being freaked out by a ghost. He inwardly scolded himself at the stupidity.

But there was no escaping that voice. It had taken on a low bass tone, an inflection locked in his memory, a sound so familiar it sent a cold flutter through his gut. He didn't know what scared him more, instincts or stone cold truth.

"There's nothing there, love," he said, trying to keep the tremor from his hands.

"No... Can't you see it?"

Temeke could see something stretched out in the grass with spiny ridge to its back, jagged sides and a gaping hole at one end. "It's a tree trunk. Promise. Let's get you home."

She walked beside him, head occasionally turning back to the secret place, eyes scanning the undergrowth as if she didn't believe a word.

FIFTY-ONE

Gabriel sat in the dining room, staring down into a plate of enchiladas surrounded by a moat of green chile. He tried to get his thoughts to behave in a logical way, mind focusing on how he had climbed into the house on Guadalupe Trail yesterday. Or was it the day before?

Easy with a screwdriver. Not so easy to sidestep a cat, tail lashing and fangs bared.

On that day, Gabriel left his shoes under the window behind a clump of juniper. He hadn't found what he came for. In all that rooting around he made sure everything was put back in its proper place. The books on the shelf, the pillows on the bed and the mattress under it. Until he heard the crunch of tires on gravel.

Instincts were as clear to a hunter as they were to the hunted. But there was always one place hunters never looked. Somewhere so obvious they'd only smack themselves. Somewhere they could see a tiny part of you if they looked hard enough.

The slow squeak of the front door told him the detective was alert and likely had a weapon. Must have seen the window unlatched. There weren't any footprints, Gabriel had taken care of that. Used his sleeve to wipe down the windowsill and the carpet to dry his feet.

He followed the detective through the house, waited until all hiding places had been checked. Mimicked every hitch of breath so precisely that the detective could only hear his own.

Gabriel slipped into an upstairs closet and gazed through angled slats at the bathroom door, open wide enough to see a figure behind frosted glass. Colored tiles added a touch of whimsy to a bland design – fitting, he thought, for a family home.

The shower, the drumming of water on glass and the crisp scent of soap. The detective must have sensed something, must have felt the air trickle along his flanks just as a shark feels the distress signals of its prey.

He didn't flinch. Not until the cell phone clattered on the sink. Then he lunged for it, faster than a snake. Naked and dripping. Muscles tense.

Gabriel had already touched that sink, the door, the towels, and he sensed the bond and fed off the adrenalin the detective had. He would have enjoyed soaking up more of that view if Adel's whiny telephone voice hadn't interrupted the trance, putting him right back in front of the plate of enchiladas he couldn't eat.

She swore she didn't have the book, but it was a lie. He could tell she was being careful with her words as if someone else was listening. And that someone else had called him later, feigned an accent so close to Adel's it took him by surprise.

Demon suddenly sputtered into life as if Gabriel's thoughts had automatically turned the dial on a mental transmitter.

"Wasn't expecting that, were you?" Demon said. "Better pop a few more of your favorite things before you have any more bad dreams. What was it last time? Oh, yes. You wait beside the railroad tracks to die. Your life, which should have been full of promise, is a bitter disappointment. You're a slave to drugs. You're a slave to everything. It is your birthright to suffer prejudice until your dying breath. But there's no alternative. Better step in front of that speeding train..."

Gabriel wouldn't allow himself to feel polluted and inferior. He wouldn't allow himself to be bombarded with a pack of lies.

"Lies? Oh, no, these aren't lies. You've been sold into bonded labor, my friend. No better than dirty rags. Human waste. The lowest of the low. University is a distant dream in your grubby little world because forty-five percent of students have no hope of graduating and the rest can't even write their own names."

"We're not stupid."

"All humans are stupid. I mean it. They fail every time. Of course, we revel in every failure and wonder why Master puts up with it, why his patience hasn't cracked. Why he hasn't cut them off entirely. Why he didn't crush that unworkable, wanton piece of clay into a tight little ball and throw it away. He should have. But they're his precious little mud people. *You* are his precious little mud heir."

Demon always pulled the jealousy card. He tried to compare himself to humans, kept pushing it further and further to see how far he could bring Gabriel down. It was excruciating to watch.

But in all the mind games Demon played, all the bloodletting, the gory acts of murder, even when Gabriel felt himself walking on a thin layer of ice that seemed to crack under every step, he was somehow fused to him. His dear and despised familiar.

"There is something else," Demon said, tapping long nails against the tabletop with the rapid staccato of a stopwatch. "You still have a monkey to catch."

FIFTY-TWO

"You know what they say, don't monkey with someone else's monkey," Temeke said, backing out of Hackett's office.

"We can't hold a suspect! Not when there's no proof. And before you go," Hackett said, lifting a hand and peering over his glasses. "Suzi Cornwell has accepted my offer. She'll be joining us in two weeks."

Temeke didn't hesitate. "Corpses always smell better in the winter, sir."

It wasn't the first time Malin had hovered in the corridor using Temeke as a human shield, coat on and arms pressed against her body. Hackett was hard to read and she couldn't decide if he processed information at a slower rate or if he was simply a nitpicker.

"Good, then you can take her to Jack's for a celebratory meal."

A roar of protest from Malin's stomach – the food at the local drive-thru was notoriously rich in green chile.

"I'm not sure Jack In The Crack is quite her thing, sir."

"Then use your imagination, Temeke. And listen. I don't want any more girls turning up dead, do you hear?"

"Right, sir. But if this is a serial killer, then it's quite likely to happen again."

Hackett rubbed a hand over his forehead. "Take one of the new cars if that'll speed things up a bit."

A heart-thudding pause while Temeke seemed to be

mulling the offer over. Knowing his suspicious nature, he was likely waiting for the blade of the guillotine to come down and Malin wondered if the car was offered in the same way a prison governor would break bad news to a condemned man.

"We have a car, sir. It goes... what? Sixty? When the wind's behind us."

Hackett was standing now. "Solve stats—"

"Are very important, sir. I wouldn't dream of taking the glory away from DCPD. But should things go wrong no doubt we'll get the blame and you'll cop the praise. Daft old world we live in."

Malin felt the electric tension in the air as Temeke closed Hackett's door. She followed him downstairs to the lobby.

"I know you're fed up with Detective Cornwell but you can't talk about her like that, sir."

"That sneaky cow was trying to undermine you, Marl. She thought you were incompetent letting Adel go like that."

A prickle of annoyance and Malin felt her voice slide up a few notes. "She said that?"

"Anyway, they don't want us on their side of town where we don't belong. So I thought you and I would do a little catch-up in the Fat Mule on 4th, because there's a waitress who'd like a word. On our side of town."

They pulled into the restaurant parking lot where a few of the Outlaw clan were chewing tobacco and sitting on bikes near the adobe wall.

"What's her name?" Malin opened a gate covered in flakey blue paint and made for the front desk.

"Melody Lane. Said she saw something hokey. Mentioned a young guy who comes in sometimes, sits by the window and talks to himself."

Temeke asked for Melody at the front desk and they were led to an orange booth at the back of the restaurant.

A woman sat drinking Coke through a straw, small and bent with a smoky rasp to her voice. Malin estimated late fifties, early sixties, blonde hair cascading down from a badly tied bun and cheeks powdered with makeup.

"We want to thank you for calling," Temeke said, shuffling next to Malin on the bench.

"After I saw this," Melody said, hand patting the front page of the *Duke City Journal* where the composite sketch was the lead article. "I knew it was him. He always sits over there. Black hair. Shifty-like."

Malin turned to where Melody pointed, saw a booth about fifteen feet away. It was a clear shot to the cash register and the coffee station.

"Shifty?" Malin asked. The stench of sweat and cigarette smoke was stronger now.

"Kept looking around like he was hiding from it all. Didn't look like he was all there, arguing with himself. Tweaking more like. Two bikers were watching him real hard, that's what got my attention."

Malin would bet money the guy wasn't scoping the place to see who he could pick up and it wasn't a drug deal. They didn't go down in places like this. The Fat Mule was a DEA preferred hangout at lunchtime.

"Any CCTV?"

"Nah. You've only got my word."

"You live around here?" Temeke asked.

"I live with my old man, Joe. Only see him once every two months now." Melody's eyes took on a hard stare, like she knew she wasn't the only chick he had. "I guess that's how it is when you're an Outlaw, always on the road."

Malin suspected Joe wasn't on the road, probably shacked up with his bike in an old Winnebago behind the Walmart on Southern. Anything to get away from it all.

"Clothes, birthmark, tattoo?"

Melody shook her head slowly. "Kid had black hair

and make-up. Course they all wear make-up now. I only said a few words, but I could see he was all knotted up inside. I don't know why they torture themselves. It's so much easier these days."

It was the second time Malin heard the word *kid* and she hung on to that image in her head. Junkyard Charlie had also alluded to the hair and that's why the young man caught Melody's eye.

There was the overnight bag Paddy had given Adel, the clothes, the wigs. That train of thought unnerved Malin and her mind lingered on it all.

"How many times has he been here?" she asked.

Melody looked up at the ceiling and closed one eye. "Five, six times. Always on his own. Stays as long as it takes to drink a cup of coffee."

"Does he talk to anyone?"

"Only me. The good news is he usually comes in twice a week. Bad news is he hasn't been here this week."

"Think he might be staying near here?"

"Hard to say. Come to think of it he always leaves on foot."

Malin shot Temeke a look, saw the faint tremor of an eyebrow. She knew what he was thinking, that these sightings weren't accidental, that the killer was getting restless and the rising publicity was making him more so. He was indulging himself with a fake identity for a time, but it would be over soon enough.

"Did you get a name?" Malin gave a little smile.

"Nah. This one's closed off, like there's nothing behind the eyes. But he did leave something on the bench."

Melody pulled a flyer from the inside of her jacket. Photographs of tractors and hay rides and the words Corrales Spring Arts & Crafts Fair, Saturday, March 18.

Four days' time.

"Well, you can't say *sir* or *ma'am* these days without

offending someone," Melody rasped. "So I don't say it all. But I ain't no bad judge of character, hon, not after thirty years working in a place like this. That was no man. But then, of course, you already knew that."

FIFTY-THREE

Gabriel fought to stay awake, drifting in a rolling lull where there was nothing but a blank space between dusk and dawn. Just the way he liked it.

A six point star lay on the floor and six candles flickering at each corner, and there a drift of bitter incense that reminded him of piñon resin. All he needed was the book to give him the words, the long, repetitive mantra he once knew by heart.

After luring Adel Martinez from her house with the offer of a shoulder to cry on, Gabriel was exhausted. Eight hours it took to prize the information out of her were eight hours he might have spent sleeping.

He sat on the only other chair in the room and tried to process what she had just said.

"Did you say I was a *freak*?" he asked, swiveling a knife on the surface of an upturned crate.

Hands tied behind her back, who could blame Adel for not responding. Her head had flopped forward like a rag doll, eyes fluttering as if she was trying to stay awake.

It was a setup. Adel never had the book. The detective did. The square-jawed, sullen-looking black man who had hunted him one night in a cornfield and along a narrow lane all the way to the main road.

Lawmen were never far behind.

Had the detective seen Gabriel on other occasions? Did DCPD's swarming network of agencies have prior knowledge of his entire life? While he knew it to be true, he found the reality of it disturbing.

"The van, you fool," Demon whispered. "All those tell-tale signs. You're dead now."

And yet, Demon had promised he would keep the van working.

Every day upon opening the front door or going about his business, Gabriel wondered if law enforcement crows would be standing outside with their all-too-familiar smiles.

Yes, disturbing.

He expelled a loud sigh and raked a hand through his hair. The basement was getting colder and both of them were shivering. It all seemed pointless until Adel lifted her head.

"Paddy... He was doing drugs." Adel looked like she was going to start crying. "Don't you remember? He kept laughing at things. He was weirded out most of the time."

Adel had a point. Paddy would have found a gray wall hilariously funny. He just wasn't *right* somehow. But he knew the difference between Alice and Adel because they looked nothing alike. Even if he was high.

"You chased him," Gabriel reminded. "Was it to satisfy your curiosity? Self-esteem? What?"

Adel winced, tried to lift her feet out of a bucket of iced water. It must have been hard with torso and hands tied with heavy duty bungee cord and feet so cold she could hardly breathe. She left Gabriel with no answers, just silence.

He looked around the dreary space he remembered so well. Wood beams stretching the entire length of the house and a water heater that soughed on and off. There was a toilet in the far corner and as far as he recalled it never flushed.

"It's where all the bad kids go," Demon whispered.

Gabriel tapped the side of his head with his fingers and

then with the heels of his hands. He remembered the beatings, the echo of his sobs. It was always him. Never *her*. Because she was perfect.

He remembered a time when she tiptoed down the basement stairs, head lowered, hoping to see him on the way down. She brought him food and she hugged him until he ran out of cry.

"What did you do?" Demon murmured.

What did I do? The cogs in Gabriel's mind tried to search for that information and all he could come up with was one word. Steal. Hunger got the better of him when he was eight. That's when it started. He stole food from the pantry and money from his father's desk. There were quarters in the top drawer, a whole jar of them, and he'd bought himself a milkshake after school.

When the jar was half empty his father began to ask questions. Never scolded *her* and Gabriel couldn't for the life of him understand why.

His train of thought was shattered by Adel's hoarse voice. Her very presence startled him because she had been half dozing, half sobbing. He was irritated. Wanted to retreat into silence with his perpetual memories.

"Did you kill them?" she stammered.

Gabriel tapped out a cigarette on the arm of the chair and lit up. He studied her face, candlelight providing sharp angles and shadow, and creating a classic 1950s beauty she never really had.

"They say a killer's motives are hidden in the psyche," he said, watching her shudder in the cold. "A place common people can't go. You'd be too afraid to see what I see."

"What do you mean *afraid*?"

"This room…" He looked up at the beams, closed his eyes for a moment. "You can love it or you can hate it. It does have a certain charm. But I didn't bring you here to discuss the Feng Shui. I brought you here to discuss the book."

"I n-never had it. They did." Adel's face was pale, pupils large and black in the light of a sputtering candle.

"You're lying." Gabriel could feel it in his immortal bones. He leaned forward, resting his elbows on his knees. "It's the only way to get rid of Demon. The only way to stop it all. The hate. The lies. You do understand?"

The candle spat a gob of wax across the floor, spreading out like a comet's tail. Gabriel thought it was beautiful. That it was a sign.

"It can't go on forever," Demon whispered from somewhere in the shadows. "This… this constancy of human failure. I should tell you there is an end to my patience."

Gabriel rolled his eyes and took a long hard drag of his cigarette. He rolled his shoulders too and sat up a little straighter knowing how Demon wanted it over with, wanted to move on to the next thing. But what Demon couldn't grasp was Gabriel's reluctance to meet those demands. He was sick of the games, the bloodshed and the rabbit trails.

Sick, sick, sick.

Because he would go to jail if he lived, and that would be hell enough. Like the tumor in his brain.

He stubbed out the cigarette and lunged for the knife, watched Adel's eyes as they flicked upward to his raised hand. And then her mouth dropped open and she began to scream.

FIFTY-FOUR

At eight fifteen on Thursday morning, Temeke pulled up outside the Delgado house, windshield wipers barely holding off a downpour. He could see Valerie standing on the doorstep through the rain and he could make out the hunched form of Adel wrapped in a blanket. They were talking to the responding officer.

"She's alive," Malin said, head thrown back against the seat rest. Then a long exhalation of breath.

"Damn lucky, I should say."

"You knew about the basement?"

Temeke reeled in a conversation they had had after visiting Valerie Delgado for the first time. The layout of the house and how he had latterly compared the floor plan to others in the street with a listing agent.

"You said something about a locked door near the pantry. Thought it was broom closet? Let's take a look at it, shall we?"

The ambulance pulled in after them, two cruisers, three SUVs and the paparazzi – camera crew oozing out from behind the sliding door of a van. Then came that daft old cow Jennifer Danes kissing a bleeding tape recorder and holding a pink umbrella. It was a zoo.

"I'm so sorry," Valerie said to Temeke as she handed Adel off to a paramedic. "I had no idea—"

"That your basement was being used as a torture chamber?" Temeke lifted the tape and ushered Malin through.

The door to the basement was open, staircase leading down into a dimly lit room. *Long... narrow. Wine racks and stone walls.* Just as Lily had described.

The stench was musty and acrid, and there was a miserable feel about the place Temeke didn't like. They kept to one side of the room, going no further than the bottom stair.

Malin took out a tape recorder and recorded all that they saw. Bungee cords, a chair saturated with urine, a pot of salt, six candles on the floor, each burned down to the wick and dried wax which had pooled onto the floorboards. Belts hung from the wall, buckles crusted with dried blood and a collection of birch switches in one corner.

"I can feel the force of your anger across the room," Malin said over her shoulder.

Temeke had no words. He winced at the sound of a soft tread on the stairs, knew who it was without looking up. He felt nothing for her when she told him about the beatings, how her husband would lock the door so she couldn't get in.

"I hated what he did," Valerie said, standing half-way down the stairs, hand steadying herself against the wall. "I begged him to stop. Tried to file for divorce—"

"But you didn't call the police," he said, turning to face her.

Valerie's eyes seemed to plead with him to understand. She was clearly groping with her thoughts like a blind man in the dark. "Alan was in every newspaper. He was New Mexico's star. It would have ruined him."

"It ruined *them.*" Temeke looked up at a tear-stained face. She was more of a criminal than her own daughter. "How long have you known?"

"About Lily? Alan's father was the same. Beating and

drilling until it was habit. I didn't realize how much he wanted a boy. Even treated her like one."

Hit her harder, no doubt, when he flogged her, Temeke thought, blinking at a single light bulb that hung above the staircase.

"I was never allowed in this room when Alan was alive. Not to clean, not even to get a bottle of wine." She paused and rubbed her arms. "I was outside raking leaves last Christmas, saw a crack in the casement window. That's how the wind got in. There was a chair and what looked like a star on the floor. Lily was down here talking to herself in different voices. Sometimes a man. Sometimes a woman. That's when I knew."

It explained the voices in the cornfield, the reason why Temeke saw only one person. "Did she have counseling?"

"Twice a week, but the sessions went nowhere. You asked if she had a boyfriend? Well, she did in a way. She had Paddy. They weren't intimate, but he wanted to be. Tried to make her jealous when she refused him, tried dating all the others. I could see what it was doing to her. She despised her own femininity and it didn't help that Paddy loved her."

Temeke wasn't convinced Paddy loved Lily any more than he loved the rest. He was a horny bastard, out for what he could get. Love? He loved himself. "Did you tell Miss Baca... the pastor?"

"She begged me not to, detective. She said it would only make things worse. Kenzie and Rosa would only get her alone and do things like they had before."

"What things?"

"Drugs. Bullying. They didn't understand her any more than she understood them." Valerie sobbed a little and wiped a tissue under her nose. "Baca didn't believe any of it."

No, she wouldn't, Temeke thought, because incidents like that went viral and schools closed down for losing their ratings.

"When the girls found out," Valerie continued, "they tied her to a chair, told her she was weird because she wouldn't take drugs, wouldn't wear dresses. She was different after that."

Like meth, Temeke thought. One toke and you were floating. This was a group of women who bonded, not by demographic chance, but by way of a spiritual sisterhood. It made separation impossible.

"Have you ever used a psychic?" he asked.

"Yes. She said Lily had been kidnapped by someone she was familiar with."

Familiar. The word kept cropping up like a bad stench.

"I called everyone. No one had seen her. That's when I called the police."

"Ma'am, did you have any idea she had moved out, got her own place? Taken ten grand out of her bank account?"

"No."

"Do you know why she would need such a large sum of money?"

"Medical perhaps?"

It was a good try and Temeke actually believed her. No face could possibly feign draining itself of blood in quite the same way.

"Medical?"

"She had headaches, detective. Took Oxycodone, I think."

Fatal in large doses, Temeke thought, feeling his stomach contracting. There was a market out there for drugs like that.

"I remember seeing her on a former case, ma'am," he said, summarizing the particulars of the case more for Malin's benefit than hers. "She was studying forensic science at Gibson. Did her internship with Pauline Bailey, if you recall. My point is this. On the night Kenzie

Voorhees died, there was a witness. He saw a young man outside Kenzie's house before the gas explosion. Said he was wearing baggy pants, a black jacket and a white hoodie. I'm guessing what he actually saw were coveralls. All our technicians wear them. It would explain why there was no DNA at the scene until we found the van your daughter was driving. There was a cell phone under the driver's seat. Had a picture of Ms. Voorhees drinking wine the night she died. We also found the spare key to Asha Samadi's house and a knife with traces of Mr. Brody's blood, the same knife she used to slit his throat. There were more red hairs on those seats than on an Irish Setter."

Valerie shrank as if she had been hit by cold gust of wind. Two tears clung to her lashes and she brushed them away with a fingernail. "She's sick, detective. Possessed. Gave herself all those bruises. Made the whole thing up."

Temeke nodded. He already knew. There was no man who picked her up, no savior. Just a figment like all the rest.

For Valerie Delgado the pain had been going on for months, years, and it would continue as long as she let it. For Temeke it was a book you closed at the end of each case, not because he had an armored heart, but because life had to go on.

The Crisis Intervention Team would have called it MPD, multiple personality disorder, where Lily had disassociated and split into parts. Hatred of women? More than being one herself, she would have hated her mother for not protecting her.

Temeke heard the scuffling of footsteps at the top of the stairs. Luis, Fowler, Maggie, Jarvis and three homicide detectives, all standing there with gloved hands in front of their mouths.

Climbing out of that hell-hole was more fresh air than his lungs could deal with and he gasped as he staggered outside.

"Good work, Temeke," one of the homicide detectives said, patting him on the shoulder.

Temeke ignored their laughs, their cheering, their self-indulgent banter. It wasn't over yet.

Bluish-black clouds swept over the west side and a rainbow broke through. It formed a vivid bridge between the mountains and the distant high-rise downtown.

FIFTY-FIVE

It was the day of the Spring Arts & Crafts Fair and Gabriel's heart was thumping in his ears. He felt more alive than he had been in days, especially with the gun nestled in his jacket pocket. It had been months since he attracted 'normal' attention, the type where a man appreciates a woman, gives her the eye, does a double take and strikes up a conversation.

He was tired of wearing dark clothes and opted instead for faded jeans and a khaki sweater. A beige baseball cap kept the sun off and flaxen hair fell to his shoulders.

He followed the woman with her languorous stride, body weaving among the crowds. Twice she looked over one shoulder and twice she frowned at him. A cop. She carried a small backpack over one shoulder, one hand nudging aviator style sunglasses up her nose. She was watching him.

There were several fiction sections on the book stand, all labeled alphabetically. Occult was third from the end, next to Vampires and Werewolves. Was this where she would leave the book?

Gabriel began to laugh hysterically, tried to put his hand in front of his mouth to mask the noise but it caught the attention of a group of school kids and a frowning teacher. His body flinched in response and he sidestepped the small group, edging his way behind a booth selling baseball hats and shirts. He smiled at the vendor and bought a red hat.

The cop may have already sensed who he was. She may have asked herself, is this the one who witnessed it all, even as Alice took her last breath? Grotesque, like the third act of Puccini's Madam Butterfly. Suicide by knife. At least that's how Gabriel remembered it.

A curtain had come down on that last ovation and the memory was all but a red haze. When he gazed at the stage he could still see a wall of steam, a porcelain tub and a beautiful red-haired girl. Had he done it? Or had she?

He could never really be sure.

It wasn't an accident, any more than walking right behind the woman toward a table of old books be accidental. No one could resist a good deal and a craft fair was a great place to mingle, eat local food, listen to local music. There were a few tractor rides, not quite as many as the Harvest Festival, but there were art shows and a growers' market, plenty to keep you busy. And there was law enforcement. Everywhere. Gabriel could pick them out in a crowd.

Corrales wasn't usually alive at this time of year and this impromptu festival offered assorted vendors that sold lavender, southwestern cuisine, old books, antiques, and a car show at the upper end of the street. All in the name of making money for Corrales Elementary School.

The cop's head turned suddenly at the happy shriek of a child. Dark glasses couldn't blot out those searching eyes, nor could jeans cover the tight musculature of her thighs.

She was damned, for one thing.

Gabriel felt excitement at that. Even Demon said he was damned for one single misdemeanor where humans, having a God willing to offer them second chances over and over again, were forgiven. There wasn't a dancing modicum of hope he would escape the fire.

Sometime in the past few years, Gabriel had resigned

himself to the fact that he had been lied to, manipulated and used, and he fought to stay ahead of the game. Moving unseen through the university, watching the students as they drifted from class to class, oblivious to the predator who dressed as a homeless person and pretended to root for food in the trash cans. He hated the word *bullied* because it was always wrapped in a shroud of pity and he didn't pity himself in the least.

He had grown strong. Different somehow. Better. And no one could change that.

"We all have choices," he murmured, recalling the scene as clearly as the one in front of him.

Alice's choice was to destroy the book because the Lilin had destroyed her, taken the love of her life. She had also chosen to take her own life, and no part of that was accidental. And so a piece of her could live on to torment the rest.

In a way, Alice had won.

Sometimes he fragmented from his true self and became Gabriel – his safe place. The place where there were no canes, no foul words, no shunning. A place where he was accepted and made whole again.

He continued to stalk the cop, weaving ahead of him now, dodging people and skirting around the slow moving cars. There was a metallic taste in his mouth and a hissing in his ears, the pronouncement of something far more exciting than just watching. The *knowing* that this woman knew she was being followed as she casually browsed the stalls, hands caressing jewelry and paintings.

The Fair was buzzing. Just how Gabriel liked it.

Until he tensed, inner radar registering a lone male about sixty yards to his left, another muscular build and a focused expression.

There was no mistaking the disciplined product of boot camp. A black man who left that training completely different than when he arrived. Forced to encounter the unknown without showing fear, physically toned to perfection and mind ready to face the enemy head on. How men like him learned to survive in the crucible of intense law enforcement training, Gabriel would never know. Proud and proven. That's what they were.

When he compared the man to the woman he followed, the metallic taste was replaced with something sour. A stirring inside his head, a deep, dark thing that had been sleeping until it opened its yellow eye, looked around and reminded him that men were the greater species.

"Time to do what Alice did," Demon said. "To move beyond a life shuttered in darkness and soar into a starless sky. You'll like it there. She does."

Excitement climbed in Gabriel's chest and the blood roared through his body. "See Alice?"

"That's what I said. So, let's get on with it, shall we?"

Gabriel placed the red baseball hat on his head and tossed the beige hat in a trash can. He edged between the crowds toward the street where a parade of vintage cars sputtered up the main drag behind a green tractor hitched to four carts.

He crossed the street to the other side, found the book stand and waited behind two dumpy brunettes.

FIFTY-SIX

Temeke was restless, but then he always was in a crowd. He had the sense Gabriel Mann was only a few steps ahead, hopefully waiting by the book stand on the opposite side of the street.

A bead of sweat ran down one side of his face and he stopped for a moment, glanced over the crowds at the families with their strollers, a live band and a lone straw hat browsing the book stall.

Jarvis was forty yards ahead dressed in jeans and an old army fatigue jacket. He was sitting at a table with Maggie Watts sharing a plate of Navajo tacos, while Officers Hinkley and Toledo were on the other side of the street admiring a 1964 purple Impala.

It was warm for March – fifty-six degrees and climbing. There were people dressed in psychedelic colors, some barely dressed at all, cruising the strip and looking for a new squeeze.

As for Temeke...*You're too bloody conspicuous*, he thought to himself, slackening his stride a little and then pausing to take in the aroma of fresh roasted chile.

Bald, black and British, he wasn't fooling anyone in his lackluster clothes and leather boots. Too tense. He attracted the attention of three young boys who were urging a young woman to touch him.

She and that dreamy expression got up too close, lips wrapped around a popsicle. "Kiss me," she slurred, lips red and shiny.

He was maddened by two intoxicated eyes and a huff of rancid breath. "I've got an unsavory reputation, love, like the toilets downtown."

Lifting both hands, he made a half circle around her, keeping his eyes on the street and the passersby. A small child pushed past him wearing green scrubs and a stethoscope made from a pair of first generation IPod headphones and a suction cup. His mouth was smeared in chocolate.

Gabriel Mann wasn't invisible, he was here somewhere and although Temeke's eyes ranged from left to right, passing over the crowd and stopping to scan the book stall, he could see no one who resembled a half dead corpse on the run.

The sun rose high in a sky where one half was clear blue and the other a blanket of gray rolling in from the west. People milled beneath the awnings, mothers carrying toddlers on their hips, father's staring longingly at the antique cars, and the elderly hovering over an open-air restaurant in the hope of finding an empty chair.

Temeke wiped his head and felt the phone vibrate inside a cargo pocket. He moved towards the shade of a cottonwood tree and listened to Malin's voice.

"Not seeing him," she said, flicking through the pages of a book she was pretending to read. "But I am seeing a *her*. Three females standing in front of a table. But here's the thing. Two of the females came off a hayride four minutes ago, heavy-set brunettes and the third, a skinny blonde, tacked along behind and then started talking like she knew them?"

Temeke heard the rise at the end of the sentence, realized he had to give his two cents worth. "Maybe she came late. Maybe she's an old friend."

"Blonde hair, as in *platinum* blonde. Five feet seven, one hundred and twenty-five pounds. Khaki sweater, blue jeans. Was wearing a beige hat. Now it's red. Something about her, sir. Watchful, you know?"

An essence, Temeke thought, pulse spiking. There would definitely be an *essence.*

He lowered his head, sunglasses hiding the direction of his gaze. A school group appeared to be listening intently to a teacher, a middle-aged man with a dog in a working harness, two heavyset women and a blonde wearing a red hat.

"Got her," he said, and hung up.

Straight back, rigid thighs, feet pointing forward as if they were pegged into the ground. She was slightly behind the other two, following but not following, browsing but not browsing.

The casualness of her pose did nothing to disguise the vigilance, gaze floating up from the book she was reading to examine the street. The posture was already mapped in his mind, even before the left knee turned sideways and the figure started forward slowly along the line of tables.

He made his way through the crowds, almost colliding with a man in a Smokey the Bear costume handing out forest fire leaflets to a group of teenagers. Temeke scanned right and left, and then straight ahead.

Under the awning he could see Malin ten yards to the left of him, Jarvis and Watts to his right, and he could sense Hinkley and Toledo behind him. They had been alerted by his sudden race across the street.

He couldn't see the blonde woman in the red baseball cap and he was baffled. His head was burning, sun glaring in his face as he studied the crowds, calculating which direction she would have taken. She had been so close, only a matter of yards, and now he had lost her.

He latched on to the most obvious conclusion and the throbbing in his chest began to slow. She knew they were there, knew they were cops, and knew exactly how to dodge them. Funny thing was, he could still feel her.

He brushed his forehead with a wrist and glanced at the hay rides as they trundled south along the street. Raw instinct made him follow them, eyes taking in each tiny detail.

Three white baseball hats, two blue, four yellow and one red, all bobbing above the hay bales in the tractor carts.

FIFTY-SEVEN

Temeke followed the blonde past the Mercantile towards Dina Nelson Road. The red baseball hat hadn't thrown him for a second and he sprinted along that country road, hearing only silence and wishing like hell he had Malin with him.

Weapon checked and holstered, he felt an eerie strain in the air as if the sun had suddenly set, leaving a darkening sky above him and rolling clouds. It was beautiful, but it was threatening too.

He called Malin, told her he was following the suspect on foot and that he needed immediate assistance. She said she wouldn't be far behind.

No, he wouldn't wait for backup. That was insane. Not when he rounded a corner and he could hear the sound of boots slogging up a dirt lane that intersected the end of the road. Gun drawn, both hands on the pistol grip, he followed her north under a thick canopy of cottonwoods.

Years of police work had taught him how to pinpoint and isolate the source of a sound, and he moved slowly, balancing on the balls of his feet. Still no sign of her.

The bushes on the side of the street were so high he couldn't see over them and every step along that sandy road was a dangerous one. He heard the huff of his own breath and wondered if she could hear it too.

Gabriel, Gabriella... whatever it was she called herself today, a girl beaten by her father because she wasn't a boy.

Beige hat, red hat. She was crazy to be out here on her own. Believing being Gabriel would help her forget and take away her guilt. Believing she could outsmart a man in a Kevlar vest and a Glock in his hand. Decades of tracking suspects left him in a state of constant motion and he would never give up.

He stood before a slight bend in the road, keeping his gun at low ready. The wind hurled sand flurries across his path, brown leaves racing and rolling, branches groaning above him. The north side of the sky was layered in dark clouds, rippling towards the southern horizon which was bathed in an eerie amber light.

Storm's coming, he thought, as he braced himself against the spiraling dirt devils, focusing on the snaking road ahead and the distant figure he thought he saw. A flare of lightning branched in the gray and flickered again like the glowing filament of a light bulb.

Had she summoned these demon winds?

From warm sunshine to peals of thunder in less than twenty minutes, Temeke had to wonder. He was conscious of the tart scent of rain as it began to tap against the surface of the road, and better still, a boot print in the dirt.

The natural cambers and bends made it impossible to get a sighting, but she had to be only fifty yards ahead walking along the side of the road and too exposed to think she was being followed.

There were potholes and spidery cracks in the dried mud and a ghostly pall on the lane that wasn't there a moment ago. He froze when he saw a red baseball cap, blown off by the wind and bobbing along the grass verge toward him.

His body tensed with the sound of scuttling leaves, but only for a second. He stooped and lurched for it, hooking the muzzle of his gun through the snapback. Temeke's instinct wasn't to touch it. There was a small bag in his pocket, not large enough for the cap, but big enough to cover his hand. Without touching the visor, he slipped it into his cargo pocket.

His pulse began to spike as he set off again, this time half running, half walking, back aligned with the hedge and grip tightening on the Glock. The steady percussion of thunder reminded him the storm was overhead now, lightning forking in a blinding flash.

With each silent step he advanced by inches, feeling the burn in his muscles. Was she armed and hiding? Because if she was, she had a better firing position. Never expect the usual, he thought. It would kill him every time.

The scent of damp wood alerted him to an old slatted barn up ahead. He approached it from the northeast corner, estimating a building of about thirty feet wide and fifty feet long. There was a four foot gap between the sliding doors and a wide aisle where pools of water had collected from the rain.

Temeke slipped into the shadows and pressed his shoulder against the stable wall. He paused and listened to the drumming rain against the roof and the occasional hoof stamping against the kickboards. Each stall had a row of bars above a sturdy five-foot wall and a door that led out to individual runs. He counted five horses inside, ears flicking forward and back, and nostrils twitching.

His trained ear caught the sound of a shoe knocking against metal and he squatted behind a tower of empty water troughs.

A pained yell.

Temeke fought a rush of nausea. It wasn't the whinnying horses that bothered him, or their intermittent kicking and strutting, as if they would break out of the stalls at any moment and trample him underfoot. It was the sound of a human voice.

He duck walked up the aisle, one step at a time, arms

extended. To his left was an open tack room with feed bins and buckets, and on the right a cloud of dust floated above a straw bale. Something had recently brushed against it. He traversed his weapon 180 degrees, peripheral vision studying the dim outline of the stalls and the bars above them.

Then a thin grinding sound, like wheels riding along a steel rail. Temeke dropped deep into his calves, leveled his weapon and ignored the throbbing in his legs.

The sound was coming from an opening in the wall about ten feet beyond the straw bale. He waited three minutes, rose up into a crouch and edged around the corner. He found himself in a short corridor where a sliding metal gate separated the main barn from a circular lunging pen. Lighting flickered feverishly through a domed glass ceiling and a layer of clouds hovered directly above.

He spun inward, saw a female fifteen feet away kneeling in a thick bed of sand, head lowered as if she was praying. She didn't seem to hear the words "Police!" Kept swaying back and forth and chanting something he didn't understand.

There was enough light in the sky to see the wig discarded in the sand beside her, hands pushed down between her thighs as if she was cold.

Temeke shouted again. This time she heard him, head raised for only a moment. He could make out the rounded cheekbones, the red hair and mouth slightly open.

"Go away," she moaned.

"Lily, it's me. It's OK."

"It's too big now." She tapped the side of her head with a knuckle. "It hurts so much. Please… go away."

"Lily, I'm here. Let me help you."

"No, no, no… Stay back!"

It was the irony of it all that would come back to haunt him. The very book Alice bought – to empower, to encourage – had damaged none other than her own precious sister.

"I meant what I said," she shouted. "Either you open the door and let me in or I'll–"

Temeke didn't hear the response that interrupted her. He heard whispers and then two voices, one taunting, the other pleading.

"I'll scream," she said. "You know how loud I can scream!"

She sounded out of breath, chest rising and falling, forehead glistening with sweat. One hand dropped to her thigh, fingers opening and closing as if she was flexing a cramping muscle.

"You said I could see Alice. You said, you said, you *said!*"

Temeke crept forward a little, feet wading through sand. And then he saw the terrible thing she clasped, barrel, slide and trigger in a rugged shade of gray.

When he was halfway across the space, she pushed the muzzle in her mouth.

When he was five feet away, she fired.

FIFTY-EIGHT

It was forty days after the disappearance of Asha Samadi and Champagne corks were popping in the boardroom. Commander Hackett was his usual ebullient self, cracking jokes with Sergeant Moran and teasing him about an array of paperclip animals now hanging behind the front desk.

Captain Fowler, Officer Jarvis and Maggie Watts were running bets on how long it would take for Temeke to go through the rest of the cold files on his desk. Toledo and Hinkley were stuffing their faces with a Glock-shaped cake that looked more like an old sock, and Malin was crinkling a plastic cup in the hope that someone would fill it. She was a splendid combination of freckles and black hair and Temeke wondered what had taken him so long to notice.

By nine thirty, the room was full and the flat screen was buzzing on the back wall. Channel 4 got to it first, Cynn Wrigley, chief editor of the *Duke City Journal,* stood next to Stan Stockard in front of the courthouse with a mic. Within minutes the networks were crackling with the suicide of Lily Delgado and the safe return of Adel Martinez to her high profile and somewhat detached family.

One network caught the Chief of Police outside McDonalds with his grandson. His suit appeared to have a generous coating of polystyrene beads on the epaulets, either that or it was a bad case of dandruff, Temeke couldn't decide which.

With the exception of Lily's death, the networks bounced back and forth between pictures of Los Poblanos Academy and Gibson University, citing the dangers of study drugs and encouraging the public to use discretion with any form of witchcraft.

The *Esoterica* was hailed as a 'dead loss' by journalist Jennifer Danes, which had increased sales online by ninety percent.

Zarah Thai's interview was short and meaningful. She said she had not spoken to Lily Delgado since starting her freshman year at Gibson, and in spite of the sisterhood, she never once considered Lily a friend.

Not surprisingly Adel Martinez had nothing to say. She was filmed crying through the open passenger window of a Jaguar XE, a car her father was driving. For some, the day wasn't a resounding success, friends all gone, memories dashed to smithereens. Adel would be continuing her undergraduate course at an undisclosed university in Georgia.

There were stills of Alice Delgado, Adel Martinez, Paddy Brody, Asha Samadi, Zarah Thai, Kenzie Voorhees and Rosa Belmonte standing under an avenue of trees, thought to be the front drive of Los Poblanos Academy, and a poignant video of Asha Samadi playing Chopin's Prelude in E minor at Popejoy Hall. A full press conference would follow.

The *Duke City Journal* showed a photograph of a body bag on a stretcher and the heading; *Suicide Girl Kills Friends. Rituals found in an Esoterica led Lily Delgado to murder and subsequent suicide. Duke City Police Department triumphs in yet another solved case.*

Temeke's back was becoming sore with all the patting and he relished the thick wad of cash Hackett had just given him. Nearly four sodding grand.

He suddenly felt crowded in and needed air. Funny how parties always seemed to go on without him and he could still hear laughing all the way down the hall. His cell phone pulsed a greeting and although he didn't recognize the number, he answered it anyway.

"Hello, David." A female voice.

It took Temeke a few seconds to register how familiar he was with that voice, how he had dreamed of it.

"Serena!" he blurted.

"I wanted to be the first to congratulate you," voice lowered almost to a purr. "I just wanted to say hi."

It was nearly April and the wind blew the sweet fragrance of freshly mown grass through the front door. It reminded him of happier days, as if she was standing right next to him.

He paced back and forth, telling her everything from the minute they found the Samadi remains to the ruin of a once vibrant family haunted by a tragic car accident and two suicides. "Mrs. Delgado will never be the same, love. Makes you realize how lucky we are."

"Blessed, David. *Blessed*."

"They say she's moving to Colorado. Can't blame her with all those memories."

"I'll be praying for her."

"And Lily... there was nothing I could have done."

She must have heard the tremor in his voice, read the despondency. "You did good."

The last word was drawn out, almost whispered, and he realized how much he missed those far-away eyes, the high pitched laughter and the wagging finger.

"I assume you'll have a long vacation now," she said, half laughing.

"How'd you guess? I could take you out to lunch, if you want."

She took a beat too long to answer. "I'll think about it, David. You take care, now."

And she was gone.

It was two long minutes before Temeke dragged himself away from the essence of that voice. He walked into the main office and found Malin sitting on one of the L-shaped desks, feet swinging, cheeks glowing and holding two cups of Champagne. It struck him he had not seen her wearing lipstick before and a third sense told him it wasn't a fluke.

"Cheers," she said, handing him a cup.

"To what?"

"To our crime squad. To you for breezing through this case with flying colors and winning the respect of your former peers. They'll be begging you to go back."

He knew she was being facetious. Homicide had shut the door on him, their fight was over and done with. This was his home now.

"You thinking about Lily?" she asked.

"She must have hated her mother for not protecting her. That's where the dissociation came from. If she lived out of her feminine self, she didn't feel safe. So she came to despise the feminine altogether. She must have hated what the girls stood for at school."

"And dating men? She was too busy wanting to be a man to please her father."

"She killed those girls and then herself. Her last act of control. It's seems unfair, doesn't it? To the human spirit."

He took a sip of the fizzy wine – hated it – if he was honest. It was dry and tasted like Alka Seltzer and made him thirstier than crap. He set the cup down on the desk, where the base left a wet mark in the wood.

"Want to know something?" she asked. "Suzi Cornwell and Captain Fowler."

"No way." He hardly heard himself speak. "Crafty old sods. When did that happen?"

"Who knew? But it might explain why she's coming

to work here."

The idea didn't bode well for Temeke, especially in light of the pass Suzi had made.

"Why did you leave the party just now?" Malin asked.

"Phone call. It was Serena."

Temeke didn't know why he volunteered the information, why he suddenly felt vulnerable sitting there with a beautiful woman. He noticed the smile fade, saw her staring down at the floor without saying a word.

She breathed heavily as if controlling her voice. "Were you OK with that?"

"Yeah."

"But you said she didn't want to come home. You said it was over."

"She doesn't want me all cracked and damaged. Not the way I am now. She wants me whole, happy and hearty. Do you understand?"

"Scars heal, sir. Really."

"I hope you're right."

She grasped his hand and squeezed it. Then she let it go. Tilting her head, she smiled with those deep brown eyes of hers. "You're a great partner, Temeke. By the way, Hackett gave me bonus. It was quite a large chunk of change. He thinks we make a good team."

"He said that?"

Malin nodded and there was certainty in that nod.

"You going back in?" she said, pointing up the corridor to where all the laughing was coming from.

"In a while."

He watched her walk away – a stronger woman this time, chin up, shoulders back and a bounce in her step. And he found himself grinning for a while. Couldn't stop. Felt like he was walking on air.

ABOUT THE AUTHOR

Claire Stibbe was born in England and now lives and works in the US She is a member of the Albuquerque Citizen Police Academy Alumni Association and a graduate of the 50th Albuquerque Citizen Police Academy.

Today, Claire writes crime fiction books set in New Mexico. There are already three books in the Detective Temeke crime series, *The 9th Hour*, a 2016 New Mexico/Arizona Award Finalist, *Night Eyes*, and *Past Rites*. She is now working on the fourth.

In 2014, Claire published her first novel, *Chasing Pharaohs: A novel of ancient Egypt*, after visiting archaeological digs in Luxor, Egypt. The debut book was a gold medal recipient at Harper Collins Publishers showcase website, Authonomy. *The Fowler's Snare*, the second in the series, was shortlisted under authors to watch.

Claire has also written short stories for Breakwater Harbor Books Publishing. The collection won Best Anthology of 2014 in the Independent Book Awards hosted by eFestival of Words.

> For more information on Claire Stibbe.
> www.cmtstibbe.com

www.ingramcontent.com/pod-product-compliance
Lightning Source LLC
Chambersburg PA
CBHW020244030426
42336CB00010B/615